Cloud Cuckoo Land

Cloud Cuckoo Land

Naomi Mitchison

with an Introduction by
Isobel Murray

Kennedy & Boyd
an imprint of
Zeticula
57 St Vincent Crescent
Glasgow
G3 8NQ
Scotland.

http://www.kennedyandboyd.co.uk
admin@kennedyandboyd.co.uk

First published in 1925 by Jonathan Cape.
Copyright © Naomi Mitchison 1925
This edition copyright © Estate of Naomi Mitchison
2011
Introduction © Isobel Murray 2011

ISBN-13 978-1-84921-034-8 Paperback

'Ασυνέτημι τῶν ἀνέμων στάσιν·
τὸ μὲν γὰρ ἔνθεν κῦμα κυλίνδεται,
τὸ δ' ἔνθεν· ἄμμες δ' ἀν τὸ μέσσον
νᾶϊ φορήμεθα σὺν μελαίνᾳ.

to

MY LOVER

'I am baffled by the quarrelling winds. One wave rolls up
on this side, another on that, and we with our black ship are
carried in the middle.'
                    Alcaeus of Mytilene in Lesbos, "the Ship of State"

Introduction

Naomi Haldane married Dick Mitchison in 1916, mid war. It was a time of dreadful chaos, and the destruction of Victorian certainties. All sorts of hitherto dependable 'truths' had vanished, and they were searching for some kind of moral or philosophical basis for living. Mitchison's studies had been mainly in science subjects, but she told us in an interview in 1984 that Dick 'was a Double First in Greats [Classics at Oxford], and was terribly keen that I should wander about the same world as his.'[1] He tried in vain to get her to learn Greek, and *did* infect her with his enthusiasm for the Classical world, suggesting appropriate historical settings for her imagined stories, and encouraging her reading. In the 'Notes on Spelling, Etc' to *Cloud Cuckoo Land*, she offers the novel as thanks both to her husband and her lover Theodore Wade Gery.

Mitchison only did things wholeheartedly, and her early books in particular are suffused with Greece and the main city states' political ideals. Apparently, indeed, she developed her first real political ideas in terms of Athens and Sparta, and continued to use these terms indefinitely, often as a kind of shorthand, although democracy and totalitarianism were loosely their twentieth-century equivalent. In *Cloud Cuckoo Land,* 1925, she made her first large scale venture into the world of Ancient Greece. Here as elsewhere in her fictions of the ancient world, the feminist Mitchison had to acknowledge that even the best Greek democracy excluded women from membership. But as we will see, Mitchison has plenty to say about 'the Woman Question' in her novel.

In our interview we talked about choosing sides between Athens and Sparta in *Cloud Cuckoo Land*, and I asked:

> Our hero has to decide what side to be on, and there isn't a right side, because even Athens is a bully at this stage. But Sparta is worse, and I think that in a lot of your books Sparta equals 'the baddie'. Is that true?
>
> **NM** Well, you see, Sparta was a little bit like Germany, and at that time we were beginning to be aware of what was happening, and although I don't think I thought of it directly, that was affecting us. We weren't going to have anything to do with the Hitler Jugend.
>
> **IM** The whole discipline of Sparta immediately makes one fear a totalitarian kind of –
>
> **NM** Yes. (I,74-5)

Her whole political ideal, often incompletely specified, was the ideal of Athens, a timeless ideal that reached its nearest perfection in the age of Perikles. What she saw around her in Europe fitted only too well to the Spartan model. It was not only the development of Hitler's Germany – when she returned from her first visit to Russia in 1932, a visit of which she had had high hopes, she wrote in her diary, 'A lot of Sparta about this.'

Cloud Cuckoo Land, only her second novel, was published as early as 1925. But Mitchison would go on, almost to the outbreak of World War Two, describing, urging, explaining, and warning about the dangers she rightly saw. Here is a quick survey of examples from fact and fiction, for adults or children.

Throughout the thirties in particular she regarded European politics according to her poles of Athens and Sparta. In *Boys and Girls and Gods* (1931) she writes that the Spartans 'are especially exciting and interesting to us, looking on from the present'. Describing Sparta, and with an eye to the present, she wrote:

> For the good, or apparent good, of the state, all kinds of cruelties and strangenesses were allowed [2]

There is a kind of sequel short story to *Cloud Cuckoo Land*, in a collection called *Black Sparta*, in 1928. In 'The Epiphany of Poieëssa' she has Alxenor's son Timas, less callow than his father was, debating the merits of possible wives. But his actual bride turns out to be a priestess of the goddess Hera, whose image has been accidentally smashed in the interruption of a sacred rite. These two can only reach a happy conclusion by leaving Greece altogether.[3] In the novel itself, the two central figures of Alxenor and Hagnon find no abiding city, and depart at the end to fight in an unknown war for Cyrus the Persian as mercenaries.

In a 1937 play for children on radio, 'The City and the Citizens', she has an Athenian father teaching his son what it will mean to be a citizen, jury duty, judging and passing new laws, voting, opposing injustice – 'Because, remember, Athens is for all, not just the rich.' Not just the rich: but in fact oligarchs rule most of the city states to their own advantage, just like Alxenor's brother Eupaides in *Cloud Cuckoo Land*. In *The Moral Basis of Politics*, written urgently 1935-7 and published as late as 1938, she still writes of Athens and Sparta and the adaptability of their small-scale political solutions to a grander modern scale.

Through its central character Alxenor from the tiny island of Poieëssa this novel dramatises and works out the rival claims of Athens and Sparta late on in the Pelopennesian Wars, when Athens has declined from its prime, but it still comes down fairly clearly in the end on the side of Athens. The historical figure of Thucydides declares:

> But even so, though she is utterly lost, starved and beaten, under the heel of Sparta, yet it was worth while, yet my city is a star to the world!. . . all the Spartans alive have no power over the idea. (196)

And in our interview the author endorsed this again: 'Yes, I'm sure. It's always worth it.' But she added ruefully, 'And a generation later the people who've been shot have a beautiful monument put up to them.' (I,76)

But perhaps the most straightforward setting forth of the two contrasting ways is to be found in a book she wrote with her younger contemporary Dick Crossman. *Socrates* was published in 1937 in a series of short biographies called 'World-Makers and World-Shakers'. Here the two states are described:

Sparta was rather special; here all the citizens were equal, and all were bound to serve the State, often in very painful and unpleasant ways, But only one in sixteen of the men in Sparta were citizens; the rest were helots, the original inhabitants of the country, who had been made into slaves by the Spartan conquerors. It was all that the one-in-sixteen could do to hold down the rest, and they only did it by using all possible means including the most horrible treachery and cruelty, and by submitting themselves entirely to the discipline of the State. This was run by a council of elders, five elected magistrates, and two kings who were the war leaders; one family of these kings was apt to be very intelligent, and they were always getting into trouble. It is no good being intelligent in a State like Sparta. [4]

Mitchison hated the ratio of citizens to slaves here. She deeply distrusted the iron discipline that taught men to exist not as individuals but only as part of a class, and then a state. She loathed the secret, gratuitous acts of violence that the Krypteia enforced on promising young men, sent out to murder helots and keep them in fear. This description is (even) less sympathetic than those in *Cloud Cuckoo Land*, where the community and togetherness of the young men of Sparta is seen at first by both Alxenor and his son Timas as very attractive: when he is alerted to the cruelty and dehumanising discipline of the Krypteia he makes a dangerous escape with his son.

Athens is indeed something else: the life of Socrates goes on:

But it was definitely a good thing to be intelligent in Athens. Here, just before the Persian wars, they had started a new idea: the idea of *democracy*, government by the people. . . . Democracy went with trade and the lively minds of town people who don't want just to do all the things their fathers do. The power in the Athenian democracy belonged to the free Athenian citizen workers, mostly men who made things themselves with their own hands or helped by one or two skilled slaves, and who traded things themselves. They had the votes, they sat on the juries, and they were the sailors who manned the ships which beat the Persian fleet at Salamis: It was during the war with Persia that Athenian democracy came into real being.

Although Athens tolerated slavery, the big idea here is that the citizens were their own masters and performed the most important tasks themselves. And it was the great age of Athenian art. But Athens was prey to takeover by oligarchs, as happened in this novel, where the 'golden age' of Perikles is already in the past. Elsewhere, Mitchison wrote: 'The peculiar genius of Athens in the fifth century had gone out, destroyed, perhaps, by the Pelopennesian War, one of the most disastrous in history.' [5]

All that is left for our characters, for Athens and Sparta and the men of Poieëssa, and Melos and Phokia and the rest, is a faint beginning to understand that they are all Hellenes: perhaps a unity of Hellenes will pave the way for a better future. From the first Alxenor had looked back to a 'good old days' when all Hellenes were brothers (13), and in the final chapter Hagnon makes peace with a former slave, Isadas, and restores his belief in his manhood, and, Hellenes together, they march off to war – but a war that is neither Hellene nor their own concern.

Cloud Cuckoo Land was the name given to a new city built by the birds in Aristophanes' comedy *The Birds* in 414 BC. Its protagonist Pisthefairos looks for a utopia, but in the event he becomes dictator of the city built by the birds, which collapses from an egalitarian state to dictatorship and tyranny. In a modern understanding Cloud Cuckoo Land is 'an imaginary situation or land, especially as the product of impractical or wishful thinking'. Perhaps, then, the title of Mitchison's novel already casts a negative shadow on young Alxenor's idealistic political beliefs about Athens – there is no such place? But the real life historian Thucydides, here a character in the novel, in the face of total defeat, asserts: 'All the Spartans alive have no power over the idea.' (196)

In the novel, everything is seen in a humbler scale, almost a domestic scale. Instead of hailing from Athens or Sparta, our protagonist Alxenor comes from the tiny, unimportant and fictional island of Poieёssa, which is and has been subject to Athens, but now an Athens past its prime. Instead of introducing Greek philosophers to debate theories, Mitchison makes Alxenor's intellectual and political growth a part of his growing up and his general relationships, in what is at first essentially a *Bildungsroman*, a novel about development to adulthood. Alxenor is found in the first chapter debating with himself whether to disown the bullying state of Athens:

Even he thought of Athens as the bully. Only – it was a choice of evils . . .   Now they had only to choose between Athens and Sparta. (11-2)

The dilemma presents itself starkly and personally: Alxenor is a member of the ruling class, and his elder brother Eupaides is a leader of the oligarchs who want to sell out to Spartan occupation. But Alxenor's closest friend Chromon is a whole-hearted and committed democrat quite opposed to this, and Alxenor feels strongly in sympathy with him. A young man in a dilemma, he seeks to reconcile the two worlds, to find a middle way.

He is also in love, in a very callow way. His object is Chromon's sister Moiro. He and Chromon have been the closest of friends as they grew up, and shared all their thoughts. His first sighting of Moiro in the first chapter is telling: he watches her at a distance, admiring her physical grace and beauty, 'feeling his hands and face grow hot as he watched.' (14) He longs to 'see her and see her until he was satisfied.' (15) They do not speak – indeed, although Alxenor is tacitly accepted as her fiancé, they have never spoken. Her first recorded words to him will be later, after she has been rescued from real danger: 'Alxenor, are you going to marry me?'(64) Marriage is the only thing that can give a Greek girl like her status and security. She has been denied Chromon's education, and shows no interest in thought at any point. Alxenor has conversed only with her brother, whom she resembles, so that he can be in love only with an idea of Moiro.

Now Chromon goes so far as to wish they were guarded by an Athenian garrison; he so distrusts the Spartans: 'they've been here too long.' (41) When Alxenor gets home to his brother's house, Spartans are there to dine, with a 'queer silent Persian', Belesys. Almost at once, Alxenor is precipitated into the story's action. Chromon wants Alxenor to spy on his brother. When Alxenor instead openly tries to persuade Eupaides toward democracy, he is laughed into silence, beaten up and locked in his room, unable to warn Chromon and the democrats of Spartan Lysander's sea victory at Notium and that the captain of the citadel has sold out. In the confusing struggle that ensued, Chromon rushed to defend the citadel, the mob went over to the Spartans on hearing of their victory, and Alxenor was left to get Moiro safely from her home, which he only achieved with the help of a Spartan boy, Archytas' lover Leon. In the melee, unseen by Alxenor, Leon killed Moiro's father. When Leon carried Moiro out of the house, Alxenor behaved childishly: 'Alxenor grew red with anger: "Give her to me – she's mine!" He dropped the child and snatched at her – "Moiro, my darling!"' (60-1) (We later learn almost incidentally that his action in dropping the child has left him disabled.) There is nowhere to take Moiro, so Leon leads them to the Spartan lodging. Moiro is lost in grief for her father, and Chromon, feeling doubly betrayed by his close friend, violently demands Alxenor return his sister and never see her again. So there is no help for it:

He could not stay in Poieëssa now, with hatred
from both sides, no friends but Spartans. Even if his
brother forgave him, as he might – laughing! – he
could not have Moiro, and she was the one good
thing he had got out of so much evil. (70-1)

(She is again a thing here, in his mind, elsewhere a
child, a little darling, a little thing). Moiro is soft and
clinging and weak and obedient. In Alxenor's time
of need it is the queer Persian Belesys who offers him
money and a passage to Athens for the three, always
including Moiro's faithful slave Thrassa.

So the three are thrust from Poieëssa. Thrassa
will prove a strong friend and protector for Moiro,
but we notice that Moiro is perpetually helpless,
weeping or sleeping or fainting. Her helpless
childishness may well reflect Mitchison's feminist
view of her upbringing and lack of education.
Thus, four chapters in, the ill-assorted pair have
left Poieëssa. Only Alxenor will return later, but to
leave again, finding it no longer a home: most of
the surviving characters will feel homeless by the
end, wandering mercenaries dreaming faintly of a
Hellenic community they cannot realise.

In Athens Alxenor has good fortune at first. He
is able to get Theramenes as his patron. Theramenes
is a historical character, called The Workers' Friend,
and Alxenor and Moiro are welcomed by him,
Theramenes paying for their wedding and making
Alxenor an oarsman. Theramenes' son Hagnon will
end up with Alxenor, marching in a Persian army.
His daughter Nikodike is another woman-victim,

but much stronger than Moiro. She is desperate for marriage and motherhood and a place in society, but helpless until, in disguise, she storms at her father in public, forcing his attention, so that she does get a husband, but not a very good one. Finally she tries to run away to fight in a war with her brother Hagnon, and is soundly beaten and psychologically cowed by her husband. Alxenor's fairly happy introduction to Athens is interrupted by a contrasting scene, when he meets Harmokydes from Phokia, who lauds Sparta to the skies:

> 'I think so well of them that I've sent my only son to be brought up among them as a foster-child of the Spartan State!
> 'Your only son?'
> 'Yes, my son Kratis; he's being made perfect too.'
> 'How long has he been there?'
> 'Three years. I've never seen him since. But I know all's well.' (107)

This idea rather shocks Alxenor – so many years separation from a son. In time he will find himself contemplating a very similar plan, and Harmokydes' son Kratis will disabuse him.

Simple juxtapositions of Athens and Sparta like this are effective without much commentary. Now Alxenor hears from Poieëssa that his brother has won the island, just before Hagnon takes him up to the Acropolis, the pride of Athens at her height. In the quotations I cited at the start, Mitchison did not put much emphasis on the Athenian creations of art and beauty, but here Hagnon, a citizen, takes Alxenor toward the Acropolis, and Mitchison follows the big set piece of the wedding with Alxenor's response to the Acropolis and the Parthenon, up the 'bare, terrible, sacred rock'. (118) Alxenor is stunned by the beauty, and 'the goddess – not his, not his! – caught him and held him'. (120) The whole reduces him to tears. From this we move immediately to the loss suffered by Athens now, telling or reminding the reader of the cost of the long Pelopennesian War:

> But a whole generation seemed to be missing, killed in battle one time or another, prisoners at Syracuse dead of ill treatment and dysentery, drowned at Cynossema and Cyzicus. Whole families had been wiped out, first by the plague, which had come early in the war after the first invasion of Attica and overcrowding of the City, and then later in the fighting that went on every year from the beginning of spring to late autumn. But the women were left, often with no kinsman to shelter them but some distant cousin, who would be bound in piety to give them housing and food, though he brought poverty on his own wife and daughters; and every one would be unhappy. There were not so many young children about the city as in old days, either; partly from lack of husbands, partly because young couples could not always afford to rear them. (123-4)

After a long and difficult labour, Moiro did manage to bear a son, Timas. But she is terrified at the thought of another baby: 'I do love you and I will do anything you want, but it did hurt me so!' (130) Her fearful unwillingness sends Alxenor to a brothel, and at this point any reader who had hopes for the marriage is liable to lose them. When cash-strapped Alxenor next leaves for war, Moiro is pregnant again, and he leaves her a despairing message that leads her also to despair: 'When your time comes – good luck to you! – if you have a boy, keep it; if you 'have a girl, expose it.'(165) It seems inevitable, as the pair descend into penury and misery, that the new baby will indeed be a girl, and so it is. Thrassa is the one who has to expose her, and the scene is rendered with great poignancy by Mitchison, herself a young mother. This awful experience leaves Moiro with little time or enthusiasm for Timas, and no desire at all for Alxenor.

In Chapter Eight Mitchison wrote a great set piece of Alxenor's first sea battle: now she can report others briefly, and concentrate on their impact. Another devastating naval defeat seems to spell the end for Athens, which depends on sea routes for its food. Alxenor is wounded, and without pay, and the family is reduced to ever greater poverty. Alxenor decides to flee, and may have to sell Thrassa – who has been their friend! - and may even sell himself for ten years, if he can only get Moiro and Timas safely to Poieëssa. But just as Belesys had unexpectedly given him money to leave home, now Thrassa picks up a purse full of money and they can take passage. Eventually they reach Ephesus, where Belesys' son (and murderer!) Gobryas recognises his father's ring and promises to help, although Alxenor does not like the way Gobryas looks at Moiro. She repulses the rich Persian, but it is a sign of things to come: she tells Alxenor, and they must be off again.

Moiro is now in a downward spiral. Now aware of her own attractions, she falls in love with Leon, the Spartan who helped Alxenor rescue her from her home. They have a passionate sexual affair, which ends only with Leon's disgusted repudiation of her when she learns for sure that he killed her father and abjectly cries:

> I would have been your slave...all yours to do what you like with. I want you to do what you choose always, kill father, kill anyone, kill me! No, don't kill me, hurt me, beat me – (262)

The rest of her story is wretched and soon told. Pregnant with Leon's child, she tries to conceal it, while she and Thrassa try several traditional means of abortion. The last and most severe of these makes her critically ill, and she dies.

It is at this point that Alxenor meets Thucydides, who asserts a belief in Athens still: 'Though she is utterly lost, starved and beaten, under the heel of Sparta, yet it was worth while, yet my city is a star to the world!' (196) Alxenor has to appeal to the Spartan Archytas, who was Leon's older lover in Poieëssa, who takes in his family, and gives him a job – rowing for Sparta! – and paid for by money from Sparta's backer, Persia. When he meets his fellow rowers, he finds them very different from his Athenian fellows, an assorted riff raff, none of them citizens. 'Mostly they seemed in terror of the few Spartiates who ruled them'(207). From them he hears of the cruel secrets of the Krypteia. Left alone in Sparta with his son, the bereaved Alxenor is perplexed over Archytas' decision to tell him about Leon and Moiro, and then his offer to let the State take Timas and bring him up as a foster-child. Just as he was at the beginning, Alxenor is in two minds, drawn both ways, to take Timas with him to Poieëssa, or to leave him to be raised in Sparta, as the boy desires. He is entertained by the Class of lads Timas would join, and meets Kratis, the son of Harmokydas the Phokian, who had rejoiced in Kratis' good fortune in Sparta. But at the risk of his life young Kratis visits Alxenor in the night: 'Don't leave your child in Sparta ' (296) He reveals a system that destroys individualism: 'they only want to think of themselves as part of the state – they're willing to give up their own selves for that!'(296) He has been deprived of art and beauty, and says even Spartan Gods are cruel and terrible, like the Apollo at Thornax, 'He is one great awful Spartan stone out of the hills up to his arms, and then – then it breaks out into that terrible head.'(299) Next day there is no sign of Kratis, and Archytas tells Alxenor that Kratis 'has gone to Thornax, to worship Apollo.' (301) Alxenor 'is afraid to the bottom of his soul', but more afraid for his son: he takes Timas on a desperate journey of escape from Sparta.

Back in Poieëssa, Alxenor is amazed to find his brother and Chromon close allies in the opposition to

Sparta, but after Alxenor kills the Spartan Governor and Chromon defeats his men, Eupaides and Chromon take opposite sides again:

> It was all going to be just like it was before, and this time he would have to decide. Not quite like, he thought bitterly, for then we were young and hopeful and eager and – oh, again, young, when all was said! (319)

A letter from Hagnon, now also homeless and causeless, draws him to become a fellow mercenary in Persian Cyrus' army. The final Chapter resolves one more issue. As a boy, Hagnon had had a Melian slave, a Hellene, Isadas. When Athens was defeated in battle, the boy Isadas had attacked and fought Hagnon, as a symbol of his slavery. But now at the end Isadas and Hagnon are both in Cyrus' army, and Alxenor brings them together in an important resolution, illustrating Hagnon's belief that they must be citizens of the larger Hellas. In this novel, Hagnon realises that Hellenes should never enslave Hellenes: in many later novels and stories Mitchison will explore and excoriate the idea that any man or woman should ever be enslaved by, or belong to another.

Notes

1 'Naomi Mitchison' in *Scottish Writers Talking 2*, 2002, p 70. Other references will be given in the text as (I,000).
2 *Boys and Girls and Gods*, 1931, p 91.
3 *Black Sparta*, 1928, pp 242-69.
4 Naomi Mitchison and R H S Crossman, *Socrates*, 1937, pp 20-21.
5 *Boys and Girls and Gods*, 1931, p 107n.

NOTES ON SPELLING, ETC.

THROUGHOUT this book, my spelling of names is quite inconsistent. I am very sorry, but I see no way out of it. Clearly, one should spell things when possible in the proper way, which usually indicates the proper pronunciation. But sometimes between Latin and English, names have gone hopelessly wrong and correction is impossible: Browning's 'Athenai' is merely irritation, though not more than his Atticised 'Sparté.' However, leaving Athenai unregretfully as Athens, one can still rescue a few names: Alkibiades and Sokrates are perfectly easy to get used to, though Kuros, Lusandros (as Browning again has him), and perhaps still more Thoukudides, seem to me to destroy all sense of ease and familiarity in reading. But it is clearly all a matter of taste.

Occasionally I have used Greek words when there is no exact or easy English equivalent. A Ker, for instance, is not quite a ghost or a spirit. It is more definitely queer and hungry and winged: there are love-keres and death-keres. But we are so steeped in the traditions of a different religion, that they are rather hard to get at. I suppose Jane Harrison knows as well as anyone.

A proxenos is a diplomatic agent for one State, living in, and a citizen of, another State. It was often more or less hereditary in one family, and must have been interesting. Alkibiades was proxenos for Sparta during various truces. But of course it would have been quite unimportant being proxenos for a place

4

like Poieëssa, and Kleiteles certainly did not take it very seriously.

I have taken the theory of triremes that is very convincingly brought forward in the Cambridge *Companion to Greek Studies*, i.e. that it was nothing to do with tiers of oars, but only with the number of men rowing at each oar. In Theramenes' ship, there were three men at each oar, except at Bow and Stern, where the ship was narrower and there was only room for two.

As to books: if I were to put in a list of all the books I have come across which bear on this particular subject and period, it would simply look ridiculous. Many of them I only read for fun, and happened to find something interesting. Obviously my chief authority is Xenophon's *Hellenica*; if I can induce anyone to read this (the Loeb translation is very vivid on the whole) and get as much pleasure out of it as I did, then I shall be – as the good books say – amply rewarded. For actual history I have gone to Cavaignac or Holm. If anyone would really like suggestions of books to read, perhaps they would write to me? In the meantime, Zimmern's *The Greek Commonwealth* is a good book to begin on.

However, the great thing is to find people who are just as interested, and better at a subject than oneself, and induce them to talk to one. If they are really good at it, they will probably like doing so. I have been extremely lucky about this. Will G. R. M. and H. T. W. G. please take this book as my thanks to them for talking.

N. M. M.

NOTE

THE events related in this book take place in Greece, the islands of the Ægean Sea, and on the West Coast of Asia Minor, about the end of the fifth century B.C. The Peloponnesian War, which had been going on for a whole generation, was almost at an end. Athens was nearly worn out, and Sparta, backed by Persian money, was now the strongest, as well as the oddest, of the City States of Hellas.

Alxenor and his brother Eupaides are members of the ruling class of Poieëssa, a small island State in the Ægean Sea, subject to Athens.

*

PEOPLE IN THE BOOK

HELLENES.—
From Poieëssa:
Eupaides.
Alxenor, his brother.

Tolmaios.

Thrasykles.
Chromon, his son.
Moiro, his daughter.
Glaukias, his brother.

From Sparta:
Lysander.

Archytas.

Leon.

Kleora.
Dionassa, her sister.

Erasis.

Ladas, a helot.

From Athens:
Theramenes.

Phrasikleia, his wife.
Hagnon, his son.
Nikodike, his daughter.

Also Isadas, a Melian, his slave.

Kleiteles.

Strymodoros.
Stratyllis, his wife.

From Phokis:
Harmokydes.
Kratis, his son.

BARBARIANS.—
From Persia:
Cyrus, younger son of Darius, the Great King.

Belesys.
Gobryas, his son.

From Thrace.
Thrassa, slave to Thrasykles.

Ditylas.

GREECE
in the
5th Century
B.C.

W E

THRACE

MACEDONIA

EPIRUS

THESSALY

Hellespont

Aegospotami

ETOLIA

ASIA MINOR

POIEESSA

Lesbos

Arginusae Is.

Sandis

Euboea

Chios

Thebes

Gulf of Corinth

ACHAIA

Athens

ELIS

ARCADIA

Corinth

Salamis

Samos

Ephesus

Tegea

Aegina

Delos

Naxos

Miletus

Sparta

LACONIA

Cos

IONIAN

SEA

Melos

Rhodes

MEDITERRANEAN SEA

Crete

CHAPTER ONE

'One is conjured to respect the beliefs of others, but for-
bidden to claim the same respect for one's own.' – Morley:
Essay on Compromise

ROUND them, and under their feet, the island
pressed up warmly against itself, rock and
earth and green turf covering it, trees and
bushes, all summer through drying and crumbling in
the sun, ringed about for ever with sea: Poieëssa,
their island, their State. By moments Alxenor felt
this; the live heat of the dust struck up through him
at every step, into his bones. Yet behind and ahead
and at either side his heart knew the water springs,
the shade, the coolness, the sheep drinking. Meanwhile he walked a little apart, watching the others.
Suddenly two lizards darted across the white path
in front of them, and vanished into the grass. A yellow butterfly went zigzagging past, into the eye of
the sun. And again Tolmaios, the eldest of the four,
repeated that trick of his, knotting the fringes of his
cloak and pulling at them; he tugged hard with his
left hand, frowning, and went on with the story:
'Well, there were the Elders sitting round the
Hearth, unarmed. You'd think he might have respected them, wouldn't you? But he didn't, not he!
Laughed in their faces and read out the despatch
from Athens. Then the soldiers came in: it was just
Melos over again. Tore them away – trampled on
the Hearth – no shame, no pity! And he looked on
all the time – I saw him myself – as pleased as a
jackdaw. Yes, that's how he served them. And
we're not so much better placed.' The Spartan,

9

walking at the other side, nodded slowly: 'Yes, that's Athens, that's your mistress.' If he meant to provoke Tolmaios to another outburst he succeeded well: 'Our mistress! Yes, with these dirty democrats of ours licking her hands. I wish I'd got one rope for them all —!' And his face grew red, and Alxenor could see the angry sweat gathering on his skin.

Alxenor was getting angry enough himself — on the other side. But he wanted more than anything not to show it, not to let the older ones and the Spartan foreigner see how they were hurting him! He even tried not to listen, but the words kept coming at him; his brother was speaking now, and then Tolmaios again. The Spartan spoke very little, but Alxenor hated him even for that, scarcely knowing why, but dimly aware that this man was despising the islanders all the time, even the oligarchs, even Tolmaios, but that they did not see it, because they wanted to be friends with him . . . for some reason . . .

Puzzling over this, he fell behind; in front of him the three were still talking, their short, mocking shadows jumping beside them over the bushes at the path's edge. It was all about people now — the democrats. 'Oh, well!' his brother was saying, 'the shipbuilders naturally, and of course our young friend at the farm!' He laughed — they all laughed — and Alxenor stopped dead, and stamped, and said what he thought of them under his breath. It was no good saying it aloud; he had done that once, but his brother had stopped him, scolded him like a child in front of the foreigner, and then told about Moiro: 'that's why he's a democrat, the young puppy!' Oh, anything was better than to have his love laughed at by a hairy brute of a Spartan! He sat down on a patch of grass, pretending to take a thorn out of his foot, till the others were well out of sight. He heard their voices for a long way in this still, burning weather; the sounds seemed to hang in the air, Tolmaios speaking again, then that rough Spartan voice, hard to bear as a rasping wheel, last his brother Eupaides, ever so deliberate, meaning to make you think how fair-minded he was!

They were out of sight; he sat up again. Now that he was not listening for the voices, he heard the grasshoppers dinning shrilly all round him. He caught one in his hand and felt the little beast butting with its hard head against his thumb. For a moment he had the impulse to crush it, show it he was master somewhere at least, but then laughed to himself: 'I'm not an Athenian!' and let it wriggle out between two fingers, and give a great leap into the bushes behind. Yes, that was it; even he thought of Athens as the bully. Only – it was a choice of evils.

He pushed his way deeper into the shade of the leaves, and at last settled down, half lying, half sitting, his back against the broad roots and trunk of a dwarf oak; through the branches the sky was deep and brilliant blue, as solid as a roof. And oh how he wished he could have belonged to some great strong city that didn't need to be anyone's ally! That was the worst of being an island – such a little island. If only the Gods had made them big, like Rhodes, or

11

else so tiny that no one would have noticed them, no
corn-ships come, and then they could have lived at
peace like those little townships in Homer. But
then perhaps they'd not have been colonized six centuries back, they might be barbarians still. No, that
wouldn't do. But what was the good of wishing ?
Now they had only to choose between Athens and
Sparta.

Gradually he fell asleep, his hands slack at his sides,
his head dropping forward from the rough bark of
the tree. That noon sky softened slowly towards
evening; the earth was hot and still. To right and
left, among the bushes of rosemary and gum cistus,
goats cropped the short turf; one or two, venturing
under the shadow of the oak, stepped with their
delicate, light hooves over the feet of the sleeper.
And a few small, brownish birds slipped in and out
of the leaves, very silent and shy.

At last Alxenor, stretching and yawning, dragged
himself out of the deep comfort of his sleep, back
with a horrid jerk to the sharp confusion and argument that had filled his mind the last thing before he
slept. He got to his feet: he was hungry. For a
moment he thought of supper at home; but the
Spartans were sure to be there. He started walking
westwards along the narrow goat track through the
scrub; below him he saw the floor of the sea, purplish
and hazy in the late afternoon, and then just the sea-
ward edge of the harbour, and a blue ship with red
sails coming in. The town itself was out of sight
down the slope, the town with his brother and Tolmaios and the Spartans. In front of him the path

rose twinkling white over the crest of a ridge; he trotted up it easily, his tunic pulled through his belt, well out of the way of thorns.

The farm lay a little ahead now, low and spreading, with olives and fruit trees all round it, grey-green and blue-green. He called: 'Is Chromon here?' to one of the slaves, who answered that he'd been in town since early morning, and his best cock with him. Alxenor went on towards the big yard of the farm, with its stacks and dung-heaps, and piles of baskets ready for the fruit. The olive in the middle was the oldest and biggest in the island; close upon ninety years of peace had gone to make it; one autumn day when it was first bearing, the ships of the Persian fleet had beaten past, tearing away for home with broken oars and tattered sails, all that was left of them, three days out from Salamis. That was in the good old days, thought Alxenor, when all Hellenes were brothers, when everything was simpler, finer, stronger – oh yes, that would have been the time to live!

He leaned against the fence, looking down into the well-trodden yard. Moiro was standing under the olive, and a hundred pigeons clustered all round her, pushing and quarrelling for the corn, settling and rising, with white wings fluttering and loosened feathers about her shoulders and bare arms. He saw her from the side, her face lively and laughing as the wing-tips flicked her cheeks, her hair low on her neck, bound with a yellow scarf and only showing brown and curly over her forehead and little ears. She scattered the corn in a wide circle, and the pigeons scattered with it. Then, as she ran forward

13

among them again, the fine, pleated linen flickered
out behind her as though she were winged too. Her
dress was yellow like the scarf, embroidered lightly
all over with small, star-shaped flowers of red and
blue; it clung to her breasts as she moved. He leaned
harder against the fence, feeling his hands and face go
hot as he watched. She threw one arm up to shake off
the clinging pigeons, and as she did it the dress slid
down her other shoulder; he wondered whether perhaps she knew he was there, and, if she did, whether
she moved in love or mockery. He knew the shape
of her whole body under the swaying, thin stuff; it
was almost unbearable to watch her any longer. He
called towards the main part of the farm – not her,
but Chromon. She flashed round at that, snatching
the double fold of her dress over her head for a veil;
then ran in, waving a hand and calling to him that
Chromon was away, but her father was there.

The next minute old Thrasykles came hurrying
out, throwing on a clean cloak over a dirty tunic; he
kissed Alxenor, and brought him along, through the
yard and porch into the house. Here he shouted for
supper, rushed out to see they were killing the right
hen, in to be sure they had plenty of onions, and
finally settled down on the couch beside Alxenor,
with an extra armful of flock cushions. For ten
minutes he talked hard, mostly on crops and weather
and their new neighbours whose goats had been
straying; Alxenor leaned back, not attending much,
but watching the old man and liking him immensely,
scrubby beard and red nose and all. He was town-
bred himself, delicate about everything, clean all

over, careful of the look of his hands, his dress, the sound of his voice. But for all that, he knew enough about country things, he could have stacked a rick or driven a plough, and he loved his welcome at this house, the friendly smell of baking bread and fresh milk and beasts, Thrasykles and his son both treating him as the honoured guest, splendidly setting him up against his own opinion, and then, often, the glimpse of Moiro. She came in now, bringing the lamp, and trimmed it carefully, as if she did not know how it made lovely, warm shadows on her face and arms; she had put on her gold and coral necklace too. Alxenor tried to get her to look at him, but she kept her eyes on the floor and would say no more than a whispered 'yes, father,' and 'no, father.' How beautiful it would be, he thought, to have his own name spoken by her, and then to be able to look into her eyes, deep and long, to see her and see her until he was satisfied.

She went out after a little, and then, when it was quite dark, Chromon came in, stumbling over a bench and swearing, his glossy game cock under one arm, and a strong thorn stock in his other hand. 'So you're here, Alxenor!' he said. 'Why couldn't you tell me you were coming and we'd have gone together! Well, has that Spartan of yours put on a clean shirt yet?'

'No, nor cut his hair either! You've had bad luck with your cock?'

'Yes, the little devil; he's about fit for the pot! Turned tail and ran his first time out!' He twitched a feather savagely out of the cock's neck.

15

Alxenor nodded sympathetically. 'My brother's got a little beauty now, a real soldier; you ought to see him.'

'Oh, your brother can afford these new Persian birds! But all the same, they mayn't be the best in the long run.' He took his own bird out and put it into its pen, and after that it was supper time.

The big, red-cheeked Thracian slave-girl brought in a great heap of salad and cut bread, then little puddings, and the chicken. Moiro just showed herself at the door for a moment, half-veiled, and Thrassa had a message from her to whisper into Alxenor's ear as she poured out the wine, only to thank him for the basket of quinces he had sent by her brother, saying she had kissed each one of them five times, and asking him to send her a slip of the quince tree to plant. Thrasykles listened and smiled at it. He was only too pleased to have such a presentable suitor for his daughter, young – too young even – not bad looking, and come from one of the richest families in the island, and it was all to the good if Thrassa got a silver piece now and then to go into her savings: she would be better pleased with her place, and speak well of the young man to Moiro and her mother.

Chromon and Alxenor had been friends from school; they had spelled out their first words together, and later had sat up in the same apple tree learning their poetry. Later still, each bringing his father's old shield and helmet, and with ashen spear shafts shiningly new, they had started their training in the same company, and for a year they had been together most of the time, marching and sleeping

16

out, learning to use their weapons, talking endlessly,
and getting to know every stone of the harbour and
citadel, every defensible crag and gully of Poieëssa,
their island. Chromon was elder by ten months, and
besides he had no big brother to laugh at him if he
tried to think for himself; when anyone disagreed
with him in an argument, he shook his head like a
young bull, and went on. He enjoyed talking, too.
At home there was no one but his father and the farm
people, who always would agree with him even before
he'd finished the sentence, and the women, who
didn't count. But he was pleasantly sure that Alxenor would always disagree enough to make it, anyhow, worth arguing.

But this evening Alxenor was gloomy; after he had
stopped thinking of Moiro, he began again on the
old tangle: he saw no way of freedom. For clearly he
looked on Athens as the tyrant, clearly he grudged
every penny their ships must pay in duties to this
Athenian empire, their money that went oversea to
Piraeus to be flung away by some Alkibiades on
some mad adventure. But equally clearly he knew he
was a democrat and hated the Spartans and mis-
trusted them: sure that they gave nothing for nothing, and, if they said they were come to free Poieëssa,
they meant first of all to put her under an oligarchy
which would favour them. And besides – he was
almost pure Ionian by blood himself, and how could
he give himself over to these harsh, stupid Dorians?
Yet, if they stayed with Athens they were bound to
sink, they had sunk already (he remembered and
repeated some of the things his brother and Tolmaios

had said), Athens was bad at letting her allies alone. She spread herself out, the great harlot, crushing the little islands to death, taking their ships and men and money, to bind her own hair with gold, and laugh and dance and sing! Who did not know of their great shining Goddess, Athene on her proud hill, all ivory and gold enough to buy a whole little island like Poieëssa, and the treasures in her temples, and the theatres and ship-yards – all paid for by us!

But Chromon, happily for himself, must be always one thing or another. Once he too had hated Athens, but now, when people were beginning to look to him as a coming leader of the democrats, he hated Sparta worse, and the spies she sent out to make friends with their rich men and all those who, for whatever end, wished for an oligarchy. He had only room in his mind for one hate; if there were two they lessened each other, and, boyishly, he did enjoy hating! So he made light of the tax, looked forward to the time when Sparta was beaten and Athens could slacken the burden on her Allies. 'And as for that golden Maiden of theirs,' he said, 'she's ours too. You've not been to Athens, but I went last year, and saw it all so fine and glittering, and every one ready to talk and give one welcome as a friend, and show one all there is to be seen and heard! Oh, it was like a feast and a market-day at once all the time, and there one was, living with it, part of it, that light-foot City that sets the world on fire!'

Alxenor shook his head, wishing old Thrasykles' home-grown wine was strong enough to make him feel more cheerful. But Chromon leaned forward,

18

swinging his cup: 'And I stood in those temples, and the marble was a live, bright thing each side of me, and the Gods were Gods indeed! And they were my temples and my Gods. You won't find that in black Sparta, not in that sprawl of mangy villages they call their city – they won't welcome you there!'

Alxenor had heard it all before; could he be, perhaps, a little tired of hearing Chromon talk, Chromon his friend? 'Sometimes I wish one had nothing to do with the choice,' he said. 'What a deal of hard thinking and loose talk that would save! Well, I must go home.' Then, 'Are we no nearer the wedding?'

'You'll have to get your brother's consent out of him first,' said Thrasykles, but young Alxenor sighed, looking out into the starry and romantic night. 'Oh, you're silly about that girl of mine!' – the father laughed and slapped him on the back –'Just wait till you've been married a year or two and then come back and tell me what you think of her!'

Chromon picked up his cloak, and followed his friend out: 'I'm coming half-way, anyhow.' Somewhere higher up, among the dwarf oaks and hazels, they heard one nightingale, then another. After a few minutes' silent walking, Chromon spoke abruptly. 'It must be queer for you having so much money, Alxenor. You aren't a natural democrat, and I don't believe you'd be one at all but for me.'

'I think you're right,' said Alxenor, 'and perhaps it would be better if I had less.'

'When I was little we were really hard up,' said

19

Chromon. 'I didn't like it, and I don't know that it
did me any good. We had a run of bad years on the
farm. There was another girl born after Moiro, and
she had to be exposed; poor mother hated that. If
one's rich one can have as many children as one
likes; I suppose you and Moiro will.'

'I never knew you'd been as poor as that, Chromon;
you always did everything like me.'

'Father saw to that; but it was different at home.
Only I think it all started me on the way I've gone.'

'It would, of course. But – I should like to be a
poet, Chromon; or a painter like Parrhasios: nobody
cares what his politics are! You know that picture he
made for Tolmaios? It's all clear and easy and balanced, like some one walking along a pole perfectly
well. Only when I try to think like that – balanced
– my brother pushes me off at one side, and you at
the other! If only I could do anything quite beautifully, I shouldn't have to think about democracy.'

'It looks simple enough to me: plain ground not
pole-walking. That's the best way to look at things
too; you'll never get anything if you don't want it
hard.' Neither of them spoke for a moment. There
was a wild pomegranate bush on the right, flowering
pleasantly late, when the fruit was already well set
on its neighbours; but now all the scarlet-blossomed
bunches had gone dead black. Alxenor even reached
up his hand to make sure they were the same petals
still, and wondered why red, the fiercest colour,
always went out at sunset, while blue flowers he
never noticed by day still showed under the stars.
Chromon, though, was thinking of something more

immediate. 'About this Spartan,' he said, 'what is he really doing?'

'Talking.'

'When Spartans talk it's not for nothing. They've been here now – what? – five days? Who else of them counts?'

'No one. He's just going about with the boy. The rest aren't anything. My brother says he's sailing almost at once. God knows what business he mayn't have on the mainland, but that's not our affair.'

'Eupaides meant you to tell me they were going.'

Alxenor looked rather hurt at that: 'Well, if you don't trust me a bit –'

'I do trust you; but you'd like me and your brother to be friends.'

'I would indeed!' said Alxenor, thinking of Moiro.

'Fire and water. If I had my way you'd have one brother less, Alxenor. But the island's all rotten, so I haven't! God, I wish we'd got an Athenian garrison.'

'You don't! Ugh, Chromon, think of them in our streets! Can't you remember what you said yourself last March?'

'There weren't any Spartans in Poieëssa then.'

'Chromon, it's all nonsense. He may be going on to Cyrus or Lysander or the Great King – or Hell itself for all we know! For any sake, don't let's get mixed up with it. What does your uncle say? Nothing, and he's quite right. And – about my brother – you're not fair to me, you know I love you twenty times more than I've ever loved him, and besides there's Moiro. Only, he is my real brother and it

21

isn't his fault if he's got too much money, and some day when things are better you'll see the good in him!'

'Alxenor, you don't expect people to stay fair when they're in earnest, do you? Even me!'

'I did. I do still. Oh well, I suppose I'm out of date.'

Chromon did not answer, and by and by the bitterness cooled down, with stars and sea and bushes rustling and sometimes a sheep bell, and the grasshoppers quieting down as the heat lifted out of the turf.

CHAPTER TWO

'There was an old man who supposed
That the street door was partially closed;
But some very large rats
Ate his coats and his hats,
While that futile old gentleman dosed.' – *Lear*

A<small>T</small> the edge of the main road they kissed, and Chromon went back to the farm, through the tangle of shadows the trees were making in the starlight. Alxenor ran most of the way into the city, beginning to feel a little cold. The streets were hotter, narrow and dark and empty between flat walls; right down at the harbour there were lights and some noise still, but not here. At once on his knock, the door of his own house opened, and he heard voices from across the court; for a moment the lamplight made him blink.

They were sitting late after their supper, drinking from red-figured Athenian bowls, and talking politics. They lay back on their cushions, in the centre Eupaides, his brother, carefully garlanded with gilt-touched roses, Tolmaios beginning to yawn, and three or four other rich men of Poieëssa. On Eupaides' right were the two Spartans, with their long hair twisted up under the ribbons and flowers of their garlands. There was Archytas the man, quiet as he had been that morning, stretched out full length, drinking little and listening to everything that was said; and the boy Leon, bolt upright on the end of the couch, cracking nuts with his strong teeth. Nobody but the Spartans seemed to notice when Alxenor slipped round to the far side and an

23

empty couch, and held out a bowl to be filled with better wine than Thrasykles ever had. Archytas looked his way a moment, questioningly, and he glared back, wondering what else the three had talked about after they went on along the path. Then Leon grinned at him, wanting to play cottabos, but he shook his head. Some one had dropped some flowers on the floor beside him; he picked them up, big daisy things with yellow centres, and a few myrtle leaves.

Tolmaios was repeating to the man next him some of the very same arguments against Athens that he had just used to Chromon, but now he felt bitterly against them. He wondered if he had some sort of engine in his soul, a tough, springy sapling, he thought of it, a thing, anyhow, that sprung back against whoever struck it. But Chromon was far more in the right than all this! He remembered now their path among the dark, cool bushes, and the two nightingales; he wished he was walking still: the moon would be risen now, and Chromon's face white and eager under it, with his eyes and lips like Moiro, and his long hands tight round the thorn stock.

Leon the boy tiptoed over and sat down beside him. 'Do talk to me!' he said. 'No one's said a word all supper but politics!'

At once Alxenor had the feeling that politics were the real stuff of life, he felt immensely superior to Leon, who clearly understood nothing but black broth. 'Oh,' he said, from the heights of his three years more, 'I suppose you don't understand all that yet. What do you like talking about?'

The Spartan laughed: 'Oh, we all know I'm just out of my cradle and you've got a white beard! I like talking about things I can do.'

'Stealing foxes?'

'Yes, and knowing how to treat guests! And running at the Isthmus, if you like!'

Alxenor came wide awake, interested: 'What, last year? I never knew you ran! You didn't win, did you?'

'Yes.'

'But my brother was over and saw the games! Leon, it wasn't you who got a thorn in your foot half-way and went on and got in first by a yard?'

'I've had worse thorns.' (But all the same, his toes, remembering it, curled up and stiffened as he sat.)

'Oh, that's just like Eupaides – he never tells me anything interesting! Didn't they make a statue of you, taking the thorn out? That must have been worth doing!'

'I was going to Olympia last autumn, but we came away instead.' He nodded towards Archytas.

'What a shame! Did you have to come with him?'

'We've been lovers ever since I was quite small and he was captain of my class. He's always seen to my training. Lysander wanted me to come once with him and watch; we aren't allowed to travel till we're older usually. Besides – Alxenor, even if you are pro-Athenian, do look at Archytas and think if you wouldn't rather have come if you'd been me!'

Alxenor laughed then, but gently: 'Oh, I know what love is.'

'But who do you love?' asked Leon.

Alxenor looked hard into the clear, friendly eyes that bore him no malice: 'It's a girl, Leon.'

'But a girl may be worth loving; I've got a cousin – What's her name?'

'Moiro, daughter of Thrasykles.'

'I think I know about Thrasykles. Politics, isn't it?'

'They're democrats – he and Chromon.'

'That seems to me just horrible, to let yourself be governed by a lot of fishmongers and tanners!'

'Chromon isn't a fishmonger. Nor am I.'

'Don't let's talk about it. How old is she?'

'Fourteen.'

'That would be young for us. Is she tall? My cousin's as tall as me.'

'Not very.   But she moves like the wind on heather in midsummer. I saw her first in the Procession, carrying a basket for the Goddess; she looked straight in front of her all the time. That was the loveliest thing I have ever seen. When I found she was Chromon's sister, I knew she must be good as well as beautiful.'

'Will you marry her?'

'I hope so. Yes. Won't you drink, Leon?'

Leon shook his head. They both sat still for a little, Alxenor swirling the dregs of wine round in his cup, trying to make them wet it right up to the line under the brim, and listening to the elders talking, wondering whether perhaps he would tell Chromon that all the Spartans were not wholly bad; and Leon quiet as a mouse, smiling a little and watching Archytas.

26

All this learning and listening, this tedious game of politics, was a matter of love and nothing else to Leon; he found it came alive when Archytas talked, when they were by themselves and he could ask all the questions he wanted. Only now it was all so tangled, mixed with wine and dead flowers and crooked talk! He wondered if he would ever be good at it, as Archytas wanted him to be; and then he wondered what the rest of the Class were doing now, sleeping out on the hills most likely, Eurotas away below shimmering under the moon. . . . He pulled himself up sharply: no good watching if he didn't attend to what they were saying too. Now there were three of them talking across to Archytas, trying to get a promise out of him; but he wouldn't! Oh, he was so much realer than all the rest of them put together, stronger, finer — I'm a lucky boy, thought Leon, very seriously, and it's worth the risk: even if the Elders didn't like me going, Lysander sent us, and it's what he says that counts; but I do wish we could come to the fighting part soon!

At last every one got up to go. The Spartans had to walk down to their lodgings near the harbour; they could not, of course, stay with Eupaides or any of his friends, as things stood; and besides, Archytas liked to be within sight of his ship and his unofficial guard, in case anything happened. Two of his own helots were ready at the door with torches to light him and Leon down; it was the coldest hour of night, the dawn wind blowing but no light yet in the east. As he went out, he turned to say something low to Eupaides, which his brother just caught: 'If

27

you would like to see Belesys yourself, let me know to-morrow.'

For a minute or so Alxenor considered sleepily who Belesys could be; then, realizing, he came suddenly awake. He had seen him once, and heard of him oftener, the queer silent Persian who had come to Poieëssa early that spring, and who now hardly ever stirred out of his house. His thoughts came as simply and clearly as water: Belesys was behind Archytas: just as he knew, and every one knew, that the Great King was behind Sparta, and building ships for her. And his brother was to be bribed. It would have to be a very big bribe because he had plenty of money already. But the Persians had more money than ten times all the tribute to Athens in ten years – when Athens was strongest. Yes, he thought, angry with himself now for having talked as he had to Leon, that is what comes of making friends with Sparta: sooner or later she brings in the barbarians. Then he went to bed without speaking to his brother again; Eupaides nearly called him back to laugh at him about it, but he was sleepy too.

The two Spartans stopped for a moment on the broad, paved quay that led towards their lodgings; they looked up over hundreds of roofs towards the citadel white in the moonshine. 'If once we could get a garrison in there – ' said Archytas, ' – no one could do anything down here.' He walked on; Leon was singing to himself; he moved as lightly as a dancer from shadow to shadow, and in the darkest of it, his feet never stumbled.

By and by the moon set, dawn rose white out of the

sea, and climbed up the eastward cliffs, and under all the leaves, and into all the little valleys, and spread itself right over Poieëssa.

A day passed, and another day; and very early in the morning of the next the Spartans were running races on the narrow lonely strip of beach between sea and cliff. Leon won over any short distance, but on the mile Archytas beat him by several yards. Afterwards, flat on their backs in the shade, they smelt of sweat and olive oil. Archytas rolled over first and rubbed his cheek against Leon's shoulder: 'The worst of races is that I can't see you unless you're beating me.' Then he got up, pulled the boy up too, by one hand, and kissed the back of his neck. Leon wriggled away, saying his beard tickled, and began throwing stones into the sea, jumping from one foot to the other to watch his ducks-and-drakes. He was sunburnt brown all over, and his hair, bleached light and hanging loose under the fillet, danced up and down across his back as he threw. Archytas was thirty years old, just out of school as they thought of it back in Sparta, tall and square with a big head, but able, through his early training, to move as quickly as the boy.

They began to throw seriously at a mark on the sand, first with stones, then with the light spears they had left beside their clothes. Leon, for lack of practice, was less skilful at this. He missed so often that his hand began to shake and he got worse still; ashamed, he stopped and watched Archytas.

The sun was well up by now; the splashing of the little waves grew gentler in the growing heat.

Archytas glanced once at the shadows, and then
called Ladas sharply to bring the clothes – his best.
The old helot brought them over, with the oil flask
carried carefully, and he put them on, a round bronze
brooch to fasten the scarlet tunic on each shoulder,
and the white wool of the himation falling over it
to below his knee. Besides that, he wore sandals,
and on his head a gold laurel wreath which King
Agis had given him after the battle of Cynossema. 'I
wish you hadn't to go so soon,' said Leon; 'must
you?'

'The Ephors have given me work to do: would you
sooner they had given it to some other man?'

'No.'

'Good: then I go where love bids me.'

'But when shall I see you again? Will Belesys be
there to-day too? He always is when I want to be
with you.'

'Patience, Leon. I want you to stay till the shadow
is round to that stone over there. I'll leave you the
spears: to-morrow you must be able to throw
straight. Go on with your running too. When the
shadow's there, come back to breakfast. You may
find me; it depends on Eupaides.'

'Very well. Oh, will you see Alxenor?'

'Hardly. But you've been talking to him lately: do
you like him?'

'He's silly – silly about Moiro. But I do like him.
I want him to wrestle with me; I think I'd throw
him.'

'You ought to be ashamed if you couldn't. Spartan
against Ionian! There are the spears, Leon: off

with you.' He turned to the cliff path, and Ladas
followed him, only leaving the oil for Leon. By now
the sand was hot and crusted in the sun. Archytas
stopped a moment at the top of the cliffs to watch, his
white and scarlet sharp and bright against the bushes.
Below him Leon was throwing the spears, as he had
been told.

The shadow crept slowly across towards the stone.
Every now and then Leon looked at it; but he was
used to being left alone and hungry. That was being
a free Spartan: only slaves and pigs were allowed to
herd together with full bellies in the shade! He did
part of his running at the edge of the sea, liking the
splash of the water up his bare, hot body, and the
pleasant uncertainty of his footing; but then he
thought it was better training to run on the dry sand,
so he came out. When he was throwing by himself,
he put his whole mind into it, so that by and by he
found he was hitting the mark nearly every time.
Then he made a smaller mark, as small as the space
between back-plate and breast-plate in somebody's
armour; but that was much harder to hit. The
shadow crossed over at last. But he wanted to be
very fair; he stayed on another little time, and danced
by himself on the beach, an old, very formal dance,
made by Alkman, a poet two hundred years dead,
every step, light though it seemed, thought out long
ago and perfectly woven into the rhythm so that the
bodies of all those young, naked dancers should
become something else, a more Divine whole. And
Leon sang as he danced, imagining other boys all
round him. His voice echoed from the cliffs:

31

'Who will race with me?
Where are we going?
Oh my cousin,
The wind is blowing –
Keep the pace with me!
Hark to the crying:
In windy weather the Hawks go flying!

Oh my fleet one,
Your eyes are bluer
Than the flashing fisher,
The wave bedewer.
Dear and sweet one,
Far are we hieing:
Over the hills the Hawks go flying!

The Dawn has known us,
And heart of cunning
The red-eyed hill wolf
Has marked us running.
Ways are shown us
By Those Un-dying:
Through storm and fire the Hawks go flying!'

Suddenly, on his right, an eagle flew out of the
cliff rocks, and up, and cried once; he ran with all
his might to see it better and to follow its rapid
flight; it seemed to turn towards the city. He wished
he could read signs, but he knew this must mean
something good, so he caught up his rough cloak
and hurried off, up the path and over the sheep pas-
tures back to their lodgings by the harbour. He

32

rather enjoyed walking alone through the streets,
best of all the fish-market which was very pro-
Athenian; they were most unlikely to attack him
unless they happened to be very drunk or excited,
but there was always just the chance, and anyhow
it was fun swaggering through with a spear on one's
shoulder, seeing them all scowl!

Ladas met him at the door of the lodgings, pulled
him in, and bolted it again. 'What's the news?' he
asked. 'Who's been frightening you, Ladas?'
'Quiet!' whispered the slave, 'the Persian's in the
back room, and there's a man locked into the cellar.'
'Why?' 'He brought a message. Ask the Persian if
you want to know.' 'Tell me yourself.' 'I wasn't
meant to hear; Archytas wouldn't want to think I
knew. The Persian is waiting in there: look, I'll
bring you a fresh tunic – I'll bring you the cloak
with the purple border if you'll stay a minute.' 'No,
I'm going as I am. I won't dress up for any barbarian. You keep watch, Ladas.'

He swung back the curtain and walked into the
room beyond, the spears still in his hand. Belesys
rose from his seat and bowed low; Leon nodded back
angrily, almost sure of the Persian's mockery. The
room was stuffy after the open, and darkened by
thick hangings; Belesys was dark too, and the hilt
of his dagger was one big, polished stone, black or
purple, you never quite knew which. His robe was
of some glowing Indian stuff embroidered all round
with little rows of stiff figures; it covered his arms to
the wrists, and his hands were thin and sinewy, and
the skin pale underneath. Below the pointed cap of

33

golden stuff, his eyes were black and moving; every day his beard was curled and scented: fine drops of oil ran slowly down it all the time, so that Leon could not help staring. Why can't we do our own work, he thought, we Spartan and freemen? And not have to ask any barbarians into our counsels, with their fine clothes and money bags, trying to make Hellas dance what the King pipes! But he knew Archytas didn't like him to say that even when they were alone; Archytas was not so sure as he was that Right and the Twin Gods of Sparta were sure to triumph by themselves in the end.

Belesys stood, fingering the jewel that hung round his neck, and smiled. 'Well, young man,' he said, 'you know the news?'

'Ladas said you could tell me: that's why I came.'

'And I thinking it was just to do me honour!' He stopped suddenly, and Leon blushed but could not think of anything to say. Then he went on again in his gentle, scarcely accented Greek, pleasanter than Leon's own Doric. 'My man Pigres was down on the quay early; he is a good servant. He saw a boat making fast, and out comes the captain, all in a hurry. "Do you know," says Pigres, "who'll pay you best for your news?" and takes him along to my house. And I here. Archytas shuts him up in the cellar without by your leave or with your leave. Never mind, I shall give the poor man good pay to make up for it.'

'Yes, but the news?'

'Oh, to be sure. A battle. You know Lysander had

34

your fleet in Ephesus harbour? All hauled up high
and dry. Well, the Athenians came out of Notium
just along the coast to row past and laugh at him –
so like them. But they were caught: he launched and
after them, and got them scattered. He has taken
fifteen ships.'

'Oh good, good! What else?'

'That was the only sure part of the man's news; the
rest was rumour. He says the Athenian admiral was
not there himself. That all happened yesterday.
And you may thank Cyrus for it, young man,
giving your sailors extra pay and getting half the
Athenian fleet deserting!'

'Yes, I suppose so. But why doesn't Archytas
want it known?'

'He will want it known – in his own time: when
everything is arranged.'

'Is he up with Eupaides now?'

'Very likely.'

'Oh. Well, I shall see you later, Persian.'

He ran out of the room, and into Ladas, who caught
him by the arm: 'You are not to go out! Archytas
said you were not to go out!' He pulled his arm
away, and hit Ladas as hard as he could; the old man
grumbled at him reproachfully, rubbing the sore
place: 'Well, would you rather take your orders
from the Persian than from me? I can't help what
Archytas said. I'd let you run out and be killed as
much as you like, and then I'd not be black and blue
half the time from your great fists.' 'You shouldn't
have grabbed me like that: it's your fault.' 'You'd
have been out of the house if I hadn't, and then what

35

would Archytas have said? I've got your breakfast
ready too.' 'Oh well, let's have it,' said Leon.
He suddenly realized how ravenously hungry he
was.

CHAPTER THREE

'Then there were heroes, Joan of Arc,
Nelson of course, and William Tell,
And Johnny Phipps who found a shark
Inside his bath and didn't yell . . .'
— Chesterton

THE morning was half over by now; all across
the island the sheep and goats were beginning
to turn from their grazing and lie down in the
shade; there was no wind at all, Up at the farm old
Thrasykles was stamping about in the yard, waiting
for his daughter; he had been ready nearly an hour,
but as to Moiro — what could the girl find to be
doing all this time? Thrassa ran out with a basket on
her arm, and over to the hen house; Thrasykles
shouted at her: 'Not got those eggs yet? You look
sharp, my girl, or I'll give you a taste of stick!'
Thrassa grinned and ran on; she didn't mind. Moiro
came out in another minute, a wide, light veil of red
stuff wrapped all round her and over her head, and a
broad straw hat on the top of it. 'I haven't kept you
waiting, father?'
'Waiting! Oh, not more than half the day! Waiting, she says!'
'Oh, father! Thrassa, father's cross; he says we've
kept him waiting! We can't have, can we? — we've
been so quick!'
'Holy Artemis, I wonder what you call slow! Have
you said good-bye to your mother?'
'Mother says you aren't to drink too much!' Both
the women laughed, Moiro first, then Thrassa when
she saw her master was taking it in good part. 'Ooh,

37

it is a long way,' sighed Moiro, as the dust rose in the path.

'Bless the girl, she'll want to ride next!'

'When Alxenor marries me I shall have a white mule. You see if I don't, father. A white mule with a red saddle cloth!'

Thrasykles only grunted and stumped on ahead; the two girls followed him, their veils fluttering behind them. Both had baskets on their arms, Thrassa one on her head as well, presents of eggs and herbs and vegetables for Thrasykles' sister Pyrrhé, whose husband was a ship-builder down in the city. They whispered to one another, and giggled and changed baskets, and wondered who they'd see. When they got nearer the town Moiro drew her veil further over her face, and left it to Thrassa to answer back when a man called after them; both of them kept a good look-out for new fashions on other women. Chromon met them in the market-place, and shepherded them along to his uncle's house, glaring at anyone who tried to jostle his sister. The girls walked as slowly as they could, trying to see all the life and bustle of the town, but Moiro in her heart was just a little frightened and glad to have her men-folk with her. It was months since she had last seen so many people.

When they came to the house, Pyrrhé was there to welcome her niece and exclaim over the baskets. 'What lovely onions and lettuce! And you've actually brought me some curly greens, you clever girl, just the one thing my old Glaukias is always clamouring for! And what a little treasure of a cheese! You made it yourself? Better and better. And I hear you've been getting yourself a husband now. Why you were still sucking your fingers when I saw you last! Come along in, my dear, and see your cousins, and tell us all about it!'

They went into the women's part of the house, laughing and talking, and her girl cousins and one or two neighbours' wives began a quick fire of jokes about Alxenor, and the little five-year-old boy ran about and pinched her legs, and nearly understood why they were all so pleased. Then Pyrrhé opened a chest and took out a thin linen dress, all tied round with blue ribbon to keep the pleats in place; she unfolded it lovingly. 'Fresh from the loom, Moiro, and every stitch of trimming my own.' She spread out the hem with its border of formal little trees in cross-stitch. 'That's more than my own girls have, but then they're not going to be married yet – lazy hussies!' Moiro threw her arms round her aunt's neck: 'Oh, it is nice to be here!'

Chromon and Thrasykles, with Glaukias, the tarry-handed old ship-builder, walked out and back towards the market-place. The streets were full of people going up and down, and most of them knew one another, and stopped to talk or quarrel or help with a bargain. Glaukias had been sitting most of the day as a juryman, but now the trials were over till next week. He explained how they'd fined a man for throwing stones at an Athenian oil-dealer – a good, stiff fine they'd given him. 'And quite right too,' said Glaukias, 'we've got to encourage trade overseas; if the man hadn't been drinking he wouldn't have done it, the fool! One of Mikon's sons, a rough lot, those stone-cutters, always up to some mischief.'

A young man in cuirass and high boots, with a sword and orange-crested helmet, came up and spoke to Chromon. He was one of the garrison on the citadel, down for the afternoon to buy food and wine and see his friends.

'Do you ever catch the Spartans spying about up there?' Chromon asked him suddenly.

The young man laughed: 'No fear! They're not so bad, though, those Spartans, at least Philermos says so. Archytas looks cleanish anyway!'

But Chromon was frowning: 'Philermos . . . Now listen: what sort of a man is he? I don't know much of him, but you've served under him six months.'

'You're going mad, Chromon! Why do you want to know? He's like most captains; out to make a bit over the rations, but I don't blame him. He's a poor man like us!'

'Poor, is he. Poor men are easy to bribe.'

'What's the matter with you, Chromon? There's nothing wrong with Philermos or any of us! Do you think Archytas is going to try for the citadel with his boy and his pack of helots? His ship's sailing to-morrow!'

Then Glaukias remembered that he had to go over to the rope-walk and see how his cables were going. Almost all the harbour side of the market-place was taken up by the rope making – the strong smell of flax. Chromon followed them there, and watched the twisting of all the dozens of ropes till his eyes ached. 'Uncle,' he said, when they were going back, 'do you ever see the Spartans?' 'Spartans!' – he spat with emphasis – 'I don't have any truck with Spartans!' 'I wish every one was the same.' 'Oh, you've got Spartans on the brain! Maybe you're right, though. Get yourself talked about if you go on with it long enough. When shall we see you leading the Assembly – eh?'

Across at the other side, under the colonnade where the booksellers and jewellers lived, Alxenor and a friend were arguing about poetry and hunting among the lateliest-arrived books, unrolling the end of a scroll just to get the taste of it, hearing the fresh paper crackle pleasantly under their fingers. The bookseller showed them Euripides' latest, his *Orestes*, played last year in Athens. 'It's all very well,' said Alxenor, ' but you won't find a man like that in Sparta!' His friend grunted disapprovingly: 'Man! Woman, you mean!' He was rich, and pro-Spartan at the moment; besides, he had been brought up to consider Aeschylus the very last word in poets, and had never seen fit to alter his opinion.

All at once Alxenor saw Chromon, ran to the edge of the colonnade and shouted across to him; Chromon heard, shouted back, and made his way over through the crowd. 'Come away to somewhere quiet,' he said. 'I don't know who every one is here.'

Alxenor stared at him: 'But you do know! There's only Amphias and –'

'Oh, I know their names. But that's not all there is. I hope I know you, Alxenor.'

'My heart's yours, Chromon, and has been these dozen years. What's troubling you?'

'The Spartans: they've been here too long. Can't

41

you find out anything? Don't you see them with your brother?'

'I see Leon sometimes; he's rather a beauty.'

'There, that's it. They're poisoning you too!'

'Chromon, don't be a fool! I'm not in love with Leon, but he's a nice boy, Spartan or not, and we never talk about politics.'

Chromon was shivering a little, though it was the middle of summer; he caught hold of Alxenor so tight that his fingers left red marks: 'I know there's something happening; I can feel it. And I'm not the only one! I tell you, if Archytas doesn't go to-morrow, he'll go the next day with a knife through his ribs! Why haven't you been down to the meetings this week?'

'I don't know. I keep on thinking about Moiro; everything else seems stupid now. I want her so.'

'Then you ought to be with us! The others won't believe you aren't like your brother if you stop away. Can't you see there's danger? If you don't, the rest of us do! We've sent a message to Samos, to the Admiral – that'll stir things up!'

Alxenor drew his breath in sharply: 'My God, though, it will! If you get Alkibiades down on us – Chromon, are you sure – oh, I wish I'd been there! What did you say? When did it go?'

'Three days ago: the *Sea Hawk* took it – to say we've a brood of rats here!'

'And the answer?'

'Any time now. But – oh, we may have sent it too late! I don't know what's happening! Here's one thing: what is that Persian doing? Can't you see?

I tell you, he wants to make us all slaves like he is, put us under the Great King!'

He stopped, panting, and Alxenor loosed himself: 'No, Chromon. You're angry, you're saying things with no meaning. The Spartans are Hellenes, and whatever they want it's no part of it to take freedom from other Hellenes. The Persians don't want us either, they know they can't hold the Islands. What they hate is Athens, and you know yourself Athens began it when she tried to take their Egypt. You must see both sides, Chromon, if you're to see fairly, and you must see fairly to see clear.' Already he was feeling all the calmer for having talked it out a little; Chromon was frightening at first; he went on in the same way: 'After all, the War's been going on for as long as one can remember, and there have been plenty of better times than this if the Spartans had wanted to do anything. You make them out all black, but really – '

Suddenly his arm was gripped again – harder: 'Alxenor, are you with me or against me?' No chance, then, of Chromon taking the middle way.

'You know I'm with you. But why are you so angry? Dear, I'll do anything you want.'

'Moiro is with my uncle Glaukias; if you choose to see her, you can. Meet me to-night at the corner by the Potteries. Only, you must have something to tell.'

'Chromon, I can't understand! Am I to spy on them in my brother's house?'

'If you want to see my sister, and to show me for certain that you're a democrat.'

43

'Suppose they catch me spying? Can't we be honest?'

'Yes, if they are. Not otherwise. Will you do it?'

'Tell me why you're all on edge! If you have sent that message off – and God knows if it isn't out of the frying-pan into the fire! – what is there to trouble you?'

'Listen. And keep to the middle of the street: there may be ears behind every wall. It was last night; I was asleep on the roof. I woke up. It was little past midnight – I haven't slept since then – so I started counting stars to go to sleep again. There seemed to be a new star low over the sea: I looked at it again. It was glowing and dimming like a live thing. Then I knew it was a signal fire on Chios. That's too far off to tell one the news for certain even on a clear night. But something has just happened. Another thing too: this morning Belesys went into the Spartans' house with a stranger from the sea, and neither of them has come out yet.'

Alxenor frowned, considering it all, beginning to look at it through Chromon's eyes. 'I'll see what I can do. I think Archytas is up at my brother's.'

'And Leon?'

'God knows: I don't. Anyway, Leon's nothing to do with it. I'll be there to-night. And you promise me – Does she sleep alone? Will you tell her?'

'I'll see. I'm not sure. Oh, go now, Alxenor, try to help me and the City!'

Alxenor knew without asking that Archytas was with his brother; there were half a dozen oddments hanging about the door, talking their nasty Doric.

44

One or two were decent looking young men enough, Perioeci perhaps, or some Laconian folk, well armed and well set-up. They barely made way for him to pass, hardly returned his greeting. The tallest of them was Damagon, son of a Spartan father and helot mother, stupid-minded and quick-bodied. The rest were helots, oldish mostly; but Alxenor thought of them all now as a guard of soldiers, ready to stick him in the ribs at a word from Archytas. He asked one of their own slaves where his brother was, and heard he was in his room and did not wish to be disturbed. 'Oh, with the Spartans?' 'I couldn't say, sir.'

He wondered what his best plan was: perhaps to pretend he had come to think like his brother and so be let into their counsels? They wouldn't believe him, he was bad at pretending. To try and find out about it all through Leon? No, Leon was not to come into it anyhow; besides, there wasn't time. Well, he thought, I must just see. The door of his brother's room was over at the far side of the court; he could see a couple of those Laconians standing outside. His own room was round the corner on his left. He went into it: at least, no one suspected him yet of wanting to spy. Once inside, with the door left half open, he could see anyone crossing the court. Suddenly he thought of a magnificent new plan: after Archytas was gone, he would go and appeal to his brother not to let himself be dragged into ruining the city! And his brother would burst into tears and everything would come right. And when Alkibiades sent, it would be all over and no one any the worse except the Spartans, and even so they might be sent off secretly, Leon at least –

Then he heard voices and listened intently; he saw them crossing the court, his brother, Tolmaios, Archytas, and – with them – Philermos, the captain of the citadel. Said Philermos, in his loud, cheery voice (and was that little bag he was stuffing into the fold of his cloak full of Persian gold?), 'So next time we meet it'll be good morning, won't you walk in!' Archytas answered 'Yes.' And the way he said it meant full stop. Then his brother spoke a little anxiously: 'Don't go out together. You first, Philermos.'

This decided him. He would speak to Eupaides and get him to tell everything; if that failed, go to Chromon with what he knew. But somehow he was sure he could move his brother, he had it all so clear, the words were bursting out of his eager mind already! At last he heard Archytas going too, he and all his people. His brother was walking back alone across the far side of the court, his hands clasped behind him, looking up at the swallows' nests under the tiles of the low roof; a bird flashed by his head and he smiled at it. Alxenor got up to go to him.

All his life afterwards, when Alxenor remembered that next five minutes, his whole body would tighten, fists clenched, face twisted up to drive it out. The thought of it would come suddenly into his mind when he was quite happy, in the middle of a party, say; then for a little time he could say nothing to his neighbour, food or wine only sickened him till

46

the memory was beaten back, till he could crush
down that self somewhere in his brain which had
so silently reminded him. But sometimes, if it came
to him in the very early morning, when everything
is terribly grey and clear, he would have to think
it out, sentence by sentence, till he could almost
hear his brother's laughter ringing in his ears. How
he had gone out into the sun, his head all swirling
with beautiful words, and stood in front of Eupaides;
and then, his brother had just looked at him,
twisting up one corner of his mouth; and the beautiful words stopped coming. Oh, why, why had he
gone on after that? Was it just that he wanted so
much to be what he pictured himself? Or did he feel
that for once anyway he must show his brother the
other side? He remembered how Eupaides had stood
quite still all the time with his arms hardly swinging
a bit, and his lips only just smiling; and for one lovely
moment he thought it was all right, he had succeeded,
he could go back and tell Chromon how he had
saved Poieëssa from the Spartans! Only then his
brother had laughed. And the whole dear plan had
tinkled down in pieces round his ears. And the
laughing went on and on and on and he just stayed
there, and felt as if he was shrivelling like a drop of
water in the sun.

He scarcely heard Eupaides speak: 'You're too
good for this world, my child!' Only, seeing him
beckon, he jumped round like an animal, and
Damagon hit him under the jaw, and his hands
sprawled in the air helplessly as he fell back. It was
all a dream for ten minutes; he let them do what

47

they liked. Then there was silence and darkness,
and at least the laughter was over.

He found he was lying on his bed in his own room,
and sat up, painfully because his head seemed so
much heavier than usual. No, he was not hurt,
scarcely bruised. What had happened last? Oh, if
the ache in his head would only stop! He lay flat
again, his eyes shut, sweating heavily till the pain
eased and he felt less sick. There was a bowl of
water on the ground beside him; he drank. One
tooth was loose and his jaw was bleeding a little.
Again he turned sick and lay quite still.

Outside in the courtyard the swallows skimmed
across and across undisturbed; Eupaides was not in
his house any more that day. The town lay still, with
shadows stretching from one house wall to the next
as the late afternoon wore on; at the end of some
shadowed, downward sloping tunnel of street, there
might be just a hand's breadth of distant sea, unbelievably bright and glistening. After Archytas had
left Eupaides he went straight down towards the
harbour and his own lodgings; the others followed
him at a little distance. His head was high and his
eyes bright; he looked as if he might have been
garlanded. There were a few people in the streets
he went along, and they made way for him as though
he were a ship moving through waves. He saw them
himself, too, as the winged Victory on the prow of a
strong galley might look out on to the sliding waters;
there they were, a coloured, moving background, not
very real, not at all important. He saw one or two
men who called themselves his friends; he knew why

48

each of them wanted an oligarchy, he knew how
easily or hardly each could be bought. At a corner
he saw Chromon leaning against a wall with his
legs crossed, watching him. He saw a pretty boy
run out of a shop across the street. But beyond them
all, and far more solid, there was a little picture of
an oldish man with a broad face and merry eyes:
stooping over a camp fire to warm his hands, and
talking . . . so that everything came right . . .
when one was younger and found life difficult sometimes . . .

He knocked on the door and Ladas opened quickly;
behind him stood Leon with a wreath of the small-
leaved wild laurel on his head, and another in his
hands. He stooped for the boy to crown him, and
they went together into the little courtyard of the
house, and Archytas sat down on a bench and Leon
stood in front of him. 'It was a great fight at Notium,'
he said, and Leon: 'I wish we'd been there.' He
spoke again. 'It may mean the end is coming, Leon,
after all these years. Think. We Spartans are masters
in our own land; there are just a few of us over all
the others; because of our birth and because of the
way we live, they are under us for ever. It may come
to be so with all Hellas: the Dorians shall conquer
once more, they will lead . . . against the barbarians
again perhaps. Yes, a great fight surely. Have you
spoken to the man yourself?'

'You told Ladas not.'

'Of course. Well, the man gave me the news; he
had been out tunny-fishing in the bay and had seen
it all himself. He was quite close when the Athenian

49

triremes, that had come to make a mock of us, were caught by the first of Lysander's fleet: the ship with a red swan painted on her. He saw the captain of that ship leap and board, first man of all to draw blood in the battle; then a spear through his heart. He saw the swan on his shield. Leon, you know who that was.'

'I think so. Was it your father?'

'Yes.'

Ladas, who had been listening, crouched down and began to sob. The man was dead whom he had never thought could die, dead in this way that made him greater, more than ever his master. Leon moved closer to Archytas and kissed him, saying: 'May we die that way when the time comes.'

Archytas put his arm round Leon and went on: 'Afterwards he saw those same Athenian ships taken; he saw their beaks sawn off. My father has been a soldier for thirty-five years.' He stood up. 'I have to think of to-morrow. Where is Belesys?'

CHAPTER FOUR

'He who sins aught
Sins more than he ought;
But he who sins nought
Has much to be taught.
Beat or be beaten,
Eat or be eaten,
Be killed or kill;
Choose which you will.'
- *The Erewhonian Oracle*

Alxenor opened his eyes. His head was still aching, but not impossibly; he could stand up now, cautiously, without being sick. It was quite dark in the room. He tried the door to begin with, but couldn't move it; they must have fastened it somehow on the outside during those first five minutes; there was an opening above, but very small, with a bar across it, even if he could have climbed. Looking up at it, he could see nothing, no stars even because the underside of the eaves came between. He listened for quite a long time, but there was no sound to tell him what was happening. It might be any hour of the night; perhaps Chromon was not yet at the corner by the potteries, or perhaps he had been waiting hours, or was gone, believing that his friend had betrayed him. Alxenor kept thinking about that for quite a long time, even while he was really trying hard to plan his escape.

He shouted as loud as he could at the crack of the door, then listened; footsteps shuffled towards him across the court outside, old Manes the porter, who wheezed through to him: 'Now, sir, don't take on like that; it won't be long.'

51

'Let me out, do!' he pleaded back; then, with a sudden idea, 'I'm as sober as an empty bucket now.'

'Ah, sir, but were you drunk before? No, I couldn't take it on myself to do it.'

Alxenor put his mouth right against the crack: 'You know my belt with the gold clasps like lions? Let me out and you shall have it.'

'That doesn't sound as if you were sober, sir! But I can't take it.'

'My silver cups, then? My ring with the sardonyx? Oh, Manes, you've carried me all about the house when I was little – don't be a brute beast now!'

'There now, I'm as sorry as can be, but your brother said I wasn't to touch the door, even, short of a fire. Come now, it won't be beyond another day, and you'll be best out of all the goings-on, as I hear.'

'What goings-on? Oh, Manes, tell my brother – No, don't. Is he in?'

'No, sir, and that's all the questions I can answer. You go to sleep.'

'But, Manes –'

'No, that's all. You've plenty of water by you; I saw to it myself. It's near dawn now. And I'm not coming back, no, not if you shout the house down.'

Near dawn. Manes was going back to his own bed by the house door: there, the footsteps were quiet. Near dawn already. The guards at the citadel changed just after dawn. He groped about in the black room, trying to remember, through the headache that was nearly knocking him down, where everything was. Clearly they had taken his sword and

52

spears, even the little hunting knife from the shelf over his bed. He thought a moment: if Manes was really not going to come for any noise – He shouted again, and threw a stone throwing-disk he had against the door. Nothing happened. Then he stooped down and began pulling at the bronze foot of his bed. It tore away from the wooden framework with a splintering rasp; he balanced it in his hand, then went to the far wall, felt his way to the right distance from it, and struck with the bronze claw. At once the plaster splattered away, filling the room with dust; he cleared it off the wall for about two feet each way, then came on the layer of rubble underneath. Here the bronze began to bend; he had to straighten it out under his foot every second stroke. Fortunately he had come on a place where it was rather loose and fell away fairly easily; he had to stop every now and then, and hold his head; or drink some more water. He knew there was a butcher's shop at the other side which would be empty now, as the butcher himself slept outside the City on his own holding; the shutter would open from inside. All at once he stumbled forward as the head of his pick went through the plaster. He shoved with both hands, and a big piece of wall fell out. Before he went through the hole he took whatever he might need from his room; looking up at the opening over the door, he saw it was misty grey outside instead of black. When he did go through, he tore his tunic badly on a piece of rubble.

There was a dim light in the butcher's shop coming through between the boards of the shutters. He put

53

his hand on to something cold and flabby and started round; but it was only a piece of meat. A sheep's carcass behind him was horribly luminous, and he stumbled over piles of hides; a kid tethered in one corner struggled at its rope and bleated at him. The shutters had a new kind of catch; he shoved at them till his hands were sore, but they would not move for a long time, then, quite suddenly, fell open.

The fresh air in the street hit Alxenor delightfully in the face after the thick smell of meat and plaster. He jumped down. There was such a dazzle it seemed as if the sun was rising just at the end of the street; no one was about; every shutter was up. He ran into the heart of the dazzle, straight for the market-place.

He ran through the Street of the Coppersmiths and down Red Walls Passage with the plaster flying out of his hair; still there was no one awake. He ran past the House of the Maidens, and in Tanners' Market he ran into Chromon, himself running up, white and sweating, with drawn sword and full armour. 'Chromon, Chromon!' he gasped, breathless. 'The citadel! They've bribed Philermos!' One moment Chromon stopped and took him by the shoulders and shook him like a child: 'Too late, you fool! Look!' Then he looked up the straight lane that led to the foot of the citadel, and just in that instant a man in armour fell from the top, and turned in the air like a toy, and caught on a rock near the bottom. 'Get arms! Follow!' cried Chromon, and bounded on. And after him ran, shouting and pray-

ing, the head of the mob, young men, poor men, with
spears and swords and clubs. He shrunk into a doorway to let them by, but a man with a broken nose
saw him: 'You swine!' he yelled. 'You drunken
bastard! Where's your brother?' And then a dozen
of them together: 'Where's your brother – your
brother – you swine, your brother?' Faces grey and
twisted with hate. 'Up there!' he cried, throwing
his arms across his face, and felt the sting of a thrown
stone. As the last ones passed he stumbled out, and
there was the citadel already glinting with little
swords!

There was no place to get arms nearer than the big
market; he ran now a little unevenly; his head was
nearly overbalancing him. I must look as if I'd made
a night of it, he thought, that's what they meant.
Ten minutes back the streets had been empty; now
already men were pouring out, and here and there a
woman half dressed and shrieking, or a little boy
with a whistle. He shouted the news to every man he
knew for a democrat: 'Quick, up! The Spartans are
in the citadel!'

The armourer's house: he banged at the door: –
'Sword and shield! Quick!' and rushed for the chests
where he knew they were kept.

The armourer caught hold of him: 'Alxenor, stop!'

'I'll pay you later!'

'No, no, but haven't you heard? Lysander has
smashed the Athenian fleet at Notium and Alkibiades
is killed!'

He stopped dead. 'Oh Zeus. The message. Who
says so?'

'A man came – just now. If Athens is beaten we can't stop the Spartans here! Let them take the citadel or what they like now, or we'll have the whole lot down on us! Alxenor, for God's sake – they'll make us slaves!'

'Chromon's there – I must go – I don't believe it – who was the man?'

'A stranger. I tell you, if you don't believe it, you're the only one! They've killed an Athenian already!'

At that, Alxenor caught up the best sword he saw, and a light shield, and rushed out wildly. The armourer slammed to the door after him, and shot the bolts, and listened, shivering, to the rising noise outside.

Alxenor had gone out by the other door on to the market-place, and there the crowd was tossing and scattering like hail on a corn-field, and beyond, in the rope-walk – fire. That checked him a moment. ' What is it?' he yelled to a man beside him over the din of voices. 'Burning out the democrats – that's it!' Alxenor turned on the man: 'You're poor, you're a democrat! Stop them! Stand fast for liberty!' But the man only stared with a burst of laughter. Then Alxenor saw how the crowd had changed round after the news of Notium; now it was all for showing the Spartans which side it was on: down with Athens, away with democracy, away with Chromon! One man would only be killed uselessly in that wild beast fight down in the market; whoever held the citadel had the city. Again he plunged round and up to join Chromon, and kill – and kill – his brother.

He saw Damagon. He meant to pay that blow of his back, kill a Spartan first; but Leon and three others came round the corner too, and as he hesitated, Leon shouted across at him: 'Oh, Alxenor! We're spreading the news! Lysander's beaten the Athenian fleet and we have your citadel! They're burning all the houses down by the potteries!' The potteries . . . last night . . . Moiro. His voice jumped: 'What, looting the shops?' 'Yes, and the women!' Leon gave a jolly, boy's laugh and came on down the street. Could he possibly not know what had happened last night? Damagon was pulling at his cloak, going to tell him! 'Leon!' called Alxenor, 'my girl's down there. Will you help me?' 'Get her away? Yes! Damagon, be quiet! I don't care what Alxenor's politics are – he's a gentleman and you're not!'

Alxenor sheathed his sword and pressed his two hands against his head: which was the nearest way? 'Whose house is Moiro in?' asked Leon. 'With her uncle Glaukias, the ship-builder.' The boy whistled: 'Old Glaukias that every one knows was for Athens! He'll get it hot. We'd best hurry, Alxenor.' He began to run, his cloak swinging out behind him, and Alxenor ran beside, barely keeping up till they got to a more crowded place; but even here all made way for Leon, and they got on fast. He spoke as he ran, over his shoulder: 'I thought you'd be in this show with Chromon. I'm glad you weren't, Alxenor.' For a few minutes Alxenor had only been thinking about Moiro, making a horrible picture of a house on fire, the crackling and screaming, a great mob of men bursting in, catching her – Now, suddenly,

57

he thought of Chromon again, and asked, panting:
'Did you see him?' 'No,' said Leon, 'not near my
gate anyway.' Something else was added to the
picture now, Chromon dead on the Citadel, tumbling
backwards down the rock, like that man he'd seen
earlier.

All at once they smelt burning; the wind brought
down on them a great puff of hot, blinding smoke.
And then they were into the mob, tearing their way
through with drawn swords. On their right a couple
of fish stalls had been knocked over and looted;
half a dozen women were still scrambling for the
great slippery flat-fish tumbled into the gutter. The
potteries themselves were blazing; no one could
come near. Alxenor saw one of the potters, an old
man with sore eyes, his beard singed half off, standing
at the edge of the crowd; quite suddenly he gave
a shrill cry and darted towards the fire, but before
he got near the wall, a long flame reached out and
licked him, and he fell.

They struggled through into the Street of the Ship-
builders. Here there was little fire yet, but the mob
was horribly ready for that or anything else; a few
were drunk, others all out to loot, others just to
smash, plenty of savages among them, Scythian and
Thracian slaves yelling and sweating with the rest.
One or two of the houses had been burst into, they
were throwing things out of the upper windows,
pieces of scarlet and purple stuff torn and kicked
through the dirt. And now for the first time there
were house-owners killed. A man with his throat
cut flapping his arms and bleeding all over the street.

Some girl screeching and screeching till one heard
nothing else – a child's voice almost.

Glaukias' house was still shut against them, quiet
it seemed, and cold. 'Is that it?' shouted Leon.
'Wait, I'll save it.' But as he spoke a little knot of
men burst forward against it, and the door splintered
inwards as if it was paper. A great yelling followed,
and a rush nearer that swept the whole door away.
Leon was in front of the rush, Alxenor behind, but
he stuck his sword into a man's shoulder and threw
him out of the way and got in too.

He had been inside the house twice before; for an
instant it stayed as he remembered it, then it was all
clawed at and changed like a shrieking face. The
women's rooms were right at the back, across a
second court; he called to Leon to follow him, and
slipped in between the blue wooden pillars. Glaukias
and his slaves were trying to hold the door to the
inner court; Alxenor began to explain: 'I've come
for Moiro – Moiro who's betrothed to me – to take
her somewhere safe –' At first Glaukias seemed not
to hear, still pointed his spear at the young man's
breast, then after a moment caught sight of Leon
behind. 'Ah,' he said, 'you've come with the
Spartans!' and bit his lip and thrust hard with the
spear. Alxenor leapt aside, raising his shield, but
even so it grazed his arm; and as he leapt the mob
at his back made another rush forward; it seemed to
sweep over Glaukias and his men; they were there
one moment, the next they were down underfoot,
broken like dry sticks. With a clutch at his heart,
Alxenor saw two women scurrying into the doorway

at the back, and a man after them; but Leon, running behind, jumped at the man, and pulled him over by the neck.

In the women's room there were three kneeling and clutching at their altar, some trying vainly to hide, and the youngest daughter standing quite still in the middle of the room but screaming as if she felt hands on her already. 'Moiro!' Alxenor cried, 'Moiro!' And suddenly saw her, flat and white against the wall, gripping the curtain with both hands. He ran to her, but old Pyrrhé rushed between and threw herself on him, clawing at his face; he caught at her arms, trying to be gentle, but she was as tough as an old ewe and kept him away for the time it took Leon to get past and catch hold of Moiro. He shouted 'I've got her!' and made for the door, and Pyrrhé, seeing a man at one of her own daughters, let go Alxenor, who tumbled over the little boy; he had been clutching at his mother's skirts, and been knocked down in the struggle. Alxenor picked him up – he would be safer anywhere away.

Leon was out in the women's court again, glaring about him, but no one interfered; they saw who he was. He held Moiro across him, one arm round her thighs, the other round her shoulders, pressing her hands against him; her eyes and mouth were wide open, but she was quite quiet; the handkerchief had slipped off her head and her loose hair blew across Leon's face. One moment the boy looked down at her, curiously, and Alxenor grew red with anger: 'Give her to me – she's mine!' He dropped the child and snatched at her – 'Moiro, my darling!' He saw her eyes flash into recognition, but she only trembled more; her teeth were chattering just at his ear.

The outer court was full of smoke already, and in the smoke they were attacked again. Moiro was whimpering now like a little dog. He had hold of her with his right arm, his left kept the shield before them both. Leon shouted and struck out into the smoke; they got through to the street.

'Where?' asked Leon, and Alxenor had no answer; he dare not take her to his brother's, and the farm was too far. Leon waited impatiently: 'Our lodgings then!' he said, and set off. Moiro had fainted; she lay over her lover's shoulder, heavy and soft, with her gold ear-rings dangling.

They hurried down by-streets and passages, out of the mob; the town seemed extraordinarily empty here. The Spartan wiped and sheathed his sword. 'I hope the child wasn't hurt,' he said. 'You were a fool to bring him out if you only meant to drop him.' Alxenor remembered that, guiltily; he said nothing; his head was making him giddy now, the cut arm hurt. He heard footsteps running after them, and turned; the slave-girl Thrassa caught them up, panting, her short dress torn and soiled. 'Oh, mistress!' she cried. 'Oh, little mistress!' and beat her breast, then, when she saw it was only a faint: 'Oh, master, master, don't hurt her!' She slipped in after them to the lodgings, and when Alxenor laid Moiro down, began to rub her hands and call to her softly, till she opened her eyes.

c

Leon took off his helmet, tossed his hair back, and splashed himself with the water Ladas brought, then put the helmet on again, and prepared to go. 'I'm for the citadel; Archytas or I may be down later, I'm not sure. Ladas will get you things.' One of his hands was covered with blood, which he carefully didn't wash. 'They used to despise me,' he grinned, 'thought I was nothing but Archytas' little friend: they don't now!' He turned at the door: 'Oh, Belesys is here – in case you don't like him! Good luck, Alxenor.'

Ladas brought out an armful of old cushions from the porter's room and laid them on the steps of the little court, out of the sun; Alxenor lay down all in a heap and shut his eyes; he listened for Moiro's voice, and at last heard it, very faint, from the room. He thought he had best leave her for a little, at least until he could decide what to do. He had definitely sided with the democrats; on that, he could expect nothing from his brother, unless – no, whatever happened, he was not going to beg for it! He would have to make his own way in the world now; Chromon would help. If everything went all right, that was. Oh surely the people would win in the end, turn out these Spartan foreigners, these beasts, from their own citadel! But what a place to be in and thinking that. Leon said the citadel was taken, meant it should stay taken. Leon was only a boy. It would be a pity if Chromon killed him, though. He turned over, groaning, and all at once felt damp fingers on his forehead and a cold sponge that smelt of vinegar. That was Ladas, tying up

62

his head, then the cut arm, as he was used to do for his own masters.

Alxenor let him do it, grateful for the feel of the wet linen; when he opened his eyes again, he found Thrassa was helping too. 'Oh' he said, 'is Moiro well?'

Thrassa looked mysterious, with a 'Hush!' and finger to her lips, till the helot had gone; then began in a loud whisper: 'Ah, sir, I thought it best; but she's taking it hard, poor lamb, very hard.'

'What, being here? With me?'

'Oh no, sir, not you – it was the other thing –'

'What do you mean? What was it you had to tell her? Thrassa, be quick!'

'I'm sure I hope I did right –'

'Oh Zeus, what is it, girl?'

He sat up suddenly and Thrassa drew back as if she was frightened, trying to spin out her importance as the bearer of exciting news: 'But about her father, sir, my poor dear master!'

'They've not killed Thrasykles?'

'Why, what a question to ask when it was your friend did it! Your foreign friend,' she added.

That was too much to believe all of a sudden: Leon . . . it changed everything. Thrassa made haste to give details, what she'd seen herself: a breast wound – he had no armour: just time to get him into a room before he died. It had happened in the smoke, coming out; Alxenor had been too blinded by it to see, and Thrasykles could never have seen it was him, only some men carrying his daughter off . . . and died thinking that. He got up slowly: 'I must go to her.'

63

He went in; he had never seen her so alone before, so much herself really, poor child, with swollen eyes, staring at him from the couch. Two of her shoulder brooches had fallen out on one side, and she did not even try to. veil herself, till Thrassa, from behind, threw a scarf she had found somewhere over the brown, straggling hair. Alxenor stood for a moment beside the couch, feeling infinitely guilty; but at the same time he could not keep from thinking that now she was here, in the same house, his at last, he would be able to look at her, touch her – he took her small hand in his: the little crescents on the nails, the veins just showing under the soft skin, rosy-brown with fine, tiny hairs standing out across the back and between the finger joints. She drew it away suddenly, and began to cry again. Alxenor had tears starting in his own eyes too; now they were together he did not know what to say to her, only 'Darling, darling,' and then, 'It was not my doing. I'm sorry, little darling, I'm so sorry for you.'

She answered nothing for a time, then sat up with the tears shining on her face: 'Alxenor, are you going to marry me?' She had never asked him a question before, hardly ever spoken to him directly; she gasped and blushed. 'You little thing!' he said. 'Of course. As soon as I can.' He kissed her face, clumsily, with a queer, sweet thrill, but she began to wail for her father, beating her breast and rocking to and fro; where her tears had fallen on to the dress it clung to her, and her bare feet were pressing against each other with grief. He wanted to kiss her again, but big Thrassa pushed him away, whisper-

64

ing to him that he might come back later, not now;
partly she saw that she had changed masters, and
wanted to start by getting a good hold over the new
one.

Now it must be an hour after noon, or more; the
airless little court was so packed with heat and sunshine he could hardly breathe. There was no sign
of the Spartans, even Ladas had disappeared somewhere. At last he called Thrassa and bade her take
every care of her mistress: 'My Moiro,' he said, not
quite daring to say 'my wife.' Then he took his
shield and sword and went out. The same ships
were still in the harbour in front, rocking very gently
up and down, but no one was marketing on the
quay side, the fish lay in heavy, sodden piles, there
were flies on the fruit. From there he looked up at
the citadel, as the Spartans had done before, but
could only tell that it was quite quiet. Three women
came slinking down past him, their cloak folds full
of stolen things from the shops. He kept away from
the Street of the Ship-builders, knowing that if he
went there he could do nothing, and it would all be
only worse than he thought of it. The rioting was
almost over, except just round the market-place;
most people had gone home, to sleep or patch up
their bruises; they would come out again in the
evening to talk it all over and wonder exactly what
they had been doing, and why.

Alxenor stopped at the corner of an empty street,
looking about him. It went up the hill, a shallow
V of rough cobbles with the gutter down its middle.
One side was almost black in shadow, the other so

bright with sun that colours hardly showed. As he looked, Chromon came out of a lane at the side and stood in the sun, leaning on a spear that had its head broken off. He was still in armour, but his helmet crest was mostly torn out and he had lost one of his greaves; his right leg was tied round with rags above the knee, and on his arms and face there were a few little gaping cuts with dry edges. As he leant on the spear he shook all over, his head moved jerkily; he began to pull at the bandages on his leg with one hand.

He looked straight across, there was a little sticky foam on the corner of his mouth. Alxenor felt his own knees beginning to shake in sympathy with that other shaking pain. He wondered when it had happened, where, and whether Chromon had tried to find his father yet. A warm wind puffed sickly between them, and the dry cabbage leaves rustled in the gutter. Then Chromon looked across and saw him, and began to tremble harder than ever. Alxenor ran forward, sorry as a woman, and put his hands on Chromon's shoulders, gently and strongly, trying to stop the trembling. 'Moiro is safe!' he said.

Then Chromon opened his mouth stickily to speak, and after a moment asked 'Where?'

Alxenor was a bad liar. 'She's — she's got Thrassa with her. I couldn't take her to the farm!'

But, 'Where?' said Chromon again.

'They're — at Archytas' lodgings. But — oh my dear, she's had no harm from them or me, nor will have!' Their faces were close together; he saw

66

Chromon's mouth turn down at the corners and his eyes narrow and full of tears; he felt him let go the spear-shaft with his right hand and begin to tug at his sword. He stepped back two quick paces, not able to believe it. 'Chromon!' he said, 'Chromon!' – trying to call to the old friendship between them that he knew . . . that was gone. 'Why?' he asked, 'Oh why? What have *I* done?'

Chromon answered him, still thickly, a word or two at a time: 'You never came. You left me. Enemy. Enemy. I hate you.' Then again: 'I went home. They've killed my father: the Spartans. You take Moiro there. Your friends.' A step at a time, leaning on the spear, his face sticking forward, breath coming hard, Chromon came across the street, out of the sun into the shadow, following Alxenor. He spoke between the steps. 'I loved you. I trusted you. You went to the Spartans: helped them. To hurt the City. Rich man.' He tried to spit at him, but his tongue was dry and sour.

Alxenor had backed away till he was right against the wall; he could hardly speak, he was so unhappy and surprised. 'Chromon, if you think that – I didn't betray you, I'm not friends with them! I'll bring her back!'

A pace away, Chromon stopped. 'Bring her back. Bring her back now. And never see her again.'

'Chromon!'

'Never. You shan't have her. I shan't give her to you. Never. Never. Never.'

'She's promised to me! She's mine! I saved her!'

67

'Bring her back.'

'Not if you say that – Chromon, you don't know what you're doing –' As Chromon lurched forward to strike, he caught his hand and dodged, and the sword only jabbed into the plaster of the wall. Chromon began to struggle with him, silently, in the empty street. They had often wrestled before, and mostly the elder had won, but now Alxenor found it only too easy. He was holding Chromon's arms and wondering how to end it, when suddenly Chromon made a great effort, arching himself forward, and bit Alxenor's face. But while he was still all stiff and tense he began to tremble again and his hands slid damply down; he fell to the ground and lay there on one side. The bandage round his leg became all at once a wet and startling red.

Alxenor knelt beside him and tightened the bandage with hands and teeth. Chromon was sighing deeply and curiously; his eyes had no hate in them now. In sun or shadow the houses were dumb at each side, but at Alxenor's urgent knocking, a man came out, Dromeos the basket-maker, and helped to carry Chromon into his house. The wife brought water; they laid him flat and took his armour off; under the breast-plate his heart was fluttering like a bird ready to go. The woman stared at him: 'He's dying surely!' but Alxenor snapped back 'Hold your tongue!' and pushed her away.

Dromeos was a democrat, but a cautious man; he had not been with the attackers of the citadel in the early morning because no one had told him

68

in time, and after that, seeing it was useless to try another attack yet, had kept indoors and gone on shaping his baskets. But he knew and admired Chromon, and sent out for a surgeon and had his own bed made ready for the wounded man. He asked what had started the bleeding again, and looked suspiciously at Alxenor, whom he knew for brother to the chief of the oligarchs.

After the surgeon had been, Chromon seemed to be going to sleep, but it only lasted a few minutes, and when he woke the first thing he saw was Alxenor. 'Bring back Moiro,' he said. 'I'll bring her,' said Alxenor, 'but give me your consent to our marrying! I love her, Chromon, I never betrayed you! Give me your consent.' But Chromon's dry lips whispered 'Never,' and he shut his eyes again, looking too nearly dead to be wakened by any pleading.

Dromeos drew Alxenor away from the bed: 'What's this you've done with Moiro?'

'Took her away into safety.'

'Yes, I know. Pretty sort of safety you rich men give our sisters!'

'It's no business of yours anyway.'

The man drew himself up. 'The honour of any democrat is my business!'

'Oh,' said Alxenor, looking at his unbruised hands and face. 'Were you on the citadel to-day, basket-maker?'

That annoyed Dromeos immensely; he spluttered: 'Bring her back now, or never have an honest man's door open to you!' His voice rose to a screech and

Chromon woke again; as Alxenor ran over he asked:
'Have you brought her back?' Then, slowly, 'When
I'm well I shall kill you, Alxenor.' He propped
himself up a little on one elbow; only too clearly
he knew what he was saying: 'Hear me, Zeus
Horkeios, hear me, Ker of my father –' Alxenor
stayed still with horror one moment, then jumped
at Chromon and covered his mouth with both hands,
himself crying 'No, no, no!' to drown the oath.
Dromeos pulled him away, but by that time Chromon
had fallen back again, unconscious on the bed, and
the oath was at least not finished.

But if Chromon woke again? Alxenor gave one
glance round the room with fingers crossed against
whatever there might be, and ran. The basket-
maker drew back from him as he passed like an
unclean thing.

Ker of his father . . . ker of his father . . .

> 'The wine is shed,
> The meal is spread,
> Pease and honey for the homing dead:
> Keres, come to the feast!'

But old Thrasykles, how had he got so thin and
angry all of a sudden? Last night and fifty years
before, he had been a man, up at the farm, swaggering through his vineyard, trying to make speeches,
laughing. And now – *now* –

When he got to the lodgings again, there was no
news; none of the Spartans were back. Moiro was
asleep. There was plenty of time to wonder what
to do, but little doubt of what it must be. He could

not stay in Poieëssa now, with hate from both
sides, no friends but Spartans. Even if his brother
forgave him, as he might – laughing! – he could
not have Moiro, and she was the one good thing
he had got out of so much evil. He took the
purse out of his girdle and counted his money,
frowning; at any rate he was not going to pay the
armourer – Eupaides could do that! His belt clasps
were worth something, so was his sardonyx ring. But
even so –

Thrassa came in to say her mistress was awake; by
habit he nearly gave her one of those very few silver
pieces, but stopped himself in time. Moiro was
sitting up, her veil drawn across the lower part of
her face; all the time, her fingers kept smoothing
and smoothing the bottom edge of the over-fold of
her dress. He could not say all at once: you must
come with me, away, over sea, leave mother, brother,
home, pigeons, playthings – no, he must be kind;
he felt immensely responsible for her. Very shyly
she made room on the couch beside her, and he
sat down, not touching her, nor looking directly
at her face, only at those moving hands. Thrassa
stood over by the door, her back carefully turned,
but ready to come at a word from her mistress. At
last he asked: 'You've slept well?'

'Yes,' she breathed, 'oh, yes.'

'And not quite so unhappy? Moiro, were you
thinking a little of me? Won't you tell me?
Did you like me kissing you? I liked it,
Moiro.'

She edged a little away from him: 'Oh please –

71

Remember father; I've been mourning for him.'

'Yes, but – he was old, he might have died anyhow, in his bed. And we're young, and I'm strong and I've carried you off – little Helen.' .

'Who was it carried me off first?'

'That? A Spartan: just a boy. I carried you almost all the way; you were so soft in that thin dress; your hair smelt of roses.'

'Did it? I was so frightened, oh so frightened. I thought I was going to die. I wonder what happened to the others.'

'I didn't see. I expect it all looked much worse to you than it really was. I'll find out some time.'

She reached down to the floor; beside her a little pottery jug of wine lay bedded in snow; she offered it to him, prettily, looking away herself: 'Are you thirsty?'

He took it from her, holding her fingers a moment in his as he did so: 'Snow at midsummer! But this can't have come from the Spartans! Moiro, you surely haven't been seeing anyone?'

'I'll tell you all about it. I – I didn't ask for it; I don't like wine very much. It was just after you were gone; this was brought over, snow and all (I didn't know anyone *could* have snow now), by a funny dark man in trousers with, oh, such huge earrings, who gave it to Thrassa and said he was Pigres and it was for me from his master Bel – something or other. What was it, Thrassa? Oh, Belesys. I didn't know if we ought to take it or send it back, but he told Thrassa his master was in this house, so we thought if you'd brought us here he must be a friend of yours.'

Alxenor looked moodily at the wine: 'Well, it was kind of him anyhow. I must go and thank him. But don't take presents from any man but me again, Moiro.'

'Oh, I'm sorry.' She twisted her hands together, then after a minute, mopped her eyes with the corner of her veil.

Just a moment Alxenor was angry with her – his wife taking presents from a barbarian man! Then he saw it was nonsense and that he had made her cry their first talk together, when she was beginning to be a little less shy, too, and told himself he was a fool and put an arm round her, poor little frightened thing, and tried to dry her eyes himself till she almost laughed. He thought then that she must be told, and plunged into it: 'Moiro, we can't stay here; we must go away, somewhere on a ship.'

She gasped: 'But why, why?'

'I've quarrelled with my brother. And with yours. I saw him to-day; he thinks I'm not a democrat; he won't give his consent to our marriage. If I stay I shan't have you, so I'm going.'

'But – but – you're not going to take me away? Chromon's angry, that's all, he'll be friends with you again soon! Oh, you aren't going to, not really?'

'Don't you love me, Moiro? Don't you want to come away with me in a great ship with a scarlet sail, dancing in front of the wind?'

73

'No, I don't! I won't come! I want mother! Don't look at me like that, Alxenor – oh – oh – oh –' She fell forward, with deep, chattering sobs into Thrassa's arms and buried her face between the slave-girl's heavy breasts.

Alxenor looked on, feeling that he must be very bad with women, then touched Thrassa's arm; she glared up at him. 'It's no good,' he said, 'we're going and that's all there is to it. I didn't think she'd be such a little fool. I've gone through danger for her, I've rescued her, you tell her I think she might thank me!' He kicked a cushion out of the way and went; then, seeing there was a bar on the outside of the door, swung it over into its socket with as much noise as he could, and left them bolted in – his!

He walked out of the lodgings and along to the little market, where there had been no fighting. The house at the corner was shuttered fast, but as he knocked harder and harder, a head looked out of the attic window; the banker was in after all. 'Oh, it's only you, Alxenor!' he said, and came down and opened, making the door fast again afterwards and lighting a lamp. 'I want some money now, against my inheritance,' said Alxenor. 'Why? You've not quarrelled with your brother again?' 'Never mind. What can you let me have?' 'It's mostly out with the ships this time of year, as you know. Were you with Chromon to-day ? Oh well, if you don't choose to say you needn't. What do you want the money for?' 'Suppose you give it me without asking so many questions.' 'I'll give you two hundred staters.

When shall I see it back?' 'God knows. You can get
it out of my brother. But I want more! It's serious.'
'And for me! Take it or leave it, Alxenor.' The
banker smiled at him, wondering what the young ass
was up to now. It was getting late.

'Very well,' said Alxenor, and waited for the agree-
ment to be written out, not bothering much about
what the interest was. He wondered if there was
anyone else he could easily borrow from, but every
one he thought of was either violently oligarch or
violently democrat; they'd ask questions. He took
the money-bag; it seemed a lot when one saw it
altogether. But, as he walked back, he began to
realize how little, after all, it was, if one had to keep
three people out of it. By the time he got to the door,
the two hundred staters seemed not much more than
nothing.

He walked through moodily. The sunlight had all
tilted out of the little court; it would be night soon;
he ought to find a ship, and at once. Where to?
Nowhere seemed very attractive. Perhaps one of the
other islands? Crete? He knew their proxenos at
Cnossos. He called Ladas: 'Are there any merchant
ships starting to-morrow, do you know? Any for
Crete?' Ladas shook his head: 'Most of the ships
that were sailing will have got off to-day when
they saw what was happening. The others are
sure to wait now.' Here was a difficulty at once,
then.

He stood there, biting his fingers, when he heard a
noise behind him and turned; Belesys, the Persian,
was standing on the edge of the steps, his hands

folded in front of him and covered by the wide sleeves of his gown. 'A stirring day,' he said, 'but I fear you have been unfortunate?'

'My head,' said Alxenor, 'that's nothing. Well, you've got a lot to answer for! You who were a guest in Poieëssa!'

The Persian smiled, crinkling his eyes, almost apologetically: 'But I'm only an instrument, after all; your brother is the real power, Alxenor, and your friends here.'

'Friends!'

He choked on the word, and the Persian broke in: 'Before you've quarrelled with me too much to listen, Alxenor, will you take this?' He pulled a leather purse out of one of his deep sleeves; it had a pattern stamped on it in red and was closed with a copper ring.

Alxenor drew back a sharp pace: 'Your dirty money! No!'

'I'm not giving it you on conditions, Alxenor: freely. You'll be hard put to it without any money, you and your little wife.'

'I don't believe you! You want something from me! I must thank you for the wine you sent my wife; she did not know she must not take presents from men.'

'So you've been scolding her for that! Well, you must go your own ways. No, don't be angry for a minute! There's a ship sailing to-night and if you want to go on her I'll give you a word to the captain.'

'Where's she bound?'

76

'Athens.'

'Athens! What would I do at Athens?'

'It's not a bad place to be a stranger in. But no place is good unless you have money.'

'Oh, I don't want your money! I don't know why you think I'll take it. I'm a democrat!'

The Persian shook his head impatiently: 'I'm just a little tired of politics. Don't you think that's possible, my friend? I give you the money because I'm sorry for you and that child you're taking with you.'

'Is that all?'

'What more do you want? That these Spartans can barely keep civil tongues in their heads when I'm here? That by and by your brother will be grateful? That my own only son keeps trying to poison me? Oh take it, Alxenor, and have done!' He dropped the purse with a little jingle on to the ground and half turned away.

Alxenor looked from it to him, stooped quickly and picked it up. 'I thank you, then,' he said, 'and I believe you. I thank you for myself and my – household.'

Belesys nodded at him kindly. 'You will find a writing there: show it to the captain of the ship; she's moored at the third ring of the lower harbour. Good-bye, Alxenor; I think we should like one another if you didn't despise me so much.'

He passed through the curtains and was gone, leaving Alxenor with the purse in his hands, feeling at the same time immensely relieved about the

future, and horribly ashamed of having taken anything from the Persian. Still, between this and his
own money, he should be able to manage for a little
. . . give Moiro things perhaps; he unbarred their
door. Dusk was dropping now; he bade Thrassa
make ready to go; she looked infinitely reproachful,
but said nothing, not being sure whether he or
Chromon would be the better master for her and
her mistress. It was dark by the time the two women
were standing together at the door, closely veiled,
waiting to go; Ladas and Pigres were there too, a
kind of extra guard, but Alxenor himself had firm
hold of Moiro's hand. As they went down the quays
she looked from side to side, but only saw two drunk
sailors, who frightened her so that she pressed close
to her protecting man.

She had never been on a ship before; she was helped
trembling up the gang-plank, and stumbled over a
rope or two as they led her down to the little cur-
tained-off space astern where she and Thrassa were
to live. The ship's captain brought them a small
lamp and fixed it on to a hook, and Alxenor sent
Pigres back for a few cushions for them. There was
only room for one at a time to lie down, so Thrassa
crouched against the planks, hearing the water bubble
just behind them; when she was a tiny girl she had
been shipped over from Thrace in a boat like this:
bigger, she remembered it. She was afraid of the sea.
But Moiro slept after a time, and did not wake
till in the early dawn she heard them slipping the
cables, and then the creaking of the oars and the
shouted orders, as they slid out past the sterns of

the moored ships, and past the end of the harbour wall, on to the fresh waves where every little foam crest was glittering pink or gold from the sunlight behind it.

CHAPTER FIVE

'Car si toute la terre est le domaine
De veillards frileux, tristes et cruels,
Le nom de Cromedeyre signifie
Peuple de la jeunesse et de la joie!'
– Romains: *Cromedeyre-le-vieil*

MOIRO lay right forward at the prow of the boat, her hair bright and curly with spray, her cheeks just lightly browned by the sun. The wind was behind them at last; she stretched her fingers over the side till she could just feel the bubbling rush upwards, against the planks, of the ripped water. The square shadow of the sail lay spread like a cloak on the backs of the light waves; but always they slipt out from behind it with a skip and a flick off into the sunshine again. And ahead there were miles and miles of them, dancing and twinkling and waiting to be caught, far ahead, and at each side, and behind, miles and days. . . . A spotted handkerchief tied under her chin kept her hair out of her eyes; her little heels were rosy flowers on the brown deck; she was humming to herself like a small, happy bee swung on a windy stem in summer, not thinking, or remembering, or more than watching through half-shut eyes the everlasting toss of the ruffled sea.

By and by Thrassa came stumbling forward across the benches, holding on all the time; when she got as far as Moiro, she sat down clumsily on the deck, feet apart, hands out stiffly behind her. She tried to keep from looking at the sea any of the time, hating the salt and lonely smell of it,

remembering the warm, greasy sheds at the farm,
packed with sheep and goats, or the steamy evenings
in the women's room when they scented themselves and sang round-songs, and ate boiled grain
spicy with mint and sage and caraway! But Moiro
still watched the sun on the waves and went on
humming till the slave-girl spoke, crossly: 'What
are you going to do, mistress? You can't go on
leaving it all to me. We'll be there to-morrow.'

'Oh I don't want to live in a house again! It'll be
nearly the same but not quite. Don't talk about it,
Thrassa, let me alone.'

'No, I'm going to talk about it. Much you'll be
let alone after we get ashore and that Alxenor stops
getting sick all the time – though I don't blame
him for that when I feel my own insides all of a
wobble every time this nasty ship falls over into a
hole! But what I do say is, he'll be after you in two
twos once we're on dry land again.'

Moiro rolled over on to her back; at once the sunshine struck warm through her dress on to her skin;
she pinched Thrassa's arm: 'Well, I don't want to
be let alone all my life – do I?'

'That's all very well, and I promise you, you
won't – not while there's a man left with two legs to
chase you! But what I'm asking you is how and
when.'

'Well, mother always said I wasn't to ask too many
questions, just be modest and all the rest would
happen.'

'Happen! Oh yes, it happens all right! Why, if
the rest of the town was like your uncle's house a

week ago, you'd have been the only maid in the place that night!'

'Oh, Thrassa – You aren't sure, even in my uncle's house! Not all my cousins – not little Kalliste!'

'Bless you, there's no harm done, even if the men do shy off a bit at first: it was the same in fifty houses and they can't have everything their own way. Your uncle'll need to spend a bit more in marrying the girls, and a bit less on his ships – and the fewer ships there are the better for every one, I say!'

'But it is funny, Thrassa, when I thought I'd be the first. I remember my aunt saying – Thrassa, is that land ahead?'

'Yes, it is! So you'd best make up your mind now what's to be done.'

'But what good will that be? He'll do the settling.'

'Not if you've got the least little bit of sense. You can get a promise out of him – yes, and a sworn promise! – that it's to be for keeps.'

'But if we're married –'

'Married! Oh, baby! How are you going to be married without any guardian or presents or anything?'

Moiro looked blank at this; she had somehow always taken it for granted that she would get married some day, and, since Alxenor had come on the scene, that he'd be part of it; she had never considered that of course the most essential part of marriage is the dowry. Still, she cheered up in a little: after all, Alxenor was in love with her, and it would be all the same. But Thrassa, whose fortune was so directly dependent on hers, and who had more experience of

82

men one way and another, seemed doubtful and kept on hinting things. Moiro began to realize that, as things were, there would be very little left of the marriage, no friends to dress her, mother to carry torches, father to give presents, no place to sacrifice. . .

Euboea was well behind them before Alxenor got on to his legs, and made his way weakly aft to find the captain. He saw the two women up in the bows, but the most he felt was a mild and empty benevolence towards Moiro. By now there was land shaping beautifully on three horizons, blue mountain shadows, the heights of Attica gradually rising ahead of them. 'I'd like some good advice,' he said, 'you know Athens; I don't.'

'Well, my boy,' said the captain, 'Athens is the place for strangers, but you keep an eye open for squalls.'

'How?'

'I'm no hand with words, but I'd say it was like this. If the people's party are in, there's war all the time, and that's no good to man or beast. And if the gentlemen are in, they'll try and grab everything for themselves, and the first they're bound to go for, is the foreigners. Have you got that clear?'

'It's a bad look-out either way.'

'Not it, because you never get any of 'em raw. See? So long as things don't go all on one wind, in a manner of speaking. But there's one man you can trust, and that's Theramenes. The Workers' Friend, I call him. You'll hear worse names for him, though, in town; they say he's not honest. Well, maybe he

83

isn't, but we're not all born little gods, and what I say
is, you can be sure he won't go too far either way.
And that's the great thing if you're a stranger.'

'A moderate: I see. Would he be my patron? – I
shall need one if I'm staying in Athens any time.'

'Yes, if you don't want to be fined right and left!
Theramenes might take you on; I've heard he does
sometimes.'

'Do you know by any chance: has he a wife?'

'Wife! God, yes, why shouldn't he – and a mistress too, or had when I was up at Mother Bacchis'
last.'

'He might take in my wife for a little, till I've got a
house and so on.' The captain answered with a
rather crude and seafaring joke, which annoyed
Alxenor very much. However, he had some more
questions to ask: 'I'm wondering what to do in the
way of – business – when I get there.'

'Well, what can you do, my boy?'

'Do!' He laughed and shrugged his shoulders:
'Nothing.'

'That's just like you gentlemen. You might go as a
fish-porter; that doesn't need brains! Or a banker's
clerk.'

'Talk sense.'

'Well, you'll find there's a lot of foreigners serving
in their navy; but that wouldn't suit you!'

'Ugh, no! Maybe it'll have to be that though, all
the same; but not at once anyway. I can see when I
get there. What about lodgings?'

They discussed various practical details, among
them, that there was to be no telling the proxenos for

Poieëssa what had been happening there; a few coins
changed hands. Already the hills ahead of them had
grown solid and coloured. That night they put into
Thoricos, where they had a few deliveries to make
and one or two letters to pick up. If the wind held it
should be a short day to Piraeus. They had taken
longer than usual crossing the Aegean from Poieëssa,
because of the calm they had run into ten hours out,
with nothing for it but to row lurching over the long,
regular swells in the hot sun, enough to make anyone sick, let alone an anxious young man with such
an aching head still.

Moiro kept well out of sight when they were in
port; she had so loved the open sea before, lulled and
steadied by the noise and sight of all that water.
But now – Athens was close on her, the new, strange
city; she would have to land, walk through the
streets, be stared at. She had so few clothes with
her; if only she had been wearing that lovely new
dress her aunt gave her when they came! If they had
given her even two minutes to get her things together! It was all very well being compared with
Helen, but then Helen was a queen and always wore
her best clothes, so it didn't matter when Paris came.
Her best ear-rings left behind too; perhaps Kalliste
would have them; though if what Thrassa said was
true . . . oh well, better not think of it. Nor about
father; though she never could quite picture him
still and shut away and nothing but a fear to his own
children; he couldn't somehow be quite as dead as
other people. And poor mother all alone; she'd stay
in that one room more and more now, never come out

into the sun or feed the pigeons, poor mother always
so frightened of things . . .

They were putting out again; she tidied her dress
and came up. Alxenor was sitting on a thwart, half
turned away, looking at something in his hand; his
hair was a little wavy, not quite black if you looked
at it carefully – shades of brown in it, and it cocked
up at the top like a baby's: nice hair. She wanted to
put her hands on it, ruffle it, feel it all soft and thick
under her fingers. His eyebrows were really black
though; as he looked closely at the thing he held,
they wriggled up and down; there was just the least
silky beginnings of a beard on his cheeks and lip:
would it be black too? His lips were redder than her
own; if only he'd kiss her quite gently at first, softly,
not burning her skin like a hot wind; perhaps Thrassa
could tell him . . .

They were coasting south towards Sunium now,
past a dozen headlands bare and clear; the captain
was whistling hoarsely. Alxenor finally put back the
seal-ring with the Persian letters engraved on it into
the purse he had been given, and then slid the purse
into the breast of his tunic. He just caught Moiro's
eyes on him before she turned quickly away, pulling
the side of her veil forward.

It was late afternoon when they got to Piraeus, and
it took an endless time of shouting and backing and
turning before they could get through the swarm of
ships and fishing-boats that blocked up the harbour.
Alxenor waited a little anxiously, thinking every
moment there was going to be a crash, and now and
then he glanced ahead to the town at the foot of the

hills with that startling citadel clear above the flat roofs; he was not sure what he thought of it, he wondered if he would ever find his way about. Chromon had been there, though; and at any rate he must show these people he was up to all their ways – he had lived, after all, in the city of Poieëssa! A quite extraordinary number of little boys rushed up, and one or two had clambered over the rails before they'd made fast even; he backed a step away from them – no, he didn't want his baggage taken anywhere! Little devils, they were laughing at him. Their silly, clipped Attic – what a tongue! No, he didn't want a pretty girl! Nor a guide to Athens, either! The captain came up and shooed them off like so many sparrows, then pointed up: 'Well, what do you make of their Maiden, young man?'

This was another Maiden, not the young Goddess all white and gold that Chromon had talked of, but hard and gleaming bronze, the Guardian of the City. Alxenor had been aware of her already; looking sidelong, with head a little bent, at the great height of her up there, he said, half to himself: 'So long as she's kind to strangers,' and then looked down from that far, high spear-point to the dock-side crowds of Piraeus, ready to burst on him and Moiro the moment they set foot on land.

Two hours later night fell with sudden coolness; Moiro, in the little room at the inn, pushed back her hair and breathed more easily; Thrassa stuck out her head past the curtain, wondering if she could ask for a lamp. In the main room beyond there was such a jabbering and coming and going that she was frightened – there were half a dozen parties of other travellers, cooking or spreading blankets, or making bargains with the inn servants. It smelt exciting after the ship, hot food and smoke and leather and lamp oil and people in a hurry and – oh, an indoor smell, at last, thought Thrassa, snuffing at it, till suddenly some one saw her and called to her. At first she didn't understand the Attic, then, telling as much by the tone as the words, dodged back behind the curtains, leaving the lamp unasked for. 'Did you hear that?' indignantly she asked Moiro, who was sitting up straight in the dark with mouth open and hands dropped at her sides. 'A nice place he's gone and brought us to! No wonder, considering the sort that travels mostly. But I never thought you'd come to this, mistress!' Moiro shivered and drew herself together: 'Then it's really – all these little rooms – oh, Thrassa, come close, I can't bear it!' Thrassa came and sat beside her on the much worn string bed against the window-less wall; she put her arms round Moiro and rocked her: 'Don't fret, my lamb, they shan't get you!' and felt strong and hard and much older than she really was.

Alxenor came in at last, with a small lamp that lighted nothing but his hands and the dull blue of his tunic behind them; he pulled the wick out a little and the flame grew, falling on to Moiro's soft, frightened cheeks, and Thrassa's rough, broad-fingered hands between him and his beloved. 'Have you got all you want?' he asked, and Thrassa began: 'No, indeed we haven't –' But Moiro, suddenly jumping up and shaking herself, interrupted: 'Yes, everything. Don't

88

fret about us. You're tired – dear.' She reached out
her hand timidly and just touched his face; he looked
so much too young and troubled to hurt her! Now
they were indoors, in the woman's place, she could
dare to help him, take his poor head between her cool
palms, make him sit down, and loose his sandals,
stroke back his hair, murmur to him silly, gentle
things. Thrassa looked on a little jealously, watching her young mistress grow up. The lamp on the
floor threw up huge smears of shadow, and lighted
unexpectedly, the underside of Moiro's chin and
Thrassa's breasts, little nails on the wall trailing up
a wisp of shade, the ceiling rafters bedded in darkness.

Alxenor, very tired, simmered in the pleasure of
feeling those little soft she fingers touching and moving along his skin; at last he was sure that it had
been worth while. He had been in a desperate hurry
ever since they landed; first he had taken charge of
the two frightened girls through the harbour side
crowd, then there had been the hunt for an even
moderately respectable inn to leave them at. After
that he was fearfully anxious to get to his proxenos[1]
as soon as possible, and he had hired a mule, knowing that he was being grossly overcharged, but not
having time to bargain, and set off with all the speed
he could for Athens, wondering what their newest
laws about strangers would be. All the three miles
along between the guarded Walls, he was admiring
the militarism of these people, feeling that if he had
been one of them, with all the newest means of war
ready to hand – he had passed the great ship-yards

[1] See note on page 4.

on his way up – he too would not have rested until
he was master of the world, nor been dismayed with
the falling of any fate upon his unconquerable hope.

After a deal of trouble he found the house of the
proxenos, but only to be told he was out at supper.
The porter was a stupid boy, unwilling to answer
questions and speaking strong town-Attic which
Alxenor could hardly understand; he would not say
where the supper party was, nor when his master
would be back, yawned in his enquirer's face, and
finally shut the door on him. Alxenor turned rather
dismally in the street, and a stranger, an oldish man
wearing a heavy cloak, Spartan-fashion but clean,
asked him what he wanted.

'I want Kleiteles, son of Drakes, and he's out at
supper and they won't tell me where. He's our
proxenos for Poieëssa; I've just come from there and
I don't know what to do!' he concluded lamentably.

The man scratched his head: 'Poieëssa? That's a
Dorian colony, isn't it?'

'Indeed it's not!' said Alxenor in all haste. 'We're
Ionians and – and Allies; we're all for Athens there!'

'That's wasted on me!' grinned the man. 'And you
don't do it well! I'm a Phokian as a matter of fact;
my name's Harmokydes. Are you here for long?'

'Well, I don't know. But I've got a young wife and
I want to be on the safe side; that's why I'm looking
for Kleiteles to-night.'

'Just as well. You can't be too careful with all these
new police regulations they're always making at
Athens. Come early to-morrow; you won't find him
up! Well, good night, and don't try the Ally-stuff on

too much, or they'll tax you double!' Off went the
Phokian, leaving Alxenor in the street, even more
troubled than he'd been five minutes before. He
tried the house again, but it was no good; he even
asked one or two passers who looked as if they might
possibly know. But his proxenos had simply vanished somewhere into this nightmare of an Athens.
It was dark; there was nothing to be done, no good
news to take back to Moiro. As he rode down again,
the clip-clop of the mule's hooves echoed between the
Long Walls; his head was full of the sound of Attic
speech. He could not see that Maiden any longer,
but he knew she was towering somewhere above him,
with her spear lifted all the summer night.

When he got to the inn door, he hardly wanted to
come in. He had been so afraid that Moiro would be
frightened still, shrinking away behind Thrassa; it
would have been so likely on this sort of day. So
when he found her kind to him, just beginning to
mother him, he sank into it and let himself become
her child for as long as she cared to let him.

The next morning he was up very early and off to
find his proxenos; the house-door seemed almost
friendly when he came to it, the one thing he knew
in Athens! They kept him waiting for some time,
just inside; looking through to the courtyard, he
could see nothing but Kleiteles' tame quails, ruffling
and pecking in the dust. Then a man came out of
the house and stood watching them; he was a short,
stubby man with a brown beard, just beginning to
go bald. Alxenor wondered who he was; it was so
odd and horrible being in a town and not knowing

every one he chose to! Two of the quails began spar-
ring at one another, ready to fight, and the man
watched them intently. Then a servant came over
to fetch Alxenor and scattered the quails again to
their peaceful scuffling. The man turned away, hitch-
ing his cloak over his shoulder, and began eating
caraway seeds out of his hand.

Alxenor came through into the inner court, feeling
very badly dressed. At the further end there was a
little colonnade with benches and cushions and a
light table of chestnut wood; there were two young
men sitting on this, and a third stood beside them,
his back to Alxenor, who could only just see that
they were handling the most lovely small white vase,
colour-washed with winged horses in pale red and
green. After a moment all three turned and stared at
the new-comer; Poieëssa seemed to be crumbling
behind him to a tiny speck of earth, he had no backing but his own anxiety. He had decided already that
this was no case for the whole truth: if once he started
explaining it might take hours to get his own part in
last week's doings satisfactorily cleared, and in the
meantime Moiro would be down there all alone in
God knows what danger. No, he must get a patron
first and then see how things stood. If Chromon had
won — as he must have! — then the proxenos need
never know, it could all be hushed up and he would
still be welcome in Athens. He did so much want to
be welcome!

The proxenos apparently had decided to receive
him, and slid down off the table: 'Who are you,
young man?'

'Alxenor, son of Timagoras, brother to Eupaides of Poieëssa; you – you may have heard of him.'

He ended unnecessarily humbly, for Kleiteles at once became quite cordial in his rather superior way: 'To be sure, yes, and what brings you to Athens?'

Alxenor looked at the Athenian, trying to make up his mind quickly what to say. 'Well,' he began, 'it's not much of a life being a younger brother – no chance of doing anything. Besides, I'm married.' Shouts of laughter, and no apology, from all three; Alxenor lost his temper a little. 'There's nothing to laugh at, and I thought you were here to help strangers from Poieëssa! Tell me what I've got to do.'

Still leaning on the table and shaking with laughter, the proxenos answered: 'Well, my young cock, you know the first thing Allies who come to Athens have to do, and that's pay!'

'I'll pay all my lawful dues. Should I have a patron?'

'You'd better!' Kleiteles seized on the other two as audience. 'Anyone want to be patron to a young gentleman with a wife? All safe for your daughters! Who's bidding for an Ally? Fine and fresh, just hooked this morning! What, nobody?' One of them muttered something about having had enough of the Allies, and Kleiteles, looking rather annoyed, said, 'Well, I'll see about it anyhow. No hurry, Alxenor; you'll be all right for a day or two; I'll speak to the police. Tell me, how's your brother? Any more trouble with the democrats?'

This would be the moment, thought Alxenor, if one was going to enlighten the proxenos; he nearly began to tell, but then decided it was better to let well alone. If once he could get his patron and position in Athens, he would be able to soften down any news that might come through: though he'd take good care that none did! 'Oh, we don't have many changes in Poieëssa,' he said, 'but about a patron –'

A slave came past, bringing a letter to Kleiteles, who excused himself and unrolled it. Alxenor stood looking round, feeling that things were going to come right after all, and perhaps it wouldn't be long before he was home again, either. The proxenos, he thought, would certainly ask him to supper parties here: very pleasant they'd surely be, and he would be able to show them that Athens wasn't the only civilized place in the world. No, indeed, he'd be able to quote from the poets too, and sing his couple of verses with the best of them; modestly at first, of course – only let them get to know him little by little. He must get some decent clothes at once; pity there had been no time that morning, it might have made a better impression; still, every one was quite friendly – The silence was lasting rather long; he glanced round at Kleiteles. Without any warning his proxenos threw the letter at his head: 'You dirty little traitor!' he said. 'By God, the cheek of you coming to Athens and waving your precious brother at me after this!'

'Oh,' said Alxenor, with some presence of mind, 'I can explain everything!'

'Explain! You'll have to be a damn good explainer to explain away thirty Spartans! And it's I who'll be blamed for what you bastards do with your rotten little island!' He choked, and gave Alxenor a good minute to tell what happened – or very nearly what happened, because of course it had to be simplified, dropping Leon, for instance, quite out of the picture, and not, certainly, mentioning that as a matter of fact he himself had not been in Chromon's fight to get the citadel back, and besides, it was so much easier to say that his brother and Tolmaios had tried to kill him for being a democrat; and so on. If only he could make it all sound quite true! The proxenos, thumped on the back by several slaves, stopped choking, but seemed quite uninclined to believe anything at all. 'Yes, if I'd had that first!' he said, most unfeelingly. 'Hold your tongue – I won't have any more! Get out! If you come here again I'll have you arrested!' So there was nothing for it but to go, with all the slaves sniggering at him.

In the street, he faced all the strangeness and loneliness of Athens; too unhappy to get any comfort from hating the ship's captain who had betrayed him. He wanted terribly to pray, or to find a friend; but they were not his Gods, and, however hard he imagined Chromon coming towards him, it would never be real; and Chromon had cursed him. . . . Next to her brother, he wanted Moiro to kiss and comfort him, looking almost the same; but he mustn't go to her with this news. He stood still, thinking how badly he'd managed it, when a slave touched his arm from behind.

'Follow me,' said the slave, 'but not too close.' Then he set off up the street before Alxenor could say a word, only looking behind him from time to time to make sure he was being followed. The slave came to a door, knocked, and was let in; a minute afterwards Alxenor knocked and was let in too. A boy took him to a seat and left him, without answering a single question. There was nothing to look at; the house seemed comfortable and clean, and there were red leather cushions on the seat; but not so much as a fly to watch or wonder about.

Alxenor jumped up at a man's voice, plainly the master of the house, giving orders to the slaves; and looked surprised when he came in, because he was the quail-watcher of Kleiteles' courtyard. There was a small boy beside him, holding his hand, twelve years old or a little more, Alxenor thought, with just the same firm, well-shut mouth, and the same trick of shifting from one foot to the other whenever he was standing still. The man nodded and spoke. 'Good day,' he said, 'you had the worst of it with Kleiteles!'

'Well, suppose I did,' said Alxenor cautiously, 'how do *you* know?'

The boy smiled quickly up at his father, with a little jump of amusement which the quail-watcher seemed to share; for he laughed: 'Oh, I know a great many things no one thinks I know! That's why they don't like me!'

Alxenor stared at him. 'Yes, but what do you want me for? And who are you, anyhow?'

'You're a stranger surely, young man, to ask that! I'm Theramenes, son of Hagnon, so now you know. And I sent for you because it would really interest me to hear what did, as a matter of fact, happen in Poieëssa.'

'Perhaps you heard what I told Kleiteles?'

'Oh that – yes. You've not had enough practice: it's difficult, you see. What did he call you – Alxenor?'

'Alxenor, son of Timagoras.'

'Yes, I shall remember now.' He sat down, the boy on the floor beside him. 'The story, please.'

Alxenor, rather intimidated by both man and boy, stood with his hands behind his back and began to explain. It was what really happened this time – trying to make it all real to Theramenes: Poieëssa, the dear little island, so out of the way but still full of life, people thinking and planning and doing things: meetings of the democrats down by the harbour, where he had slipped in and sat in a corner, ashamed of his good clothes: Chromon alone at midnight on the roof, watching the light south-east over Chios: the dark, quick-footed servants of the Persian seen under the shadow of a wall at dusk: and the beautiful Leon, stared at all up and down the streets, but caring for no one but Archytas.

At first it annoyed him that Theramenes seemed unresponsive, hardly looked at him all the time; but then he saw it was just a manner, and understood, and did not try to interrupt it. He ended by showing the Persian seal as some little proof; there was still a fair amount of gold pieces with it. Theramenes nodded at him gently: 'So you've been trying to take the middle way, like the donkey between the haystacks. And by God you've got the donkey's stick all right! You're damned lucky not to be in a worse mess; if Kleiteles wasn't such a lazy hound of a fine young gentleman he'd have had you arrested – and

97

serve you right, my child! Now listen: I'm going to
be your patron as you seem short of one. Not because
I'm sorry for you, or any nonsense like that; but you
seem to think a little, even if you haven't any common
sense, and – well, I like foreigners. Now, don't go
and be grateful! Moderate men like you and me
oughtn't to be; it gives one side too much hold –
don't you think so yourself?'

Alxenor put his hand to his hot cheek and breathed
deeply: 'You do mean it? You aren't laughing at
me?'

'As a matter of fact I quite often mean what I say.
You've heard something else? Yes, they've got a lot
of silly names for me here.'

'I heard you called the Workers' Friend.'

'Did you indeed, that's a rare one! But very likely
you'd rather not be a worker?'

'Oh, I must be. Only, I want to get married first.'

'Married? But you seem to have the young lady
quite happily to yourself as it is? Oh well, it's your
own look-out. Perhaps it mightn't be a bad thing if
she came up here till it was all settled.'

'Well, I'll try to be a worker, for you're being my
friend in all conscience! Shall I send her up to-day?'

'I'll tell my women-folk to be ready for her. Now,
I'm busy. We'll settle up about the tax and all that,
this evening. Good-bye till then.'

The boy jumped up and took Alxenor as far as the
door, then ran back: 'Father, he is so pleased – he
went pink right round to the back of his neck! I'm
glad you helped him; he's nice, and he does like us!'

'M'm,' said Theramenes, pinching his son's ear.

'How long do you think that's likely to last? He'll hear some other name for me to-morrow! But all the same, Hagnon, I think our City's best chance is to make friends with foreigners. I'm feeling rather gloomy about it to-day; it comes of talking to that young ass Kleiteles who thinks he's fit to govern us all just because his great-great-triple-ass-of-a-back-grandfather managed to have an affair with some goddess and a shrine put up to him! But anyway, it always interests me to find a moderate man, even if he does come from some comic little island. He's had his reward so beautifully soon; I'll get mine some day too, but not yet, not quite yet, Hagnon. And we'll both have been right, this Alxenor and I; but we shan't get anyone to thank us. It doesn't look well to be a moderate. By the way, you'd better tell your mother the girl's coming; I hope she's reasonably pretty after all this fuss!'

Moïro, fluttered and pink, hardly dared to peep out at the streets and temples they passed. She fingered her necklace to make sure it was safe, shook the dust off her skirt, pushed back an end of hair under its handkerchief, and wondered whether she was looking tidy. Thrassa carried the bundle – so dreadfully small, only just the change of things that Alxenor had bought her to-day. It had been duly impressed upon her that her host was a person of great importance; when they came at last to his house, she felt her poor little heart jumping with shyness.

Alxenor had to leave her at the door of the women's rooms, with a quick squeeze of her arm and a whispered 'Darling!' Then a maid shut him out and led

99

her along to the chief room, deliciously cool on the north side of the court, with painted chests against the walls, Egyptian hangings, oil and perfume jars, and a few sweet-scented flowers. A girl, who seemed just a little older than she, was standing by the loom, but not working on it, only looking, frowning, at the ground. When Moiro came in, she gave a startled, rather clumsy jump, like a colt, and ran out, calling 'Mother!'

A moment afterwards Phrasikleia came in, the tall, deep-eyed, kindly wife of Theramenes; her dress was dull blue, elaborately girdled and pleated, embroidered all over with a white vine pattern. Her grey-streaked, light hair was pinned high behind the plain, silver band that rose to a crown over her forehead. Moiro ran over to her, and knelt down prettily, looking up at her, then kissed the edge of the blue dress.

'Stand up, child!' said Phrasikleia, 'and welcome to Athens and our house. Let me look at you.' She tilted Moiro's face towards the light. 'Have you a mother alive?'

The girl suddenly flushed, and her brown eyes were full of tears. 'Yes, at home – and – and – this is the first lady's room I've been in since!' She tried to wink back the tears, but they slid out and splashed on to the floor.

'I know,' said Phrasikleia gently, and turned: 'This is my daughter, Nikodike.' The clumsy girl had been standing silent, one arm round a pillar, her back to the light; she came forward slowly, with eyes deep-set and dark blue like her mother's, and her beautiful, half-grown body moving uncertainly. She looked at Moiro for a moment, then suddenly smiled and took her hands: 'You're going to be married,' she said, 'oh you lucky, you little lucky! None of us get married in Athens now!'

CHAPTER SIX

'Smile then, children, hand in hand . . .' – Flecker

IT was settled that Theramenes should go through
the form of adopting Moiro as his daughter, so
that she could be married from his house with all
the proper ceremonies. Of course it could not be
much of a marriage, even so, but still Alxenor supposed that the children would be citizens when they
got back to Poieëssa, and that was the main thing.
As far as Athens was concerned, it didn't matter
much, as they were foreigners and outlanders anyhow. He arranged that they should lodge with a
very decent stone-mason and his wife, Strymodoros
and Stratyllis; they would look after Moiro well
when he was away; he was beginning to get that
pleasant feeling of property in her already. For the
moment at least, he thought, he would have to be a
sailor; wasn't he, after all, an Ally of Athens? Of
course it was not what he would have chosen, but
there was no dishonour about it; when he was
home again he could be proud of what he had been
doing.

Moiro and Thrassa, in the meanwhile, were very
busy with their sewing and embroidery; they found
they had a great deal to learn from the Athenian
women, though in her heart Moiro thought she liked
best some of the old island patterns that her mother
had taught her. Her own work was very fine, but
slow; she would always have liked to go on and on
at the same dress, making it more and more delicate
and perfect. But Phrasikleia said, quite rightly, that

Alxenor wouldn't notice, and of course she was going
to do what was most pleasing to him.

There was one sister much younger than Nikodike,
and three little boys, the eldest Hagnon, whom
Alxenor had seen the first time, one of about seven,
and the youngest only just walking; two others had
died when they were quite babies. Nikodike was a
quiet girl on the whole, but every now and then a
gusty mood would seize her and set her talking
fiercely and rapidly; she thought about things perhaps three times as much as any of the other women,
which was unfortunate for her, being a respectable
Athenian. Some of the things she said were quite
shocking to Moiro, who was, for one thing, so little
used to town life. Nikodike was nearly sixteen; she
could not write at all well and she had nothing to
read; her weaving and sewing were not very good,
but she could cook and do accounts on her fingers,
and she could sing as well as if she had been trained
like a flute-girl. She had been betrothed twice; the
first time, five years before, it had been a political
matter, but her father's views shifted, and it came
to an end. The second time was more than a year
ago, to young Learchos, twice winner of the torch-
race, whom she had seen and was prepared to love.
But he was killed at Byzantium that summer, and
since then there had been no talk of marriage.
More than once Phrasikleia had spoken of it to her
husband, but he had bidden her hold her tongue and
leave it to him. Nikodike had even spoken to him
herself, bursting in on him at supper, driven by a
horrible thought of herself in five years, ten years,

103

childless, forgotten, withered, nothing to live for –
But Theramenes, angry with the girl's voice, the
wild, unhappy face, all this disturbing bundle of
emotions plunged on to him in the middle of supper,
had jumped up, shaken her well, and pushed her
back to her own part of the house, and her anxious
mother who knew it would only mean a scolding for
herself later.

And now this girl who had come into the house, this
child Moiro, who knew so much less about life
than she did, was going to be married! Phrasikleia
had been definitely glad: 'One marriage in a house
brings another,' she had said, and began at once to
plan out the wedding day, the bath, the sacrifices,
the feast. And besides, Nikodike liked Moiro herself; for that matter no one could help liking Moiro.
She was so young and fresh and modest, and so
pleased and delighted with everything, and she'd
had such a hard time, poor dear, and hadn't she
– in a way – suffered it for Athens? – her father
killed by a Spartan, her home broken up! Oh yes,
it wasn't her fault if she was being married and not
Nikodike.

They had nearly a fortnight – till the next full
moon – to prepare for the marriage. The younger
children of course loved it; there'd be cakes and fun
for them, every one would be pleased; fat old Plathané would come with the garlands and tell them
stories and let them see her warts. And perhaps,
perhaps, thought Hagnon, I shall be allowed to stay
up late and see them off.

The slaves liked it too, though they grumbled to

Phrasikleia, and gave her more bother than usual. The serving-boy, Isadas, who would have to take round the cups, wondered if he would be given any money; there was more chance of that if some of them would only stop late and get a bit drunk. He wanted badly to buy his freedom, and then – perhaps – go back. He looked at Alxenor, coming in and out, and wondered what his island was like; he thought he might ask him some time. It must be littler than Melos. He could not remember Melos very well, not the place at least, only the feel of it, so warm and happy, sitting somewhere, on a step perhaps, and putting grapes out of one basket into another . . . a small child very busy . . . some one he loved calling him from indoors . . . It would be different if he went back now; he could never find all that again, he would be disappointed; only, perhaps, if he thought enough about being disappointed, it might be the other way round, the surprise of finding it wonderful after all. They said they'd colonized Melos – afterwards; but he knew the truth of that: the soil would have none of them, the old Gods had come and whispered into their ears. His aunt, who had been carried off with him, used to tell him stories, things that had happened to those Athenian colonists; she had heard somehow; she always knew what came to Melos. Besides, if there were any of them left in the island, after Sparta won the war (not that he loved Sparta who had deserted them!), when Athens was beaten, her temples smashed the way his had been, that Maiden thrown down, trampled on, then . . .

'Isadas, Isadas, wake up, get that table out of the
way!' 'Yes, mistress, I was just going to.' He didn't
often think like that; it must have been this other
islander coming. He was only an Ionian, though,
and Melos was Dorian, strong and golden-headed.
He couldn't get that table to move; it must have got
stuck somehow.

All those first days Alxenor used to wander about
Athens, familiarizing himself with streets and
markets, wondering who every one was. The whole
thing seemed to be turning its blank side towards
him, as if he had strayed into somebody else's family
party; longing to be part of it, he was delighted
whenever he saw the same face twice, or found himself suddenly in a street he knew; the only one he
avoided was the street where Kleiteles' house was!
He wished he had ever asked where Chromon had
stayed when he was here; most likely with some of
the ship-building folk at Piraeus. Various people
spoke to him, though hardly ever the ones he would
have liked to talk to; they usually asked him questions
about who he was and what he was doing, and often
wanted to sell him something. Once or twice the boy
Hagnon took him out and showed him the sights,
but he was even worse at asking questions than
the grown-ups, and at first Alxenor was rather afraid
of his patron's son. The second week he met Harmokydes the Phokian again; he asked him into
his lodgings and sent out the landlady for some
wine.

'How are you enjoying it now?' he asked.
Alxenor looked puzzled: 'It's an overwhelming

kind of place – still. I thought I was used to Cities! But this is different. They talk so much one hasn't time to turn round.'

'Ah,' said Harmokydes, and poured out the wine. 'You ought to go to Sparta. Oh, don't look so frightened – there aren't any informers here, they stick to the barbers' shops! Besides, we've got a very decent proxenos who always looks after me. Yes, they're fond of the sound of their own voices. But in Sparta a man thinks before he speaks, and while he's speaking too. And they don't write poetry nor polish their nails, and the Gods don't go changing all of a sudden. Ah, that's the place for anyone with sense enough to know what a State's for!'

'Sparta may be all very well if you're one of the real, true-born Spartiates,' said Alxenor, 'but what about the others?'

'Well – what? Good food and trade and houses and money; they needn't care if they've no part in the State. And if they do, aren't they just the spoiled blocks the artist throws away before he gets his perfect Nike? I tell you, Alxenor, they're very near to having perfect men in Sparta! You mightn't see, but I know – I've been very lucky – they showed me. I think so well of them that I've sent my only son to be brought up among them as a foster-child of the Spartan State!'

'Your only son?'

'Yes, my son Kratis; he's being made perfect too.'

'How long has he been there?'

'Three years. I've never seen him since. But I know all's well.'

Harmokydes sat smiling with half-shut eyes, thinking of his small son growing up better than his father. But Alxenor drew away, a little horrified. He had often thought of the children he would have with Moiro, small naked boys, playing — as he had pictured them — along the narrow beaches of Poieëssa, sons to gladden the house when he grew old, and to pray together over his tomb when he was no more than a ghost. To send away one's only little son — and to Sparta!

The evening before the marriage they brought water from the spring Callirhoë for Moiro to bathe in. Nikodike, wringing out the bride's soft, dripping hair, thought to herself: when shall I give my virginity to the spring? When can I be a woman too? And Phrasikleia thought, sighing, of her own wedding day, the great day in her life when for a little time the girl becomes something for herself, some one important for once; and then it's all over, so soon, so soon; and never comes again.

Poor Moiro had very little to vow to Artemis; only the lock of brown hair, no toys or dolls like most little girls going away from home. That made the other women all cry, but Moiro herself felt that going to Alxenor was more like going back to those dear times than anything else she could ever find now; he would surely talk to her about it all. That night she slept sound and quietly, but Nikodike sat watching her, on the edge of the mattress, wide awake for hours.

By daybreak the next morning Isadas was down at the market, waiting for the fish to come in; a little

later the cook began to discover all the things he
absolutely must have within the next half-hour for
the party. Soon Nikodike and the children were
hanging long garlands everywhere between the
pillars, smilax, myrtle and lavender, with flowers in
little bright bunches against the dull or glistening
green, carnations, asters, corn-cockle and poppies;
they looped them up as quickly as old Plathané
could make them, and she worked like magic, sort-
ing the blossoms, pinching and tying and smoothing
the delicate things with her fat, rough fingers and
talking like a magpie all the time. Phrasikleia
watched by Moiro till she woke, and then kissed her,
with a hundred good wishes, and dressed her fresh
and gay in all the pretties, thin, fine linen of shift and
robe, little gilt brooches to catch it up on shoulder
and arm, white sandals with yellow ties – Then
Nikodike and the maids brought in the girdle and
veil, and Moiro thought them all so kind: it really
was a wedding after all!

Then Thrassa must do her hair, all soft and fluffy
from the spring water, and the veil must be pinned,
and the myrtle wreath, and all the neighbours' wives
must come in and admire her, and wish her a Warm
Bed and No Sleep, and Sons and Grandsons, and the
Word of the Kind Goddess. And almost at once it
was time for the banquet, before really one could
have had time to think or wonder or look ahead
much. They waited, sitting together, holding hands,
whispering, every one's eyes smiling at her whenever
she looked up, listening to the noise of the men
feasting in the next room; now and then she would

hear Alxenor's voice for a moment, and every time
she blushed and shivered, and perhaps Phrasikleia
would pick up her hot little hand to rub it against
her own cheek. There had been things to eat all
day, little cakes and fruit handed about, and some
light wine for the older women; and the figs – oh
how they'd all laughed about the figs! Moiro herself hadn't eaten much, though they'd brought her
all the tit-bits – and of course she must have a
sesame cake!

Most of the neighbours had sent in something, if
it was no more than a piece of honeycomb and a few
nuts. But there, they were all just as good to her as
they could be. She hardly missed the wedding it
ought to have been, with her own mother and the
cousins and all; she hadn't a moment to be sorry,
except that they couldn't know, with this wonderful,
thrilling day whirling round her, and all these gentle,
merry Athenian women, ready to laugh or cry with
her, their kind eyes crowning her queen of the house!
Only Nikodike, her head thrown back as she listened
eagerly to the songs from the men's room, was queer
and rough a little, she thought; but oh, not really, for
the girl ran up suddenly and hugged her hard,
pressed against her with hot, wild mouth and breasts,
whispering to her, till Moiro whispered back: 'Oh,
it'll be you *soon*!'

Then Phrasikleia smoothed down her dress again,
the gold embroidered hem of the mantle drooping
downwards in a dozen folds from breast to knee,
gleaming under the long veil, as the women led her
into the room of the feast. She shrunk together, not

daring to look about at all, their whispers hardly reached her; but at last they could all sit down again, settling themselves on benches by the wall, and she pressed her hands on her heart and raised her head, a little, and saw Alxenor, crowned too with myrtle, and looking almost strange on her host's right hand. And then he smiled across at her, just stretching his arms, so that she felt all soft towards him and murmured his name under her breath; but the time to lift the veil was not yet.

The boy Hagnon, solemn-eyed and gentle like his mother, went round from guest to guest, saying 'I have fled from Evil and found Good'; and he gave a sesame cake to each one as he spoke, feeling himself a priest full of blessing to shed out on them. Most of the guests were silent a moment, little moved by the old ceremony, but much by the untouched grace of this boy in his short white tunic, going from one to another and taking himself away without a smile for any one man more than his neighbour. But one or two of them were only wondering whether they could get a word with their host that evening; now that Alkibiades was banished again, one couldn't be sure what was going to happen or who was going to rule. Diomedon, one of the new generals, a young man, keen on his work by all accounts, was there; he and Theramenes were being very polite to one another; his wife had brought Moiro a little jar of scent.

It was dark by now, but not indoors with all the lamps and torches throwing light across from one wall to the other, the shadows of the garlands between the pillars swinging as some one passed, and the changed colours of the dresses and faces, warmer and more exciting. All at once the women stood up, and Phrasikleia led Moiro into the centre of the room. 'Courage!' she whispered, and threw the veil back, so that all the men should see what they could of the new bride. For a moment Moiro trembled, then, feeling the strength and comfort of all the other women backing her, she stood up straight with her hands clasped in front of her, thinking she would be fifteen in winter and must try not to be a baby. Then Alxenor was standing facing her, quite close, with an open ivory box in his hands; Moiro gave a little cry, lifting her eyes for a moment to his – a necklace! She hoped he hadn't been too extravagant. He laid it at her feet, and then rolls of linen, and a beautiful tall oil jar with winged figures on it. She was overwhelmed with his kindness and her own worthlessness, with nothing to give him in exchange but herself, and in her heart she vowed herself again to obedience and faithfulness. Then he took her hand to lead her out, and Phrasikleia went before them with torches. No one spoke among the guests, and then Hagnon began to sing their marriage song:

'Oh gently, gently, ye silver horses,
And stay your courses
For a little while.
Let darkness cover
The loved and lover,
And lamp-warm shadows the maid beguile.

They will not harken
Though rain-drops darken
The star-bright waters of the well-head clear.
No sound shall hasten their strict embraces,
Their ardent faces
Shall find no fear.

With stingless arrows shall Love possess them,
His wings caress them,
That close they lie.
Oh fair the wedding,
And fine the bedding,
The Gods' own Eros will satisfy!'

Alxenor's lodgings were not far off; Theramenes
had lent him two white mules and a cart with gilt
rails. There was singing all round them, and every
one they met in the streets joined in. Stratyllis
opened the door to them with a shower of sweets,
and helped Moiro down from the cart and over the
threshold into her new home. Then Phrasikleia
kissed good-bye to the bride, and went back to her
own house to see to the clearing-up of the feast, so
as not to let the servants waste it all; and then she
must praise Hagnon for his singing, and see that
the children were all tucked up, and try her best to
comfort Nikodike, and at last undress quickly and
get to bed before her husband could grumble at her
too much for being so slow.

CHAPTER SEVEN

'For man has reason, woman rhyme,
A man scores always, all the time.' – H. G. Wells

THE next day, by rights, the bride's father should have sent presents, but Theramenes couldn't be expected to rise to that: the wedding feast had been quite an expense, though of course the guests were his friends, not Alxenor's, and he had done a certain amount of business. He was glad to have seen something of Diomedon; not that he liked him, certainly – the man was clever enough, but he had no real ability, for politics or war either, and besides he had been seeing a bit too much of Alkibiades that spring. But then there were rather few people that Theramenes did like; one of these few was his son Hagnon, to whom he used always to talk more freely than he did to most people. For him, this young Hagnon, with his clear child's voice and beautiful quick intelligence, meant all he hoped for the future of Athens, those times when he thought Athens could be saved after all.

A few weeks after the marriage he took the boy down with him to Piraeus to look over his ship, which might be sent for any time, to join the chief admiral, Konon, at Samos. They stood together in the great, dim ship-shed, with the warm air all round them heavy with the smell of tar from the coiled ropes stored along the walls. Gradually the boy's eyes got used to the half dark, and he began to see down the aisles at each side, shapes coming clear out of the shadow, piled oars and masts and benches,

114

a spot of light on the curve of each of twenty great
iron anchors, here leather flaps and oar-loops, there
three-toothed, bronze rams, wrapped up in hay and
corded for safety, further on ladders going up to the
loft above where the sails lay dry and ready. At the
far end the wide door was half open, and the sea
beyond was deeply and amazingly blue. It was quite
quiet in the shed: all those great silent things waiting
to be brought to life. Hagnon tiptoed over and
began fingering a green painted figure-head which
stood propped against one of the pillars staring in
front of it; then he tried to lift a few turns of cable;
it was heavier than he had thought.

Theramenes broke silence: 'You can't remember
the start for Syracuse?'

The boy looked up: 'Not really, father. I do remember afterwards, though: when you said everything
was coming to an end – I kept on expecting it every
night. But it hasn't happened, has it!'

'Don't be too sure, son: not while every loaf of
bread you eat comes from overseas! The Gods gave
us a second chance after Syracuse – and a third
when Phrynichos was killed; they won't have a
fourth up their sleeves.'

'We won't want a fourth – we'll know who to
trust now: not another old Nikias anyway!'

Theramenes laughed harshly and suddenly: 'Nikias
wasn't such a fool: besides, he paid for it. But
there's no reason – no reason at all, my son – why
any time we shouldn't get ten worse generals than
Nikias. Look at the way they're chosen – look at
them now – look at Diomedon!'

'But Diomedon's clever, isn't he?' said Hagnon, surprised. 'Every one says —'

'Every one says! That's how battles are lost. Come and look at the ship and don't talk nonsense.' He stumbled out into the sun, scowling at his ship. 'There it is, Hagnon, all the expense of her that I've got to stand out of my own pocket, or they'll pick me to pieces in the Assembly, and what do I get for it? Just one miserable vote, the same as my green-grocer! And then your mother expects me to go marrying the girls off!' Hagnon followed his father out without answering, and jumped on and off one of the wooden mooring-posts; the future couldn't scare him for more than half a minute on a day like this.

The trireme lay rubbing her side gently against the wood-sheathed harbour wall; a couple of men were on board, below deck, watching to see if any of her seams leaked. And Alxenor was with them, asking questions; Theramenes had taken him on as one of the crew, and he wanted at least to know what was what. 'Getting on all right?' asked Theramenes. 'How's the wife?' 'Oh, busy as anything,' said Alxenor. 'She's the best little weaver and sewer – oh well! Perhaps Phrasikleia would come and see her one day? She'd love it.' He did not tell Theramenes that they both thought there was a baby coming, and Moiro wanted her mother, and he himself found it rather alarming.

Theramenes began going into the question of cost with the men on board: so much for pitch, so much for timber, the girdling cables must be renewed, something extra for them beyond the government pay if they got it done reasonably . . . He found some caraway seeds at the bottom of his purse and nibbled at them, doing accounts in his head. Hagnon went up to Alxenor: 'Have you seen everything in Athens yet?'

Alxenor shook his head: 'I've been too busy; things take a long time if one's a stranger. Most days I've come down here – hoping for news from my City.'

'And what is it?'

'My brother's won – God's curse on him and the Spartans. I want to know who's dead now, but the ships that come here can't ever tell me: it doesn't matter what happens in a little island like mine! Well, I suppose I shall go home one day. I saw Kleiteles last week, but he didn't see me – lucky!'

'Oh, don't bother about Kleiteles – father doesn't care what he says!'

'Oh, I see. Politics here are very difficult, aren't they?'

'Well, if you aren't used to them. Of course I am. I say, Alxenor, shall I take you up to the Acropolis?'

Alxenor was very glad to be taken; it is a little difficult always in a strange city to know just where one may or mayn't go; near temples and strong places, especially, one is apt to do something which might be misunderstood, and if there is a young wife waiting at home, one has to be more careful than ever. They got a lift up from Piraeus on a cart. 'It must be funny being a foreigner,' said Hagnon, chewing a piece of grass.

'It must be wonderful being an Athenian!' Alxenor answered. 'There's nowhere like Poieëssa really; but we've kept out of things; we had to, we were so small. And you here – you're what the world's pointing at; there's nothing you do that isn't marked down at once hundreds of miles away. You might lie awake at night and almost hear the islands whispering about you!'

Hagnon laughed: 'You are funny, Alxenor! I wouldn't be anyone but an Athenian for all the treasures in Asia, but father says things used to be better in old days.'

'I think people's fathers always say that. But it's extraordinary seeing everything like this after – Well, six years ago no one in Poieëssa thought you'd stand another summer. But your Maiden brought you through: no wonder you treat her well.' He looked up at those pale, dazzling pillars: 'I wonder how many foreigners come and envy you every year!'

'Father always has lots of foreigners. There was a funny old man called Prodikos, who came and stayed with us last year; he was from Ceos, I think.'

'Isn't he a Sophist?'

'I dare say. He used to stay in bed half the morning. Father thinks I ought to learn philosophy.' He jumped out of the cart, which was beginning to take them out of their way, and Alxenor followed, wondering what Chromon would have thought of him.

They went up, step by step, the boy leading, talking over his shoulder. It was all bare, terrible, sacred rock, no grass, no trees, the heat of the sun and the sky heavy above them. At the top, the rock grew into walls, the walls were crested with the gleaming of temples, the crown of Athens.

At first Alxenor had been thinking of their own citadel at Poieëssa, and the very old, black stone Goddess that only showed herself on some days in the year, but whom one was aware of all the time in her square wooden house, up there looking away down through acres of clear, moving air to Poieëssa harbour and all the little ships. Then, after a time, this citadel and this Goddess began to force themselves on him. Hagnon had very skilfully managed to catch a lizard, and now he sat on the wall, swinging his legs and holding it in his hollowed hands. Alxenor walked straight forward by himself, trying not to feel just a worm under the shadow of that bronze spear; but She looked away, the Guardian, the Watcher, utterly impassive all the time, so clearly divine that he need not trouble about his own little feelings. He bit his lip and turned to the boy; the lizard escaped in a tiny green flash, and it was good to be reminded that there were things like lizards in the world too. 'We'll go to the Parthenon now,' said Hagnon. 'Some people say the carving is awfully old-fashioned; but I don't know – I like it.' He kicked at a stone and blushed pleasantly. 'I suppose I'm not old enough to know about Beauty yet.'

Alxenor stood still with his back to one of the columns; looking in, out of the dazzling midday, at first it seemed all dark; then, gradually, as his eyes got used to it, there was a shaping and gleaming far down, in the heart of the temple. They went in; it

was cool and still and very high. On each side of
them were the offerings to Her; and at the end of it
all She stood, facing everything. Alxenor began
thinking to himself, hard: so that's where our taxes
went! But it was no use; the calm and beautiful face
of the Goddess – not his, not his! – caught him and
held him. The delicate ivory of her neck rose out
of the gold breast-plate as soft and gentle as the
flowering of any young maiden going with her
mother to sacrifice: if one could imagine a maiden
who had dared all things and was afraid of nothing,
because She knew – oh, he was being a fool! He
turned away uneasily; Hagnon said nothing. At the
far end, where they had come from, was the great
opening, narrowed between the flat, beautiful curve
of the two pillars, and outside so much light pouring
across that he could scarcely see the outline of the
hills. They walked out of the temple again, past the
smooth, honey-coloured marble; then he left Hagnon sitting at the corner of one of the steps, deep in
shadow of the porch, facing eastwards to Hymettus,
and began to walk round the colonnade himself,
following the frieze, muttering half aloud: old-
fashioned, yes, not enough feeling in it – stony. It's
done by the yard. It wants repainting – they ought
to be able to afford that! He passed one or two other
foreigners wandering round, and two young citizens
sitting together on the edge of the step, holding
hands and talking; he hated anyone being there but
himself. Gradually he came round again to the
eastern end, where the Gods sit, watching and blessing the Athenians.

'What's the matter?' said Hagnon, looking round. 'Are you going to be sick?'

Alxenor dropped down beside him into the corner, shaking all over: 'No, it's all that.' He stopped, then went on with a rush: 'I didn't mean to let it. I knew it meant to, only I tried to throw mud at it, but that's no good – it's got me!'

Hagnon put a small, solid arm round his neck: 'Do you know you're crying, Alxenor? I don't think you do know.'

Alxenor shook his head angrily: 'Oh, it's so beautiful one can't stay near it – it beats on one's soul like being under a great wave! There, now I can look again.' He stood up, one foot on the upper step, resting his hands on his bent knee, peering in; and then went on, a step or two into the temple; again he got the same shock from seeing Her there in the dusk, so strong, so perfect, so much realer than life.

Hagnon looked up, as he came back slowly. 'That's because you're a foreigner,' said the boy. 'She's our Goddess.'

They stayed by the parapet a little longer, looking down over the theatre and the low, crowded houses; the Long Walls showed up clearly with sharp black shadows, and beyond them Piraeus and the sea and the lovely slopes of Salamis, sun-warm now in the late afternoon, and then more sea, and Aegina far out on the horizon. It all seemed utterly safe and calm, under the Maiden and the citadel. Alxenor came down rather silently, not noticing much where they went, till all of a sudden house-walls had closed in round him again, and the smell of the streets.

Then, before he was yet well out of the dizziness the
Maiden had cast on him, he found himself back at
the lodgings, and thanking Hagnon for guiding
him. Once in the inner court, Moiro ran up to him
and threw her arms round his neck; he kissed her
half-heartedly, and she wondered what was the matter
but didn't like to ask. She did try so hard to be a
good wife and find out all the things he liked to eat,
and was always ready to help Stratyllis about the
house. Of course she hardly ever went out; Thrassa
did all the marketing. But sometimes older married
women came to visit her, and once or twice Alxenor
had allowed Stratyllis, who was sufficiently respectable, to take her to see a procession.

Alxenor was away for a few weeks' cruise that
autumn, and glad of the pay. Moiro hated to let
him go, terrified lest anything should happen to
him, and indignant too, that her husband, the young
flower of Poieëssa, should have to go and pull at an
oar with common sailors. As for Alxenor himself, if
he felt that a little too, he managed to hide it all
right from his mates on board. They had good
weather, and the hard work and interest of it all
made him feel less sea-sick; they never even sighted
an enemy all the time. While he was away, Phrasikleia came round several times to see Moiro, and
again in winter, when the poor girl was feeling ill
and cold and lonely. One day late in January, she and
Nikodike came, and a couple of slave-girls bringing
some presents for Moiro, among them some of her
own old swaddling clothes – she hoped, and was
nearly sure, she was too old to bear any more chil-

dren herself. Moiro loved seeing Nikodike; for ten
minutes they chattered and laughed and joked with
one another like babies; then Nikodike seemed
suddenly to dry up, she hunched her shoulders, and
looked at the floor. 'What is it, darling?' asked
Moiro; but Phrasikleia knew. 'Oh, it's not your
fault,' said Nikodike heavily, 'but – oh, I do want
a child!' She laid her open hand on Moiro, and after
a moment felt the faint kick against her palm: 'Oh,
Moiro, I'm getting so old!'

Living was dear in Athens in those days. The place
was full of farmers with no farms, just charred olive
stumps and the scattered stones of house and byre.
There were plenty of old men, ready to talk about
the good old days of Perikles which seemed now so
incredibly remote, and plenty of mere boys who had
scarcely seen a summer's campaign yet. But a whole
generation seemed to be missing, killed in battle
one time or another, prisoners at Syracuse dead of
ill treatment and dysentery, drowned at Cynossema
and Cyzicus. Whole families had been wiped out,
first by the plague, which had come early in the war
after the first invasion of Attica and overcrowding of
the City, and then later in the fighting that went on
every year from the beginning of spring to late
autumn. But the women were left, often with no
kinsman to shelter them but some distant cousin,
who would be bound in piety to give them housing
and food, though he brought poverty on his own wife
and daughters; and every one would be unhappy.
There were not so many young children about the city
as in old days, either; partly from lack of husbands,

partly because young couples could not always afford
to rear them.

But still, Athens went on magnificently; a stranger
at first sight would see nothing wrong: not till he had
lived there six months or so, as Alxenor had. By
that time he had found out how things stood in
Poieëssa, how completely Eupaides and Tolmaios
and the Oligarchs had won. Chromon was still alive,
though, brought back to the farm with a wound that
left him ill and lame, even after weeks of lying flat
on his back, powerless against his enemies. But they,
feeling secure enough, had not had him killed, nor
any other of their fellow-citizens for that matter;
there were some dead on both sides the first day, but
not very many, no one except Thrasykles that he
knew very well, though he remembered them all a
little – passing in the market-place, the training-
ground, borrowing an oil flask, helping to mend a
piece of armour . . . Archytas and Leon were gone,
but had left behind a Spartan garrison. But nobody
cared much in Athens: Poieëssa was such a little
place, and they had their hands full enough with the
rest of the Allies – such as were left.

One day towards the end of April, Thrassa came
hurrying over from the lodgings to fetch Phrasikleia. It was a long business for Moiro; half-way
through she began to cry for her mother, and went
on till it was over: she never expected to be hurt so
much. Alxenor walked about outside, terribly sorry
for her; he had been getting used to her now for
nine months, but this startled him back to the time
when she was still the unattained, the spirit of

Chromon, his dearest friend, in a maiden's shape. He vowed a kid to Artemis for her and the child's safety. They called him in at last to say it was over and to lay his son in his arms; he held it tenderly and awkwardly – he had never imagined it so little and ugly and pitiful. And Moiro's face was still white and relaxed with pain; she was unaccountably angry with him about his extravagant vow – which hadn't helped her; it was only his wanting to think he'd borne part of it – and he hadn't!

He did all the right things by his child; on the tenth day it was named Timagoras after his father, but they called it Timas for short; he thought it was getting less ugly. Moiro was frightened of the baby at first, but not after she had suckled him; he had dark hair and was downy on his back and arms; she loved seeing him unswaddled. She and Thrassa tied coral charms round his neck and on the cradle, and every one they knew was asked to come and see him. Phrasikleia brought him a rattle and bells, and Nikodike cuddled him up to her till her breasts began to ache with wanting him for her own. Stratyllis was delighted to have an olive wreath hung over her door again; her own sons were both at home that month, but one had been wounded two years before, and the other was a sailor: so one never knew.

Thrassa brought her friends to see Timas too, and loved showing him off as if he'd been her own making. She found several fellow country-folk at Athens, maids going marketing for their mistresses and very willing to stop for five minutes' chatter – the mistresses would want all the news themselves

when they got back. And there was also a policeman, a rather ridiculous man called Ditylas, who
looked tremendously strong and ferocious, but was
really terrified of getting involved with an Athenian
citizen in the course of his duties; Thrassa had at once
been impressed by his red beard and yellow government trousers and bow and arrows. Then one day
he had caught a thief in the act at one of the fishmonger's stalls and every one within a hundred yards
had run up to see. The thief claimed loudly to be a
citizen, so of course half the crowd backed him
against a mere Thracian slave; but most of the
women, including Thrassa, were more law-abiding
and backed up the policeman. The next day they
nodded to one another, and a week after they'd
arranged to go for a walk one evening; and one day
Thrassa brought her Ditylas to the lodgings and
carried Timas into the outer court to be admired.

The next week Isadas came with a message to
Alxenor from Theramenes, telling him to be ready
to sail the day after; Thrassa lamented, and gave
Isadas a cake; then he asked if he might bring his
aunt to see the baby. Thrassa, who liked him, said
he might, and went to help her mistress to do up the
bundle with a change of clothes and some food for
Alxenor to take with him. Three days later the aunt
came, youngish still, and dressed in red with a white
border; her name was Hasychia. When she unveiled,
Thrassa saw the woman's painted face and had no
need to ask her trade; she was even rather shocked.
All the same, Isadas was a nice boy, so she said
nothing and took the baby out of his cradle, careful

126

to keep him in her own arms all the time. Hasychia smiled at him timidly: 'He's not old enough for sweets, is he?' she asked. 'No, of course he's not!' said Thrassa, indignantly. 'Don't you know *that?*' 'No,' said the woman simply, 'I don't often see babies.' Thrassa sniffed at this and told Isadas to pick up Timas' rattle. Then Hasychia began to speak again, more surely and rapidly now: 'He will be lucky – he has a lucky face; he will travel and see strange countries and come home in the end, home at last to his Island. And it's well for him that his home's not here, and well for him that he's no kin to the Grasshoppers, and well for him that's he's got no dealings with the Maiden!' She stopped suddenly at Thrassa's astonishment and almost whimpered: 'There, I didn't mean it! I'm clean silly sometimes, I think.' Thrassa stared at her: 'Well, you talk like it anyway!' and danced the baby in her arms, with 'Come away, my lamb, my precious, don't cry, there's a lovey –' When she was gone, Isadas took his aunt by the arm: 'Can't you take care? How do you know that woman won't tell? You'll say something once too often some day!' Hasychia shook her head: 'They all call me crazy now, they do. They're about right too. But still, I can see further than most.' 'God send you see true about – this. If only those pig-heads in Sparta would wake up one year!' 'Ah, I don't know about Sparta; that's too difficult for me.' She began to shiver. 'I want to go home. Take me away, Isadas.'

Alxenor came back from his cruise early in June, thoroughly sick of his shipmates and his roughened

hands and his salt-cut knees, looking forward to
civilized food and talk and music, most of all to the
soft touch and voice, and gentle breasts of his wife.
He shouted now like the others when they saw the
sun-tipped spear-head over the Acropolis, and looked
out as eagerly for the nearing landmarks. The two
oarsmen in front of him were talking about what they
were going to do when they got ashore, a complete
programme for the next two or three nights; wine
interested them, but women more; one of them
recommended a house to the other, a place with a
good clientele – the captain of the ship went there
himself. Alxenor had been listening half-consciously, but this last remark woke him up, and he
began considering the new aspect of Theramenes.
However, just then the boatswain called them to
get on to their oars sharp and start the paean; they
liked coming into harbour in style.

He waited with his bundle half an hour to be paid
off, wondering how Moiro and his son were, and he
bought her a necklace of glass beads from one of
the many dealers at Piraeus. Half-way to Athens,
Theramenes caught him up, riding, took the bundle,
and told him to hang on to the girth, so he got to the
city pretty quick, hot with running and pleased as a
boy at the beginning of holidays. He hammered at
the door of the lodgings, and the stone-mason himself
let him in, with 'Well, you're looking a proper man
now, Alxenor!' 'Oh, my beard!' Alxenor grinned,
'not bad, is it? But how's the baby?' 'All well to go
by his noise!' said Strymodoros, chuckling, then,
more gloomily, 'My eldest's warned for service

again. God knows how I'm to get on in the yard with
nothing but a pack of slaves and foreigners. There
now, I keep on forgetting you're only a foreigner
yourself! I'm sure I could lay hands on a hundred
citizens a sight worse men than you are.' He talked
his way into the house, one arm through Alxenor's.

The two women were bathing Timas; the steamy
room smelt of oil and porridge and half-washed baby
clothes. Moiro cried out joyfully at seeing him, but
could not run to him at once because of Timas on her
lap; she sent Thrassa off to get something extra for
supper, and laughed at her husband helping her
with the swaddling clothes. Supper was a delicious
meal for Alxenor; after days and days of salt fish
and beans sitting on the damp and splintery benches
or on some stony beach ready to rush back to the
ship if the look-out man whistled, it was exquisite
to lie among cushions, bathed and comfortable, with
Thrassa waiting on him and Moiro on a stool beside
him, looking up with bright eyes, rosy and chattering, in her prettiest dress, full of pleasant feminine
gossip you could attend to or not, just as you liked:
every one was well; Stratyllis had a new cooking
stove; yesterday Diomedon's wife came in – her
husband had just given her a different kind of scent
to anyone else's in the loveliest little jar, wasn't she
lucky? – but not so lucky as Moiro was now! Nikodike had been round last week: no, she wasn't even
betrothed yet. He stroked her hair and put his finger
through the little curls at the back of her neck; how
good it was to have a home of one's own! He was
feeling hungry as well as greedy, and Thrassa did

129

her best with the cooking; Strymodoros sent in
some of his own wine, and Moiro made him a wreath
of ivy and larkspur and blue ribbons.

At the end he lay back with a sigh of satisfaction,
stretching his bare arms and considering what next.
Moiro was suckling the baby, her dress unpinned on
one shoulder, and her head bent over him so that
her eyes were hidden by the soft, brown hair.
Alxenor reached over and touched her on the
breast; she threw her head up like a startled horse:
'Oh please!' she said, but he kept his fingers there,
and the baby choked and began crying. She looked
reproachfully at her husband, but he was laughing.
'I can't get used to you in your new beard,' she said
nervously, 'you look so old!'

'Well, I'm not such a baby as I was,' said Alxenor.
'Come to bed, sweetheart.'

Moiro fidgeted: 'To you?'

'Not to anyone else! Take those silly clothes off,
little love. It's months since I've been near you with
Timas coming and all.'

'Oh, have you thought –' she drew back, redden-
ing, 'I – I can't. If anything happened – he's only
ten weeks old! And – and – I do love you and I will
do anything you want, but it did hurt me so!'

Alxenor stared at her: 'You don't know what you're
saying. Here am I, just home, come out of danger
and hardship and toil, back to you, and you keep me
off as if I was a mad dog! You little block of ice, come
here and be warmed! Tell Thrassa to take that
baby – be quick, Moiro!'

But instead of being an obedient wife, she rocked

herself about, clinging to Timas: 'Oh I know, and I'm a worthless creature, but do wait!'

Alxenor pulled her over to him, baby and all: 'Silly, don't be frightened; you're safe enough while you're suckling him.'

'Oh, but I'm not – Phrasikleia says –'

'It's her, is it! Zeus, she'd better take care, coming between a man and his wife!' He began kissing her neck angrily, and she half yielded, but the baby, upset by all this, started wailing, and she snatched herself away and stood in the middle of the room, sobbing, not able to say a word. Alxenor sat up straight among the cushions, with his bare sun-brown chest heaving. 'You don't mean it!' he said. 'You don't really mean it, Moiro darling!' He wanted to be her master – with his new black beard and all – but when she went on crying with her face wet and crumpled like a little girl, he was still angry, but too sorry for her to use force. She stood there, with her lips trembling and her hair streaky across her cheek, and her blue dress hanging down from one lovely soft shoulder and breast. She cried low and steadily, and the baby yelled in angry, echoing jerks; Alxenor jumped up, snatching at his cloak, and ran out of the room.

Once in the street, the noise was all shut away and he could think again: but what to do now? He felt incredibly ill-used by that ungrateful little brat of a wife of his. What did she expect? – that a man should come home from a horrible, ugly, soulless time earning her bread for her, and then just sit and look at her as if she was a goddess and too holy to

be touched! What did she think a man was like?
He'd kept himself down and been like a brother to
her all the last weeks when the baby was coming,
and afterwards when she was ill, never thought of
going to another woman, and this was his reward,
when she was perfectly well again and fit for anything and as pretty as – Oh God! said Alxenor,
stamping, and began to curse her and himself and
every one, till again he felt a wave of self-pity coming
over him. Well, she'll be sorry for it some day: he
felt the ribbons of his silly wreath tickling the back
of his neck – what's the use of wearing it now! And
then it suddenly occurred to him that after all he
would enjoy himself, and he remembered the address
of the house he had heard that morning.

They'd been having supper there too, a proper
feast with flute-girls and acrobats and as much wine
as one could carry. He went in, fine and tall and
young with his eyes still angry; he looked about for
anyone he knew, and saw Theramenes, hairy about
the chest and legs, putting his hand down the back
of the girl next him who squealed and wriggled but
took it all in good part – not like some! 'Well,' said
Theramenes, 'and what are you doing here, young
man?'

'Sick of rowing your ship for you, Theramenes.'

'Sick of Moiro too? Oh, don't glare at me so – you
look like Diomedon. Dear Diomedon! Let me in-
troduce you to some of these distinguished young
ladies. This is Korallion, but she's promised to me
for to-night, aren't you, darling? And there's
Theodoté with her hair coming down – I hope it

won't come off! She's rather expensive though. Still, you've got your pay to get rid of. I'll tell you a secret – it won't be long before you're earning some more, my boy. And here's our hostess, the adorable Bacchis in person! Maman, let me present my young friend Alxenor, one of our gallant pre-servers!'

'Yes, I dare say!' the old woman sniffed. 'But he'll do if he acts as handsome as he looks.' She drew him away with a finger on his elbow, and looked at him hard: 'Come to forget something, dear? Money, is it? No, a friend – has she turned you off? – the little cat! Never mind we'll forget all about it. Now, who would you like to know? Let me see . . .'

Alxenor was considering his pocket by this time, but she was very sympathetic. The charming Theo-doté was quite out of reach, but there were others. He had never seen anything of the sort before, and was prepared to take geese for swans – after all, this was an evening's sport, he hadn't seen a woman since he was in Athens last, and anyway it was chiefly to spite Moiro. He joined a party of young men, none of whom he knew, and was accommo-dated with a dancing-girl. He did not try and talk to her, or look at her close, but he handled her and felt her yielding softly against him like a bird whose neck he could wring if he chose. She had a sweet voice and sang him some of the latest songs – her dancing was not so good and she didn't care to be seen in the full light. Later on, he found he hadn't got to be gentle with her as he was with Moiro, she seemed to like whatever he did, and made him feel

133

magnificently her master, which was all he wanted now Satisfied, he slept.

He woke late in the morning, feeling tired and not too well pleased with himself. The woman came in with breakfast of brown bread and honey and some thin wine; he looked at her, not quite sure: 'Was it you?' he said. She smiled at him: 'Yes, dearie; but we none of us look our best in the mornings, do we? Will you come and see me again one day? You're such a nice boy!' 'Perhaps,' he answered uneasily, 'later on. And – and – thank you. I must be going now; shall I –?' 'Oh yes, to me. And something for the porter, won't you? My name's Hasychia, if you want me again. What's yours?' He hadn't the experience, as she perhaps saw, to give her a false name or none, so he answered with some embarrassment: 'Oh, Alxenor – I'm a foreigner, you know.' But Hasychia exclaimed, delightedly, 'Oh, it was your sweet little baby I saw! How is the darling?' Alxenor jumped up hastily: 'Quite well, thanks. Good-bye. No, I don't want the wreath.' And he went out as fast as he could, and hurried away from the house, but not before old mother Bacchis had asked how he enjoyed himself, and would he come again. Theramenes, she said, had left early – he usually did – and gone up to the Council: yes, it was beautiful weather, for her part she couldn't see too much of the sun.

He thought he would have a bath at least before going home; Moiro would be anxious – well, let her, serve her right! But even after the bath he didn't quite want to see her at once, though he certainly

134

had nothing to be ashamed of, he was sure of that.
He went up towards the Agora, but he could not see
anyone he knew, and he did not want to spend any
more of his money; he hung about the outskirts of an
argument for a few minutes, and priced some shoes
for want of anything better to do. Then he remembered Theramenes hinting at another cruise the
evening before, and thought it might be just worth
while to go and see what the Council was talking
about. It was a public sitting and he slipped in
easily, and leant against the wall; there were very few
others looking on, three or four older men, and a boy
in a long travelling cloak, with a broad felt hat pulled
down and hiding his face. The round, vaulted building was dim and stuffy, and not too good for hearing
in; they were listening to a report from one of the
harbour officials, read out by a herald without any
stops, but quite half of them were not attending at
all.

Theramenes was sitting nearly opposite, on the end
of a bench with his head in his hands; once he leaned
back and whispered to the man behind him. The
report was apparently about the bad state of repair
of some of the docks, sent up by the magistrate in
charge; nothing very surprising in that, though.
Alxenor was just going away again, when abruptly it
came to an end. Nobody paid any attention for a
moment, and then Theramenes grunted and heaved
himself to his feet, yawning; the President nodded to
him and he started to speak. After a few minutes the
Council woke up; he was a clever speaker, and what
he said was sufficiently arousing. He was making

the dock report a text for a speech on the general
incompetence of the Athenian fleet and admirals;
he skirted lightly round Erasinides and Diomedon –
nothing anyone could take hold of – and began to
emphasize the danger they were in from the new
Spartan admiral, Lysander's successor, longing to
make an even better record: already he had gone
to Miletus and levied some huge sum, he was said
to be doing the same at Chios. And meanwhile
what was being done at Athens? Well, look at this
report. Here one of the others began shouting at
him, and for two minutes the place was like a pit of
wild beasts, but Alxenor stayed, wondering how
serious Theramenes was, and what he was really
after. The speech went on, calling now for more
men, and money for the ships, support for Konon,
and an attack on the Spartan fleet before they were
ready. But most of all men, not slaves and foreigners
that no one could trust, but free Athenians – And
then suddenly Alxenor saw the boy in the travelling
cloak run out into the centre of the hall, fling up his
arms and cry out in the face of the Council: 'Yes,
take them, take them! Kill them as you've killed
the rest, but don't wonder you've no grandsons!'
And then, rising to a cry, an invocation, 'Oh, maids
of Athens, playmates of mine in childhood, where are
our husbands? Ask them, ask him –' and she flung
it in the face of Theramenes ' – Bring back our dead
husbands !'

For a moment the whole place had been startled
into silence, but then Theramenes knew it was his
own daughter, and Alxenor guessed, and the Council

saw it was a young woman and fair game. She stood quite still, shaken with passion and sincerity, not yet afraid. Then they came rushing at her, grey beards and crooked hands and little angry eyes. She turned to run, but was caught in a knot of them: 'Veil yourself!' they yelled at her, pinching her bare arms where the cloak had slipped, pressing against her hot and panting with horrible high laughter, calling her filthy names. Somebody slapped her on the breast, and she screamed, terrified: 'Father, father!' struggling to keep the cloak round her.

Theramenes had been too shocked to run forward at once with the others; now they were between him and his daughter – he felt more shamed than ever in his life before, he tried to think how he could hush it up. Alxenor, butting his way into the crowd, wondered if somehow the girl could know about last night and realized it was ridiculous – she couldn't possibly. He was tough with rowing and they were mostly oldish men; he dragged her through them and bade her run. Somehow they got away, dodged down a street or so, Nikodike still clinging to the cloak, and stood safe and panting. Alxenor told her severely to follow him, and she said nothing but obeyed. At the lodgings, she went into the women's rooms, very silent, and Alxenor went round to Theramenes' house to find Phrasikleia.

She came hurrying out and he told her shortly what had happened; she gasped, hand to mouth, her mind darting between her daughter and her husband, wrapped her cloak round her and went. Nikodike was sitting on Moiro's bed, dreadfully

137

calm and dry-eyed; she hardly answered anything to all their questions – she had done what she wanted. 'But why, why?' asked Moiro with clasped hands. 'Darling, how *could* you do such a thing?' 'You gave me your child to hold yesterday,' said Nikodike, then: 'Don't cry, mother, it wasn't your fault.' But Phrasikleia, now that she was sure her daughter was safe, had time to be frightened herself, and sobbed: 'I don't know what your father will do! It's dreadful – what can I say?' 'I don't mind,' said Nikodike, coldly. 'Father can do what he likes; it's all one to me.' Moiro looked on horrified, her mouth open; it was as if something dreadful had happened to the whole world, first Alxenor, then Nikodike. And Phrasikleia stood up, wiping her eyes, though her lips twitched a little still: 'I'll be made to mind, if you aren't,' she said. 'He'll blame me. . . . But it's all because of the war.'

CHAPTER EIGHT

'So that when we elders hear
Your loud knocking at our doors,
Pardon us if we appear
Dressed in dirty pinafores.'
    – James Dale: *A Song for the Seventies*

A LXENOR was ashamed and cross with himself;
he never wanted to have another night like the
last one, only – it was her fault, not his! And
Moiro had discovered how dreadful it is to be a
modern woman and do things against the will of
one's men-folk, and he wasn't asking for more than
his rights – what had he married her for? – and it
wasn't as if she didn't love seeing and feeling him,
his beautiful, strong body melting her own to its
will; as for the risk, that must be taken; he took far
more going as a sailor in that horrible ship – for her
and Timas. So that evening he said nothing and she
said nothing, and both tried hard not to remember
anything else that had happened, and they went to
bed together. And so all the time he was back. It
was hot, dry August weather, and there seemed to be
more and more stars every night.

It was queer, he never thought of Athens as a
besieged city; few people did. And yet King Agis
and his Spartan army were all the time on Attic land,
at Dekeleia, not twenty miles away to the north:
waiting, in case anything happened. As it was, they
were no worse than some sore thought at the back of
anyone's mind; there they lay, and there was no
budging them. Sometimes they came down and
burnt the crops and had to be chased back again, but

139

they were not nearly strong enough to attack the walled city itself, or come very near for that matter, even if King Agis had been a younger and less desperately cautious person. But still there was no getting rid of them: and north again was Thebes, all hostile. Well, it was better for citizens of Athens not to think of all that, while life went on still, in the sun and sea air, and friends could be together, and beauty being made. Most of the richer ones, at least, lived in the present, on the knife-edge of time, and the future they saw was misty, and coloured with reflection from their great and sudden past.

One morning Theramenes and his son were up at the Agora together, Hagnon walking behind, quiet and upright, carrying his father's cloak and purse. It was a school holiday; four hours earlier, when the grass was cool and dewy in the dawn, he and the others had gone out, and sacrificed in a meadow. He still wore his best tunic of fine red linen with the plaited leather belt his sisters had made for him, and his heart was still clear and God-filled. The life of the market-place swept round him, lifting him higher yet with its thought of Athens, the home and joy of his own Gods, the Far-Looker, the Queen of the Seas. Going easily through the colonnades, up one side, and then across again, they passed one after another dear and beautiful buildings, made, some long ago, some almost yesterday, by men who had loved their City, and done their utmost to make her yet more worthy of love, her and the Gods. And she made her citizens glad of her, and even the young boys felt themselves dimly the best of Hellas, and

140

wished for goodness and wisdom and the grace of Athene the Maiden. So Hagnon stepped gently behind his father, smiling, and the sunlight tilted fuller and fuller into the market-place.

. Theramenes had spoken to a dozen or more of friends and acquaintances, avoided a few, and was looking for others; he saw one of the Generals, young Perikles, a little oppressed, as usual, with the burden of his father's great name and reputation, looking older than his real age. At the corner he stopped to buy sweets, honey and nuts flavoured with pepper or wild liquorice, and gave a few to his son. He was considering who he should marry his daughter to; she had cheapened herself and could not expect too good a match; and yet in a way, he admitted logically, there was something to be said on her side; she didn't mind her scolding or punishment either. It was harder to deal with one's women-folk than even the Athenian Demos herself, beautiful, crook-lipped hussy – he glanced half-laughing over to that magnificent, impudent painting Parrhasios had so brilliantly made of her in the portico – not to be driven, surely, and hard to lead: lovely, exquisite playmate so long as she got what she wanted, but when you crossed her – wild cats were easier to tame! He stopped again under one of the big plane trees, reading the notices that were nailed up on its trunk, and Hagnon waited beside him, looking up at the light through cracks in the roof of heavy green leaves.

Theramenes turned at a light tap on his shoulder. 'Well, Kleiteles, and where are you off this fine morning? – as the fox said to the goose.'

Kleiteles was in full armour as a cavalry captain, with fine gold-inlaid breast-plate and greaves, and curly purple cocks' feathers in his helmet; he looked serious: 'Haven't you heard? – the Herald!' Then pointed: 'There!' And all at once the people in the market-place began scurrying and crowding down as they always did for a proclamation.

'What is it?' said Theramenes, 'bad news?' And Hagnon suddenly dropped out of his dreams to listen and shiver.

'Yes,' said Kleiteles. 'They've got Konon.'

'Dead?'

'No, but shut up in Mitylene harbour with all the ships – except thirty and they're taken; he's short of food and everything. That damned Spartan's been too quick for us.'

Theramenes nodded. 'Who was with him? Erasinides? I thought so. But Konon's too good to lose. When's the Assembly?'

'At once. You'll speak?' Kleiteles asked, anxious and excited, feeling something terribly important had happened and would go on happening, wanting to push it on himself.

'Maybe,' Theramenes answered almost absently, thinking hard, then turned to his son: 'Get home, boy, quick. You'd best say nothing to any of the women yet.'

The Assembly met for the next two or three days, making out its decrees with admirable sureness and despatch, now it was too frightened to amuse itself with much talk. People remembered Theramenes'

interrupted speech about the harbour report, particularly when he and his friends mentioned it
casually, and he got more credit than usual. There
were a few ships ready or under repairs, but most had
been with Konon when the Spartan admiral had
first attacked him and driven him to shelter at
Mitylene; still, another twelve were sent out under
Diomedon to see if they could help. More were put
in hand; for three weeks all the citizens seemed to be
down at Piraeus in the ship-yards; Strymodoros and
his eldest son let their stone-cutting go, broke con-
tracts and went to work all day on the hulls. Athens
could recover after defeat by land, but nowadays
almost all her food came by ship, mostly from Thrace
and Scythia, through the Hellespont, so if she was
beaten at sea she must starve at once; she would lose
her empire and be ruined.

Every sort of resident foreigner was pressed for
service; slaves who went as rowers were promised
their freedom, though many would have gone even
without that, through goodwill towards kind masters
and a just State; and they felt it somehow a fine thing
to be enrolled – Carians or Scythians or whatever
barbarians they were – to fight among Hellenes in a
Hellenes' battle. Theramenes called his house people
together and told them; two fellow-servants of
Isadas' went, and one of them, a tough old shepherd
from the Thracian hills, wanted him to go: 'Even if
you're not old enough, I'll swear you're as strong as a
bull! What, six weeks' rowing and then your freedom – come on, lad!' But Isadas, smiling Greek-
like with little even teeth, answered: 'If I knew it was

143

only a week and no danger, I'd yet not buy my freedom with helping Athens!'

Alxenor was promoted to bow oar, as he took care
to let every one know. The pay was better, which
meant a great deal to him, as he or Moiro had used
up nearly all the Persian's money and what he had
borrowed, and his oar-mate was a citizen, a grizzle-
haired old man who had fought at Delium; he was in
debt to Theramenes, and apt to drink too much.
The bow-oar itself was scratched all over with names
of men who had used it. Of course in ordinary rowing it was not so important as Stroke, who set the
time and started the paean; but when it came to a
charge, prow-on, a good deal depended on Bow's
steadiness and courage. Also he might have to ship
his oar suddenly, or use it against an attacking trireme without waiting for orders.

They started off in the first days of September, a
hundred and ten ships, a huge fleet, packed with
soldiers. They had to take the risk of leaving Athens
almost undefended by land, but they knew their
Walls were enough to stop King Agis. There were
hired bowmen and light-armed troops, and slingers,
with their own hoplites as well, and even dismounted
cavalry, among them Kleiteles and his friends, with
their fresh-painted shields hung out over the cat-
heads.

Crowds of friends came down on to the quays, to
join in the prayers and see them off, old men, women
and children. Thrassa held the baby and Stratyllis
had an arm round Moiro who knew there was sure
to be a real battle this time, but tried hard to be

144

brave, till, when all the ships were past, and the beat of oars and paean less wildly beautiful and insistent over the stretching waves, she felt Stratyllis begin to shake and sob, and could not stop her own tears. They walked together up those long and lonely three miles between the Walls, and at home the rooms waited dishevelled for them, the bed still unmade, remains of his breakfast . . . Phrasikleia had seen fleets off before, but never quite so anxiously; Diomedon's wife, who was quite young, came round that afternoon to cry about it; her husband had been badly beaten trying to help Konon, and only just escaped with two ships out of his twelve; now he had been given a fresh command of fifteen.

The fleet sailed straight for Samos and there got some Allied reinforcements; then they went north, close to the Asian coast. So far they had not sighted the Spartans. The weather was only moderately good, and for the first two days Alxenor had a miserable, shivering return of his old sea-sickness, and could scarcely manage his oar. But as they passed Chios the sun came out again, the cross-wind dropped, and in an hour or two he was all right. He peered out westwards across the sea, but they were thirty miles off Poieëssa, and nothing to be seen.

Theramenes came up past him to the prow, and looked out, with one of the helmsmen standing beside him. 'Where are we making now?' he asked, sucking his lips. 'That bunch of islands?' 'They're the Arginusae,' said the helmsman. 'Not much shelter there, to my idea.' Theramenes glanced across at the blurred sunset: 'Yes, it's a bit changeable; can't trust it to

stay fine a day this time of year. Do you think we're
in for a storm?' 'Like enough,' said the helmsman,
gloomily. Alxenor asked his oar-mate what he
thought, but did not get much of an answer. In the
meantime there was dinner to come. They landed on
the islands, made fires, and stretched and washed,
and wondered what the plans for to-morrow would
be. Alxenor ate up the last of Moiro's sausages with
his rations that evening.

The whistles woke them the next morning at daybreak; the Generals were sacrificing already, and by
the time they had each had a drink and a piece of
bread, the Herald was giving out that the signs were
favourable. In twenty minutes they were all on
board, sails stowed, leather screens up along the bul-
warks, and all the soldiers ready in place. At first
there was nothing to be seen, but gradually people
began to whisper and point: the Spartan fleet was
coming to meet them, spread out in open order, a
horribly long and even line, waiting for the chance to
break through. Alxenor had never seen the ship so
well prepared before; he tried to keep cool and quiet
like the old man next him, but found it almost impossible, his mind was so bubbling with excitement, fear
overlaid with intense curiosity. He could hardly bear
the slowness of their pace, he wished he was Stroke.
But between times all his perceptions were very
sharp; he watched Theramenes nervously spitting
his caraway seeds to right and left; he could see
every quiver of the helmsman's hands down the
length of the ship, and he noticed how all the time
the waves were getting up, slapping sharply against

the dipping oar-blade, and breaking every now and then into a dash of spray.

He wished he knew how close the enemy was; the next trireme on his left was as near up as she could get without shortening stroke. They were on the right of the Athenian fleet, Diomedon on the left; the two wings had sixty ships each, close together in a double line trying to keep themselves safe from any outflanking or breaking-through by the Spartans, whose hired sailors were better than their own. The centre was safer, as it was still in shallow water close to the islands, so there was only a single line there. At last the boatswain began calling all the rowers over by name, to steady them and get the time well before the charge. Alxenor's knuckles were white with his grip on the oar; his breathing was deep and short; he knew it was coming.

There was just a moment's silence; the soldiers were staring tensely ahead, frowning and whispering. Then 'Go!' and all thought and anxiety blinked dead out and instead came the pure physical strain of the rowing, the jerk and jerk and jerk of the short stroke, keeping it even in the waves, rising the effort every moment. 'Time, Bow!' The boatswain shouting: 'One – two – three – four –': in with the paean. How soon now? Nothing to see. They were nearing and nearing a noise, crashing and shouting that drowned the paean. There was an arrow stuck quivering in the edge of the bench in front. Sling bullets. Backwards into a battle. 'Victory, Victory!' – the paean of Athens ringing through his head. Suddenly 'Bow – oar in!' He shipped it with one quick, practised

147

pull, his mate helping, and so all along the benches.
Then over the leather screen above him he saw for a
second the teeth of a Spartan ram; it swept past and
the two ships ground together.

The Spartan had been trying to ram her amidships,
but their helmsman had been too skilful; now they
had grappled, and each side was trying to board.
Alxenor picked up his oar and shouted. 'Keep down,
you fool!' cried his old oar-mate from half under the
bench, pulling at him, but it was no use. Theramenes yelled orders to his men from behind, keeping
an eye on the rest of the battle too. A man came
tumbling head over heels on to the deck, almost at
his feet, jumped up, helmet off, half dazed: 'Kill that
Spartan!' shouted Theramenes, and Alxenor swung
the butt-end of his oar down crash on the man's head,
which split bloodily – first dead to Poieëssa!

The ship next them, with Lysias, one of the Generals, on board, had rammed and sunk a Spartan, and
now came to their help; in about a quarter of an hour
the fighting was over, the enemy killed or prisoners,
and the ship ready to tow. The Athenian right wing
had well outnumbered the Spartan left, and beaten
them thoroughly; on the rest of the line things were
about even. But the Spartan admiral was drowned
and they were hopelessly disorganized by the end of
the day; the north wind was rising; they set sail, and
it drove them battered and flying to Chios or Phocaea.

Alxenor helped to chain some of the prisoners, and
got a cut on his own head seen to. His oar-butt was
in a mess, but he rubbed it clean with salt water; he
had taken a gold ring from one of the prisoners, but

could not wear it rowing, so hung it round his neck. The day had started brightly, but first a thin veiling of cloud had come over the whole sky, then it had thickened, always out of the north, and now there was sharp rain on the sea, and the long, narrow war-ships tossed and pitched and quivered like live things through all their timbers. But very soon they were back in the shallow water by the islands, one ship shouting for news to the next. Theramenes landed in the rain, and went hurrying up to the high rocks where the Generals and most of the ship-captains were holding a rapid counsel, half of them pointing down at the sea. There were more than twenty of their own ships helpless out there in the rising storm, rammed and holed, half under water, battered about, oars and timbers washing out of them, men still clinging to the masts; and even more enemy ships mixed up with them, sinking and drowning half a mile off.

Almost all the Generals had slightly different plans; Erasinides was sulking, Lysias and Diomedon curs-ing each other, Perikles, very wet, was trying to knot a bandage on his hand. Lysias turned sharp away and caught hold of Theramenes: 'Ah, you! – look here, we're going to finish this for good and all! – we're taking half the fleet to Mitylene to smash up the rest of them; you and Thrasybulos take the other half and do what you can out there –' he stared for a minute at the roughening sea '– I think: my brother – if you can, Theramenes.' The orders were con-firmed; they all ran back to the shore; but even in the five minutes they had been gone everything was changed. The north wind was full on them; the triremes were all out of line, smashing against each other; some were being beached already, one had been caught and knocked right over into the surf. They were narrow, unsteady things, easy for a wave to twist broadside on and swamp. Further out, the sea was a grey, heaving dragon, eating the wrecked ships, one by one.

Theramenes called to his men to get to their places and shove out; not a quarter of them even began to obey. 'He can't expect us to face it!' said Alxenor, rather pale. 'He can't make us! We're free men – I've got a wife and child!' 'That's right,' said his oar-mate abruptly, 'stand up to him; I'm not going.' They ran up and joined the shouters round Thera-menes; the helmsman was pointing at the sky, call-ing the Gods to witness, and Stroke, usually rather a silent man, talking at the top of his voice: 'It's not I don't want to get the poor chaps safe, but what I say is, Captain, why us? Ten to one we'd all be drowned too before we were half-way out! Make the slaves do it, not citizens!' 'Yes, the slaves, the foreigners –' Some one got hold of Alxenor, but by this time he almost screamed: 'You shan't push me to death! I won't! I've fought for you once – do your own work now!' No one listened, though; they were all getting more and more frightened. Theramenes knocked his way out of them and turned: 'Very well: leave them to drown – voters!' He called Thrasybulos and they hurried over together to the Generals.

Alxenor hunched himself up under his cloak, shivering; two of the others were shielding the fire with their hands, waiting for the stew to warm up. They had made a sort of shelter against the side of the ship with timbers washed ashore and one of the sails. All along the beach the rest of the ships were drawn up too. They had to speak loud over the hissing and booming of the sea. He got up, trying to tighten his head bandage with sticky, cold fingers. Some one close to the sea cried up 'Here's another!' and he ran down. It was tossed about, just out of reach, in the first of the big waves; he had a long stick with a nail at the end, and waded out, and after a time managed to hook it into the clothes. They turned the body over. 'It's only a bowman,' shouted the other man, over the sea noise. 'The ones with armour won't come in yet.' Between them they dragged it up the beach; there was a whitish, gaping wound on its shoulder, all the blood washed out. Already there were some ten or twelve bodies in a pile there, but no Athenian yet, only foreigners or slaves; the one man in armour was a Spartan who had tied himself to a bench and been swept in that way, but drowned like the others. It would be five days before most of them were in.

Before eating, Alxenor washed his hands and said a prayer against the Uncleanness of the dead things. Looking out to sea, he could make out nothing because of the mist and spray close in; he wondered if there was anyone alive out there still. They all crowded together in the shelter, eating the warmed stuff, sullenly, cursing and muttering at each other; something ought to have been done – but not by them! What was the use of a victory if they felt like this afterwards? Alxenor said to himself that they were only Athenians – he'd done more than he was paid for already: killed a Spartan. For the hundredth time he began to think of what was likely to happen to Moiro if he was dead: no, it wasn't his business anyway! But here one was, safe and fairly dry. How the dead must hate one.

The Generals had been forced to give up their plan too; to-morrow would be in time to relieve Konon. In the meanwhile they put up their trophy, sadly enough. 'He ought to have tried again,' said Erasinides, suddenly. Lysias looked round at Theramenes too, but shook his head: 'Not in this weather. You saw his men; he did his best with them, but they're half of them foreigners these days; they just went rotten. After all, he was a general before any of us. The Gods were against us. I hope – they didn't have too long to bear it – out there.' 'If you hadn't all turned down my plan, we'd have got off at once before the men began to be frightened!' said Erasinides again. 'But of course you all listened to Thrasyllos: you always do!' 'That's neither here nor there,' said Diomedon fretfully, fingering his beard. 'What I want to know is, what are they going to say at home?' 'That we've beaten Sparta!' 'All very well, Lysias, but will they take it like that? I know them. What shall we put in the despatches? No, there's Thrasybulos prowling round – God blast him!' And the wind swept, whistling over the bare rocks of the Arginusae Islands, and the helmet plumes of the Generals were sodden with the rain.

But the rest of the Spartan fleet never waited for the

storm to finish and the attack to come; they slipped
away from Mitylene, and the next day Konon sailed
out and met the other Athenians setting off from
the islands. There was still much wreckage drifting
between the long grey waves, but no living thing.
They sailed all together to attack Chios; but they
were not overwhelmingly strong, and there was no
really brilliant mind among them, no Alkibiades this
time, to leap on Fortune and hold her. The Generals
were anxious too, they dared not take risks with the
judgment of Athens hanging over them. So after
all, nothing happened. As long as the Twin Gods of
Sparta had their divinity backed by the Great King's
treasure, they would not be the losers in the end. But
Athene's gold was all spent, and taxes came slowly,
trade was difficult; she was Goddess of bare hills
with difficult marble quarries, and small rocky valleys of olive trees and goats grazing: that was all.
She had no friends among the barbarians.

At Athens they melted down the ten golden Vic-
tories that Perikles had bidden be made, one for each
Tribe, twenty-five years ago. It was terrible for the
magistrates who had to lay hands on them and watch
by the furnace; for days they felt they had seen the
Luck of their City die. But at least no one yet spoke
of stripping the golden dress that Pheidias had put
on their Maiden in old days.

Theramenes was home before the Generals, which
was just as well for him. Alxenor came home too,
and sold the gold ring for twenty staters. He would
need the money; both his own and the Persian's was
almost all gone. And Moiro was not looking as

pretty as she used to be: peaked and downcast, with lines coming on her forehead; she was pregnant again after all. Timas had to be weaned, and did not take kindly to porridge and goat's milk; Thrassa said he was teething, but really he was not old enough. For a time he did not grow at all, and used to cry half the day; Alxenor could not stand it and went out whenever he could. The lodgings were not very cheerful, either; Strymodoros and his eldest son had come back safe, but the youngest was drowned. Kleiteles was dead too, and many of his friends with him, unburied and far from home, no more to talk and love and be wise or merry, no more to ride their little tossing stallions through the Athenian streets.

The weather stayed bad all that autumn; the first days of November were sunny, but the wind buffeted cold and rough round the street corners, and those who could stayed at home. When the women were visiting one another, they wore their husbands' thick woollen cloaks, and the hostess would have a hot drink ready, and chestnuts to roast. But Moiro had to be careful of the housekeeping money; she did accounts every day, with Thrassa beside her, ticking off the things she'd bought that morning on her fingers, and beads on a string to help her counting. She did her best, but she had always been used to living on things from their own farm at Poieëssa, and now there were little oddments to be got most days for the baby, and often she had to ask Alxenor for more money. He tried not to scold her, but it was worse when he looked anxious all the time; he was not used to saving either.

154

Phrasikleia would help sometimes; but she had her
hands full already, with her husband back, and the
children growing up – and everything that was happening in Athens these days. One morning she
called Hagnon into her room; he stood by the loom,
fingering the shuttles, while she sat on her stool and
talked to him as if he'd been grown-up, telling him
how anxious she was about his father, that he was not
eating or sleeping properly, and she knew something
was on his mind; but he would not quite tell her.
'Can you help me, son?' she ended.

Hagnon considered, carefully clearing his mind,
very much flattered, as she had meant him to be.
How much he loved and wanted to help them both –
father and mother! 'Don't you think perhaps father's
frightened of something?' Phrasikleia nodded, and
the boy went on, gaining courage, 'Isn't it just since
the Generals came back? They're saying it was
father's fault about our men not being saved after the
battle. But of course it wasn't! Only they're trying
to shift the blame on to him. So now he's had to say
it was their doing.'

'But is that all?' said Phrasikleia. 'He's cleared
himself by this time – or as good as done it. There's
no danger for him now, surely.' She sighed sharply.
'I wish I could get out and see for myself a little
more. One lives in twilight.'

The boy began running the wool thread up and
down between his fingers; he spoke excitedly: 'But
isn't it like this? – after all, Father told us just afterwards, and Thrasybulos was saying the same thing
everywhere: it was the storm coming on suddenly

that stopped them, nothing to do with Erasinides or any of the Generals. And if it was just that, but one had been speaking against them, swearing oaths against them in the Assembly, well, wouldn't one be afraid of the Gods? Isn't a false accuser under the anger of Zeus? Wouldn't one be afraid of punishment? —' Suddenly he stopped, realizing from his mother's face, the evil things he had been saying, only half-consciously, about his own father: and also that they were true.

In another week it was Hallowe'en, the day before Apaturia, the Feast of the Dead. Moiro was sitting rather miserably in the lodgings with a piece of sewing, and no fire to keep her hands warm, when Alxenor came in. 'Moiro,' he said, 'have we got any black clothes? — something for mourning.'

She jumped up: 'Oh, why? You haven't heard from home?'

He shook his head and laughed: 'No! It's that clever old fox Theramenes; the trial's on and he wants to get every one hating the Generals first. So we're all to wear mourning and cut our hair and go and cry for our cousins who were drowned at Arginusae!'

'But we didn't have any cousins drowned!'

'No, silly, and nor did half the others we shall be with. Theramenes won't mind though!'

'Oh, I see. But I thought Phrasikleia told me he said it wasn't the Generals' fault?'

'Never mind what she said: this is politics. And anyway he's my patron and a good friend too. I don't care whose fault it was! I was there and

156

Phrasikleia wasn't! Where are those black clothes?'

'I'll go and look. Don't be angry with me, Alxenor!'

'I'm not. I was only thinking. Go and find them,
there's a dear.' But when she went out, he beat his
hands on his breast, saying under his breath the
Words that have strength over dead things; he
remembered that stony beach at the Arginusae, those
sinking ships out beyond; he thought of all the evil,
powerful little Keres swarming wet out of the sea,
over to Athens now that their day had come, finding a stranger to hate and light on, far from his
Gods.

Moiro came back. 'This is the best I can do. But
we could dye your old blue wool – it wouldn't take
long. Oh, did you say – I was to come too?'

'Yes, if you can. You're feeling well enough,
Moiro?'

'Oh, I'd like to come! I know I can find some
things. I can stay near you, can't I? It's nice of you
to take me; I do get lonely without you; it's such a
big city.'

He kissed her: 'Poor little girl! We didn't think it
was going to be like this two years ago, did we? I
thought I'd be able to give you everything you
wanted. Never mind, it'll all come right some day.
Theramenes said we could go back to dinner at his
house afterwards, and I expect there'll be something
for us to take home, too. I wish you weren't feeling
so tired, Moiro; I'm sorry.'

She smiled back at him bravely, shaking her brown
curls. 'That's nothing really. Besides, it's because

157   F

you love me – isn't it? I wouldn't mind at all, if only – if only I could see mother sometimes.'

'Darling,' he said, beginning to cry too, 'I wish I hadn't brought you! I wish your uncle had killed me! I wish I'd never seen those damned Spartans!'

They hugged one another, crying like babies, till they both felt happier and less frightened. Then Moiro went into the other room, feeling better than she'd done for weeks, and told Thrassa to run out and get a cupful of black dye in the market while she put the water on to boil. And Alxenor, rather ashamed of himself, washed his face and walked down to the stone-yard to help Strymodoros with squaring a big block; now that he was likely to be at home for some months, he worked at stone-cutting most days in exchange for his rent, and got quite clever with it after a time.

Strymodoros had a very high opinion of Theramenes. 'It would have been a different matter,' he said, 'if he'd been General instead of that bundle of rotten sticks! Look how well he did five years back!' Alxenor, trying to remember, could not think of anything particularly successful that Theramenes had done then, but still, things might have seemed different according to whether you lived in Poieëssa or Athens. Strymodoros and his wife were keeping Apaturia in all earnest this year, because of the youngest son; but they hated the Generals enough to be grimly pleased with the two sham mourners. The elder son had been on Arginusae beach too; but by now he had managed somehow to persuade himself

158

that the blame was all on Lysias – a man he had disliked for years.

Theramenes' plan was completely successful. The
mourners came dark and wailing into the Assembly;
at the same time the Generals were accused again,
this time with every atom of hate that could be
gathered against them, the Athenian people urged
alike by the accusers and the mourners to sentence
their Generals to death, now, now, at once! Alxenor
watched, one arm round his wife, as the Assembly
went wild with speeches and shouting and counter
accusations, and a great clamour to put the vote for
the death sentence. Suddenly, a scurry below them,
the centre shifting for a moment as some one got to
his feet, crying out that it was not lawful, that each of
the six Generals must have a separate trial – and,
down on the right, Theramenes twitching and biting
his hands with fear lest this should be allowed, the
people given time to change their minds, the Generals
let free, he himself the victim! No, it was all right.
Lawful or not, the Assembly would have its will,
shouted down the speaker, and terrified the Elders
– all except one – into putting their motion: life or
death for the six. Then, as the voting began, a
curious stillness came over the Assembly; nothing but
the Heralds' voices down below, and whispering, and
the noise of feet going past the voting urns.

It was getting late; Alxenor sent Moiro back, but
stayed on himself, trying to make it all out. He
began to wonder what they were feeling like, those
six in the middle, Diomedon who had been at his
marriage feast, young Perikles who had been nearly

drowned in the battle . . . and after all they had won! But *he* couldn't get up and tell the Athenian people to look before they leapt. Now it was beginning to grow dark; the buildings all round were fading into dusk; against that dimming sky the temples high above them on the Acropolis seemed faint and brittle as old sea shells. The voting went on, for life or death, and still Alxenor stayed. At last the Heralds stood up and announced the finish of their count. For a moment there was utter silence, then the Assembly broke into such a roar of joyful hate that Alxenor flattened himself suddenly back, gripping the wall, till it died down a little. Then the Eleven came, and took the Generals away.

Alxenor went hurrying back to his supper at Theramenes' house, all at once hungry and very thirsty. There were several of the sham mourners there, all rather silent, eating hard, with their black cloaks thrown off on to the floor. As he was standing by himself in the corner, biting into a meat pie, Moiro suddenly ran up to him from the women's rooms, pulling Nikodike after her, laughing and blushing, a fold of her dress caught up between her teeth as a half-veil. 'You tell!' 'No, you must!' 'Oh, I can't!' So Moiro leaned up and whispered to him: 'She's going to be married quite soon! It's all arranged.' 'Oh, good luck!' said Alxenor, 'I'm very glad!' And he was really pleased about it; she was a nice girl, pretty and brave and kind to his wife, and he thought her father hadn't been too fair to her. Besides, it was pleasant to have a marriage to look forward to, after to-day.

160

Theramenes came towards him, a bit pale, and pulling nervously at his beard; he looked at Alxenor without seeing him properly: 'I had to,' he said. 'Them or me. And I'm too useful. I'm the Workers' Friend.' He laughed jerkily. 'You like moderate men, don't you? I did try at first. But they sent a letter about us, Thrasybulos and me. His fault too. Them or me.' He smiled absently at his daughter, running a finger down her hair. 'That's it, if you must have a democracy. And it seems as if we must. Them or me,' he repeated. 'Them or me.'

Alxenor took Moiro home, with a little basket of food under her arm. He was thinking in some dim back part of his mind that now the Keres would have gone to rest again, satisfied.

The next day he went off as usual to the stone-yard; work was slack and the two slaves belonging to Strymodoros, who usually did the rough chiselling, were hired out to the State for ship repairs. The square block had to have a final polish, but after that there were only a couple of very small jobs on hand; there was little money in Athens now for public building or private either. The eldest son and Alxenor set to work on the stone, while Strymodoros stood by the wall, making a charcoal sketch for a gravestone he had to do during the next month. He frowned and muttered to himself, scrubbing out a line with his thumb: 'Looking bad, things are. First you know, we'll have those dirty Spartans back on us. What with one thing and another. Scurrying us out of our wits: God knows who mayn't get the hemlock next time!'

161

Alxenor cocked an eyebrow towards the son, questioning, and got back: 'Yes, I was there too. May be all right – if votes show. Shan't get Lysias messing us all up again, anyway. But as to the others – well, what do you say now, father?'

Strymodoros grunted. 'I ought to have trusted to my own trade; tried to keep the Laws – he did.'

'Who did?'

'Oh, Sokrates. Wanted them not to put the motion; only the rest gave in. But if they'd stuck it – like they ought, or what's the good of being Elders at all? – we couldn't have voted, and to-day – Oh, well no use crying over spilt milk. You didn't hear, did you, what Diomedon said, just when they were taking him away? "Men of Athens," he said, and he looked all round at us, "may our City be more happy and glorious for this. We cannot give thanks for our victory now; but you must, to Those we prayed to and who answered our prayers: Zeus Stayer of Armies and our own Lady Athene." Then they took him away. I wish I hadn't voted.'

The son went on angrily rubbing away at the stone. 'All the same, if we'd left those fine gentlemen alive, there'd be some one's head to pay anyhow! Theramenes is a better friend to us than they'd ever be, Gods or not! That Perikles trying to look like Father!'

'Well, he never did me any harm for all that,' said Strymodoros over his shoulder.

'No, and Lysias didn't do you any harm either – leaving my brother to drown! You've got as much memory as a haystack, father, and that's all there is to it!'

But here Alxenor thought he'd better interrupt,
and asked about the new porch that some one said
Archedemos was going to have built in the Agora at
his own expense, and who was going to get the job.
It was all in the air still, though. 'Nobody knows
what's going to happen,' said Strymodoros. 'The
war's been going on long enough, and a bit too long,
if you ask me.' Then they began to talk about the
Plays next spring, and who was going to pay for the
choruses, and whether comedies were best written by
an old man or a young, and so on till dinner.

Winter went on, and Alxenor was not earning any
pay; certainly the expenses were small, for Stratyllis
helped them as much as she could, and so did
Phrasikleia. But still one had to live. Sometimes
Alxenor would begin to think about going back to
Poieëssa, but even there he couldn't be certain of
anything; he would have to be under his brother
again, not even able to do what he liked with his own
wife and child; and if Chromon was still angry?

Nikodike was married just at the turn of the year,
and there was a fine marriage feast, with the bride-
groom's father sitting next Theramenes. It was a
little bit of a surprise to Alxenor to find he was such a
definite oligarch, a travelled man who had been on
embassies, had met King Agis privately, and was
prepared to joke about Lysander's artistic tastes. He
had written a little himself, and knew Aristophanes,
not well but enough to be able to laugh at Theramenes about some of the jokes on him that would
appear in the new play. His son, Diokles, on the
other hand, was not very intelligent and had a

thorough dislike of poetry; he thought Nikodike was pretty and hoped she would spin well and not quarrel with his mother. He had heard of the incident last summer, but was quite sure he would be able to keep her in order now; these women weren't so hard to manage once they'd got a proper respect for you. Hagnon, though, despised him as only a clever small boy can despise a stupid young man, and took no pains to hide it. As for the bride herself, if it wasn't the marriage she had dreamt of, well, no one gets everything they want. Perhaps he might be better when she got to know him; at any rate, he was a man and must be clever at lots of things . . .

Alxenor had to go off again in March, sorry to miss the play with the jokes about his patron, but very glad to be doing something and earning again. He got an advance on his pay and left it with Moiro; he was sure to be away over May anyhow. The last week or two before he went, he was as nice to her as he could be, and made love to her as if she was a fresh girl, not a sick, white, frightened woman who often wouldn't even kiss him back. He had something to tell her, but when she was ill and cross with him he was too sorry for her to say it, and when she felt better and put on her best dress and loved him back and was his own little girl again he couldn't spoil it all and make her cry, poor sweet, gentle thing. So he wrote it one day from an island harbour where their ship had put in, cursing at his oar-mates as they knocked into him, going by to the pleasures of the town, telling him to come with them, not be so mean with his money. Moiro, Moiro, when my letter finds you, how you'll curse me! 'When your time comes – good luck to you! – if you have a boy, keep it; if you have a girl, expose it.' He wondered if he could tell her how nearly he had bidden her expose it either way, and then hadn't the heart to; but letters were hard enough to write anyway, without saying exactly what he was feeling. All the same, he hoped it would be a girl; he couldn't see how they could afford another. Besides, he didn't much want a daughter anyhow.

In due course the letter came, and Moiro read it slowly, shaping the words with her lips, hardly realizing what it was about till the end. Then she went dizzy and fainted. Stratyllis, who was in the room, kneading flour, picked up the letter and read it too, while Thrassa was attending to her mistress. 'You're not the only one,' she said, almost roughly to Moiro. 'He's been as good to you as a man can before. Now, about this; if it's got to be done, do it at once. The worst's when they let you keep it for ten days.' But 'Oh,' said Moiro, rocking herself about, 'doesn't he know what bearing a child's like without this!' Nikodike came in the same day, and said it was sure to be a boy and everything would be all right; she was going to have a baby herself, and was feeling glad and hopeful about all the world.

Moiro's time came early in May; she knew what it was going to be like, and was not very brave. It was terrible for the other women to listen to her. Afterwards she lay for a few moments, quiet and spent and torn; then, when she saw by their faces and at last was told, that it was a girl, she held her breath for a minute, gathered herself together, and then screamed at the top of her voice, worse than ever she had screamed for pain before. Thrassa began to blubber in sympathy; Phrasikleia turned away, her hand over her twitching face; at last Stratyllis took up the baby and dumped it down by its mother. Then the screaming stopped, but Moiro clung to it, digging her fingers feebly into its shawl, glaring with a real and horrible hate at the others. When they came near to tend her, she bared her teeth at them, too weak to talk, until at last she dropped exhausted into sleep.

'Shall we do it now?' said Stratyllis. 'Better not let it suck at all, poor thing.' 'Oh, must we?' Phrasikleia whispered back pitifully. 'Won't she go mad to wake and find it gone?' 'Better now than later; she'll get over it so: less to forget. I know.' She went over to the bed and gently lifted Moiro's limp hand, and took the baby away. 'Shall I put in a pillow?' said Thrassa, seeing her sleeping mistress begin to fidget and grope with her fingers at the empty place. But Phrasikleia stopped her: 'No, no! We owe her the truth anyway.' And soon the mother was sleeping sound and heavily again. Stratyllis took it through to the next room. 'Have you got the things ready, Thrassa?' She wrapped it in the oldest set of swaddling clothes and Thrassa brought a big earthenware jar, and held it, sobbing and sniffling, for the baby to be put in, the little dark, mouse-soft head showing in the jar's neck. 'It's no use waiting too long,' said Stratyllis, 'it'll die soon, and you've got plenty to do here.'

Thrassa took up the pot and went scurrying out, terrified lest that screaming should start again. She looked about her, then turned down towards the Agora. It was late afternoon and pretty crowded; she knew she mustn't leave it to annoy people full in the middle of the street, and wondered where she would find a good corner, where perhaps some rich, childless old man would pass. . . . Suddenly she saw Ditylas, her policeman, and called out to him in their own barbarous tongue. He came up grinning, then looked into the pot: 'Not yours?' Thrassa explained angrily, and asked where she could leave it. They carried it together to a likely corner and waited themselves in the shadow of the house opposite. It was such a thin, long, heart-breaking cry that came from the pot; Thrassa clung to Ditylas, shaking. 'Never mind,' he said, 'they don't feel, not so little as that.' And he made up his mind to stay with her till it was over. That was brave of him, because if one of the Clerks of the Market had caught him hanging about with a girl, he would have been whipped.

Some people didn't notice; a few did, and passed on quickly, with a glance perhaps at Thrassa, pitiful and angry. No one stopped. By evening the little thing had finished crying. Thrassa went back; it was like a bad dream one couldn't wake from.

Stratyllis met her as she came in. 'No luck of course? No. She's awake now. Don't talk about it.' There was only one lamp alight in the room; Phrasik-leia sat by the bed, her hands folded; every now and then an owl hooted mournfully somewhere outside. Moiro lay quite quiet, her brown hair in damp,

167

straight tags on the pillow, her arms flat at her sides, her breasts already beginning to swell and ache with the useless milk. The hate had died out of her now; she said nothing when Thrassa came in, only turned her eyes, and looked, and then looked away.

Afterwards she got well quite quickly and recovered her old prettiness; she went out and visited her friends; she laughed and sang and curled her hair and began to use rouge for her cheeks, only Nikodike advised her not to. 'You've got plenty of colour already,' she said. 'Besides, what's the use with Alxenor away?'

'Oh, I don't know,' said Moiro, trying the effect with and without in her friend's little silver mirror. 'I must do something.'

'Well, I don't think he'd like it, Moiro. Besides, once you start you'll find yourself spending money on creams and scent and all that. And we can leave those things to the sort that's got nothing else to do: we've got better!'

'That's all very fine for you, Nikodike, with a big household to look after – oh, I know about your mother-in-law, but still it's you who have to do all the hard work! But me with my two rooms! Even after I've helped Stratyllis do hers there's not half the day gone. We can't afford wool enough for me to be weaving all the time!'

'But Timas!'

'Oh well, baby; but Thrassa can look after him.' She couldn't somehow explain that it gave her a pain now every time to see the one child alive and fat and happy, while his sister lay dead and rotting in some

168

corner, not ever to laugh and play and be kissed by
her mother or know any kindness from the world she
had just seen. Nikodike understood though; she
changed the subject and began showing her new
embroidery, sure that Moiro would suggest something better, and that it would please her to. They
fingered the shiny, flaxen threads, comparing colours,
their heads together. 'You are lucky to have all
those needles!' said Moiro. 'I've only got the one.
Alxenor said I must just do with it.'

Nikodike sighed: 'All the same, your Alxenor and
one needle is better than some husbands and a dozen!
You'll be all right again when he comes home.'

'Shall I?' said Moiro. 'I always used to be, but this
time it seems different. I'm grown-up now. One
wants to live another way, doesn't one?'

CHAPTER NINE

'Passant, combien de printemps
Pour croire encore a la vie?'
— Romains: *Europe*

THE palace at Sardis was on the other side of
the town, away from the Greek markets and
temples and civilization; they knew the way
there, though. Always when the Prince was staying,
he had his Median soldiers drawn up in the cool
hollow of the arch in two companies of ten each; the
gate was oak plated with bronze, and beyond was
the outer court with stables and kitchens all round.
The Spartans crossed it, and went on into the inner
palace.

First there were curtains, heavy crimson damask,
embroidered in gold with branching Babylonian
trees; Belesys clapped his hands, and they were
pulled sharply apart from inside. Then there was a
long, narrow, painted room, strewn with sharp-
scented leaves, and a guard of black men, tall and
shiny, with tunics and head-dresses of curled ostrich
feathers and red tassels on their spears. Then,
through a square, wide doorway, a garden of
cypress and azaleas, with the Prince's peacocks
stepping and sweeping from tree to tree. The two
Spartans whispered to one another, grinning, and
Archytas wished Leon was there to see. Then there
was another set of curtains, the same, and through
these sun and air again in the most charming little
courtyard, half Greek and half odd. The house
beams were long, winged, lion-women; they rested
on slender pillars of some reddish close-grained

170

wood, their shafts lightly carved with palm and lily leaves, their capitals picked out with gilding; the floor was of marble, green and white, with steps down to a small, square fountain, where hundreds of bright fish darted through swaying stems of water grass, and little tame, green-breasted ducks swam up and down. The two seats were made of the same carved wood, cushioned with green. A flute lay across one, and its guardian was a tiny gay parrot that cried out in Persian when it saw the curtains twitch.

Belesys motioned them to stop, and went on himself. Lysander puffed out a deep breath and ran a finger round under the rim of his best helmet, which he seldom wore as it was not comfortable. Archytas whistled to the parrot and got it to walk on to his wrist; it was like a jewel of carved jade and coral in the sunlight against the polish of his breast-plate.

They were alone for nearly ten minutes, but neither felt he could talk much to the other. The palace was all a-rustle wherever they looked with coming and going of listeners and whisperers. Besides, there was nothing to say.

Then quite suddenly the little square was crowded with courtiers pouring in, the long, bright Persian dresses, the hanging sleeves, the stiff, golden caps, the dark wink of ruby or sapphire as the ringed hands moved in greeting, and the ducks flapped their wings, crowding into the middle of the pond. Lysander spoke cleverly to one and another, remembering names and faces, which was worth money, which was jealous of him, which he suspected of being in Athenian pay; in some ways they were easier to

deal with than his own friends. Archytas stood a
little behind him on the left, the shield side, admiring
and trying to copy his admiral, but stiffer and much
less good at hiding his natural dislike of the easterns.

Then all at once Lysander smiled with real pleasure,
took a step forward and saluted. The courtiers
parted with swishing and clinking, and fingers
touching eyes and breast. Young Cyrus came strid-
ing through them, his cloak flung out behind, and
took Lysander's hands and began talking in fluent
and emphatic Greek; then suddenly turned on his
heel and snapped out an order at the others, who
slipped out rapidly, all but Belesys, and left him
looking eager and searchingly straight into the grey
eyes of the Spartan admiral.

Then he threw himself down on the seat, his legs
flung out, kicking at the cushions: the gold circlet
held firm over his dark, short hair, the thong-laced
trousers and tunic of fine red cloth, belted close,
his arms and neck bare, the Seal-ring one square of
deep and sparkling blue on his left hand. After a
minute he remembered he was not among his court
any more, and motioned Lysander to sit. Archytas
stood behind, fondling the parrot, ready to prompt
his admiral on figures; Belesys went out for a
moment, then came back with pen and ink.

Cyrus did most of the talking; he was anxious and
excited, and for a little the Spartans wondered if he
was drunk. But it was only that he had got a message
to say his father was very ill and bade him come to
Media to see him; and now he was beginning to
think of the succession – his brother against him –

the Satraps, Tissaphernes worst of all – oh what a tussle it would be, and what a prize! In the mean-time he must keep the balance here; it would be terrible if things went back while he was gone, Athens got command of the sea again, threatened Ionia and Egypt! 'Lysander!' he said. 'Oh, Lys-ander, what will you do while I'm gone!'

'I'm thirty years older than you,' grunted Lysander, not really angry, because he liked and admired the young Prince, and anyhow it would have been stupid to be angry just now, but gruffly enough to set Cyrus jumping up and running over to his seat and kissing him.

'Oh, best of old foxes!' said Cyrus. 'Every one knows you're the cleverest soldier in the world, but do remember that the Athenians are down enough to be desperate, and desperate men suddenly go and win battles against all rules! You can have as much money as you like if you'll use it the way I want; I know you'd rather beat Konon with one ship and your own dozen best friends, but think of me and be reasonable! Don't attack till you've got twice as many ships as they have, and keep safe, for I can't afford to have you killed! I can give you ten men's weight in gold, but worse luck I've got no gold-hearted men to give.' He jerked his thumb contemptuously after his Persians: 'Straw and paint, that's all they are now – ah, how did we ever win our Empire! But oh, remember, my Lysander, boy I may be, but I've an old head – promise by all your Gods not to give battle till you outnumber them!'

Lysander grumbled and glared, but thought it

173

perfectly sound; if this was the Prince's mood, so much the better. He wanted ready money. Archytas whispered to him details of arrears of pay to be made up. Cyrus assigned him all the tribute which came to him personally from his own cities, and sealed the document that Belesys prepared, then gave him almost all he had in the palace. He spoke again seriously: 'Suppose my father (may he live for ever) dies, and suppose – but one's a far cry from the other – I become the Great King, we shall still be friends, Lysander! I love the Hellenes. You'll come to me when you're banished from Sparta!' Lysander gave a start – the boy was seeing a little too far this time! – and protested angrily, till Cyrus soothed him down again with 'No, no, I'm wrong, I'm sorry, it will never happen, I said nothing!'

Then suddenly he turned, laughing, to Archytas behind: 'So you've made friends with my Lord-High-Everything!' The parrot called shrill at that: 'Prince's men, prince's men!' and Archytas, embarrassed, bent his head over it, stroking its smooth wing feathers against his lips.

Belesys came up and whispered something, and Cyrus frowned, fidgeting with his dagger, then took two gold bracelets off his arms and gave them to the Spartans. 'Remember!' he said, and slipped out, Belesys only just in time to pull back the curtains for him. Lysander tested the bracelet with teeth and finger-nail; it was soft, fine gold, and he was childishly pleased with it. Archytas was wanting to put the whole day into a letter to Leon, but knew that somehow between here and Sparta the words would have got pale and cold, the colour and life gone out of them, no love between him and Leon, but stiff foolish sentences that meant nothing. He put the parrot down on to the back of the seat.

The same evening Belesys brought Lysander the money; they counted it out slowly between them. Afterwards he stayed on for a little, talking to them both, eating lettuces dipped in salt. He felt safe with the Greeks; that son of his could not get at him here; no need to try the food on a slave – and then not be sure. 'Why don't you have him killed?' said Lysander. 'I would.'

'Oh well,' Belesys smiled at them, 'I am not so strong-minded as you. He is my only son, you see.' They nodded assent to that, understanding. 'And besides it might bring things into the open between Tissaphernes and my master Cyrus. We must not have that.'

'But aren't they going to the King together?'

'Dear Lysander, they love one another vastly. Just as my son and I do. And while they are away together, I mean to keep things safe here for the Prince ; but that's mostly on you. Well, you'll not need to make enemies at home with asking for money now!'

Lysander went out to make some special arrangements of his own about safeguarding the gold. The talk shifted to old days at Poieëssa; Belesys asked about Leon.

'He had to go back to his Class,' said Archytas, sighing. 'He'd got to, of course. It wouldn't have been good for him staying with me any longer;

175

young things must have regular discipline and training, and not too many strange doings. He'd been
away a year; that was enough; I expect they gave
him a bit of a rough time when he got back, poor
dear. Well, you can't bring boys up on milk and
water.' He would have liked to talk to Belesys about
Leon, get the Persian to say what a wonderful boy
he was, let them recall together the beauty and courage, the way he shook his hair back and stamped,
the small brown hands closed on a spear shaft . . .
But that would have been unfit between himself and
a barbarian. Instead he asked Belesys if he had ever
heard what became of that young Alxenor he had
helped to escape. 'Oh, you were quite right to do it,'
he said, 'though it annoyed me at the time.'

'I remember,' said Belesys, chuckling, 'your poor
Ladas got the worst of it!'

'Oh, he's used to that! But I must say I think now
you did much best to get him out of the way; he'd
only have complicated things with his brother. A
nice young fellow, as they went; Leon liked him. But
you've heard nothing since?'

'Not a word. How should I? I hope they are
happy now. The brother seems to be succeeding.'

'Eupaides thinks he can do what he likes with
Poieëssa now. He'll find his mistake one day. But
not, I think, till we have no more need of him.'

'When you have won your sea-fight?'

'That's it.' Then the admiral called him; he
jumped up: 'I'm wanted. Tell the Prince we will
remember!'

A few days later they went down to the coast.

176

Lysander gave his men their arrears of pay, signed on several hundred more skilled sailors, and picked up the new ships that had been building in two or three of the coast towns. The Athenians lay over at Samos, just within sight, getting their fleet ready too. Lysander looked out that way, feeling like a boy who sees the apples ripening.

Cyrus rode east and north into Media, with his dear friend Tissaphernes, the Satrap of Ionia, always close by where some one could keep an eye on him. And at last they came to the hill town where the Great King fretted and moaned in his golden bed; his brother was there too. Summer went on, bleaching the plains below them; the princes waited for their father to die.

About a month after the court had moved from Sardis, Belesys was poisoned by his son Gobryas, and died. Gobryas took over household and money, and wrote a letter to Tissaphernes, who carefully burnt it after he had sent back an answer. In most ways, Gobryas was a pleasant young man, very fond of horses and hounds, and hospitable to every one.

There was a small half barbarian town called Kedreiai, on the coast; its chief men had allied it with Athens years ago, but the people had gone on with their fishing and trading and pastured their goats on the hills above it, and not thought much about the war. They did not like the Athenian ships coming, because they took so much without paying; but still, Athens was a great city with a golden Goddess, and one did what one's chief men bade one. There were two ships there when Lysander's fleet sailed past

Cos and into the gulf; but for them, the town might have made terms for itself, but the Athenians threatened and praised and persuaded and heartened them up to stand against Lysander. The second day he took the town by storm; some of the people escaped, among them about half a ship's crew of Athenians; the rest were sold as slaves. Then Lysander sailed to Rhodes, hatching more plans in his head.

Kedreiai was not a very important town, and Konon did not care particularly; he was preparing an attack on Ephesus. But it was a pity about the two ships, though one was an old thing and not fit for much anyhow. Most of the men who had escaped got back to Samos one way or another; one boat-load brought Alxenor, wounded in the arm and feverish. He was sent back to Athens after a time with some more useless ones; they were told that if they reported again when they were well, they might get some of their back-pay.

It was the middle of July when Alxenor landed again at Piraeus. He did not know what had happened at home since he had been gone. Moiro screamed when she saw him, he was so thin and ragged and bloodless looking, with limp hanging fingers of his hurt arm. But oh, living still, her man! He spoke weakly, looking at her; she was her own pretty, slender self again, so clean, so gentle: 'What happened, wife?' And then she went stiff, the hands stretched out to him fell at her sides: 'It was a girl.' 'A girl. Then – then you did it?' She bowed her head.

She brought him in ; he suddenly found himself

wanting very much to see his son; the baby had forgotten him of course, and howled at being seized
on by a strange man. But soon he got to know him;
Alxenor was not well enough to work with Strymodoros, so he stayed at home a good deal and played
with little Timas, and gave him his dinner, and was
delighted and thrilled with his first words. He and
Moiro were ill at ease with one another, she jealous
for her dead one, hating to see Timas petted; he angry
that she wasn't kinder to him, wounded and all.
They took good care never to risk another child,
and that made things all the harder, as now they had
to give up the other room, and all sleep and live
together in one.

Strymodoros let them have that free in return for
the help his wife got from the women. Moiro and
Thrassa could usually get a meal from Nikodike if
her mother-in-law wasn't looking; Alxenor could
often have one at Theramenes' house, or if not, try
his luck – but not too often – with one or another of
his old shipmates; only they weren't much better
off than he was, and after all he was only a foreigner.
That was the worst of it when one got down to hard
facts: not being a citizen; so that if by any chance
they did die of starvation, it was nobody's affair and
Athens none the worse. Everything that could be
sold was sold; the only thing Alxenor kept was the
ring he had from Belesys; he felt it might some day
be even more useful than their immediate bread.

More than once, Moiro had asked him why they
could not go home; whatever they found there, it
would be better than this. It was not her affair of

course – he was master in his own house; but he answered her gently, saying he was sure things would get better, this was an unlucky time to choose, soon they might go, soon. . . . Once even he wrote a letter in her name to Chromon, and she signed it; but ships were uncertain; it never got to Poieëssa. And besides, his real answer to her would have been 'Too late.' They might have gone back a year ago, in honour at least, if not rich and great; it might have been all right, they might have been happy, without this dead baby between them. Only he had been too proud then; and now – there was the cost of their passage anyhow. It was not so terribly hard to live from day to day, but it was almost impossible to raise a large sum of money.

By August the wound was practically well; he went and reported to Theramenes, who was not with the fleet this year. Theramenes was vague and said he would see what could be done about back-pay, but of course that was the State's affair, not his, and in the meantime what about the tax on foreigners that he had not paid yet? Alxenor explained humbly that the tax depended on the pay, and pressed the matter as far as he could, but dared not quarrel with his patron. He left the house very gloomily; he did not care to go back to Moiro with no plan, so wandered down towards Piraeus, hungry and almost desperate. He asked at the harbour whether any of the ships were bound for Poieëssa. The captain of one, sailing next day for Samos, offered to put in there on his way for an extra thirty staters; but Alxenor's promise to pay on arrival was not good enough, so the captain bade

him be off for a cheat and beggar, and threw fish
heads at him when he tried further persuasion.

He turned again and walked up between the Long
Walls, chewing bits of dry grass. Half-way he
suddenly got very tired, and lay down full length
in the shade and slept, first lightly, waking every
now and then with a start of hunger, then heavily.
It was dark when he woke.

He sat up and shook himself; they could sell
Thrassa of course. He hated the idea, and knew it
would make matters even worse with his wife, but
it was the only thing to do. He looked at the stars,
and judged it must be near midnight: better go home
perhaps. They might have some food there.

He thought he heard something below in the harbour, and stopped a moment, listening, but could
not tell what it was, and tightened his belt and went
on up towards Athens. It was warm enough; he
thought of August nights on the downs above
Poieëssa, and almost cried for Chromon to be with
him again. Once more he heard that sound of wailing from below that seemed to fit into his thoughts.

Then came the noise of feet running and stumbling
behind him, and he turned; he could see in the starlight tears streaming down the man's face. 'What is
it?' he said, startled out of his dreaming, and the
man cried harshly at him: 'The *Paralos* – the *Paralos*
is back, and we're beaten! Oh God, oh God, we're
utterly beaten!' 'How, how, how?' Alxenor gasped,
shaking him. Not Konon?' 'Yes,' said the man,
realizing it again for the hundredth time as plainly
and terribly as when he had heard it first. 'They've

beaten us. All our ships but nine. This is the end.
Athens —' And he flung his arms up over his face
and rushed on, sobbing.

And as Alxenor still stood there, scarcely able to
think, another passed him, and another, crying aloud
at the disaster, the death of friends and kinsfolk, the
shadow of the doom of Sparta falling on them
already. 'How many ships gone?' he asked, plucking
at an old man's sleeve, who answered there were a
hundred and fifty taken. 'Two hundred,' said
another. 'All our fleet. Oh, lost, lost, lost!' and
trailed away with the rest, weeping, towards the
City. Alxenor followed them, dazedly.

As he went up towards Athens, the crowd got larger
and larger, hurrying and moaning, each man separate
in his own grief and fear; there was no comfort in
being one of many at a time like this. Now there
were women among them, mothers and wives of the
dead at Aigospotamoi, sobbing quietly, too stunned
to shriek.

When they got to the Agora, Alxenor looked round
again, astonished to find that he was one of so very
many. They were all very quiet here in this holy
place under the tranquil sky of stars. Only the men
from the *Paralos* were speaking, the citizen rowers
who had brought Athene's ship safely home. They
shuddered with narrow eyes, thinking of the others,
all the beautiful, gay, high-prowed warships, and
their fine, gallant sailors, crows' food now in the
Hellespont. They told how it all was: Lysander's
cunning, the Athenians scattered, unsuspecting —
not time to man the benches before the rams were

on to them! Konon had escaped, they thought, none
of the other officers. Every one knew the temper the
Spartans were in now; they could not hope to get
any prisoners back.

Yet here in this familiar place, it was hard to believe
that the end had come, hard to believe it was all
behind, Marathon, Salamis, the Empire they had
made, the hopes and the glories, all gone, all nothing,
Athens finished. Unmerciful they had been, proud
and cruel: ghosts of murdered Hellenes cried on
them from Melos and Aegina, Torone and Histiaia.
Now Fate had marked them: their corn-ships clipped
off with the shears of the Old One. And slowly,
slowly, the tide of famine would rise round them,
death staring at them for many days before the inevitable surrender. The war had been going on so
long that every one had forgotten it must end some
day. Now it was over.

After a time Alxenor went home, stunned with
disaster. If by any chance he could get his wife and
child out of Athens now. . . . They were all asleep
in the room; no one had told them. He bent over
Moiro, young and gentle with his baby son beside
her, and he kissed them both lightly so that they did
not stir, and found some pease porridge they had
left for him, and ate it, and tried to think what he
could do.

Towards dawn the people in the Agora began to
thin out, drifting away to the homes that were theirs
still, knowing there was no more to learn yet. Theramenes went across to his son-in-law's father's house
to talk things over; foreseeing the siege and the

famine, Phrasikleia felt deadly anxious about her daughter and went straight to her. Only Hagnon stayed on in the market-place, crouching against one of the plane trees, intently watching the creep of dawn light once more on to his City.

He turned slowly, at a step beside him: 'What are you doing out, Isadas? Get back!'

Then Isadas rocked himself on the balls of his feet and looked down at his master: 'You'd better not give me orders now, Hagnon!'

The boy stared at him, a little frightened, but not much: 'You shut your mouth or I'll have you whipped! We're not beaten yet!'

Isadas laughed. 'Now you listen to me, Hagnon son of Theramenes! You're for it now, you and your Athens. The Spartans are coming to smash it all up, smash, smash, smash, and kill your father and rape your sisters, by God they will, – and your mother if she's worth it – and sell you for a slave, yes, by the Twin Gods and whip you too! And see if I don't help them!'

Hagnon got quickly to his feet and jumped for the Melian's throat, and nearly had him over; but Isadas hit out, and for five minutes they fought, silent with hate, under the plane tree. Isadas was three years older, and heavier, and a Dorian; his skill and quickness were little use to Hagnon. Isadas knocked him down and held his hands, and kicked him when he bit, then seemed not to know what to do. At last he let Hagnon go and watched him struggle up, uncertainly, then, moved by some odd impulse, knocked him down again. This time the

184

boy was slower at getting on to his legs and shook a good deal. So Isadas spat in his eyes and turned and ran off, bounding down through the dawn, talking to himself, off to the hills until the Spartans come!

Hagnon stumbled over to a well and washed his face carefully; his best tunic was torn and covered with blood and dirt. It was nearly light. He wondered if there would be school all the same in the morning.

Half an hour later, when there was enough day-light to see a little, Alxenor woke the women, bade them take Timas, and follow him down to the harbour. There was little to take with them, the bedding, a few clothes, an oil flask and a bag of meal. He told them to come very quietly without saying good-bye; for some reason he was afraid of being stopped. They tiptoed out, the women carrying the bundles, and he the child. Speaking more to himself than the others, he said: 'A good thing there's not another of them,' and hushed little Timas up against his shoulder, and saw that the blanket was pulled well round him. He had no very definite plan in his head, he must trust to luck when there was nothing else to trust to. He vowed a golden ship to the God-dess of Poieëssa if they could be saved. He meant to go to the captain of the ship which was sailing for Samos, and see what could be done; he would certainly have to sell Thrassa; if necessary he would sell himself for a term of years, but his wife and son must get to Poieëssa. He said nothing to them, afraid to have Moiro and Thrassa screaming and

185

sobbing at him, only hurried them down, helping
his wife with her bundle. The Guards at the Long
Walls let them by with curses for dirty foreign rats.
And they were not alone. Already people were
streaming down towards the sea, mostly women and
children and old men. Any Athenians with good
friends in Ionia, were sending over their women-folk
as the best chance. It looked bad for Alxenor.

Only, just then, Thrassa, stumbling along under the
weight of bedding, suddenly gave a queer choked
cry, and stooped and snatched up something from
the ground. Alxenor, trying to push through in front
without hurting his baby, did not notice; but Moiro
saw, and for a moment the two women looked into
each other's eyes, trembling. All at once Thrassa
knelt down in the dust of all those flying feet: 'It's
me!' she said, 'me, little mistress, not him!' And she
shoved the purse into Moiro's hands. The three of
them made a little eddy in the crowd, standing close
together with the bundles on the ground between
them. Moiro began crying again, but differently
this time, and Thrassa said nothing, but breathed
hard and gulped. Alxenor looked round half fearfully: 'Anyone might have dropped it! We can't
ask! For the child, anyhow.' Then, 'I wonder – if
it was our Lady of Poieëssa.' Suddenly he took
Thrassa by the shoulders and kissed her; so did
Moiro. Then they went on.

The money was in silver mostly, good thick
Athenian Owls, and some odd bronze; there were
two or three Lydian gold pieces as well, and a few
chain links and bits of coral, some four hundred

staters in all. He had to pay every bit of it to the
Samian ship's captain now — there were so many
clamouring to be taken — and he knew he must land
in Poieëssa penniless, in debt as far as that went, and
have the shame of begging from his brother; but
still it mattered little compared to the fact that they
were actually on board. Before they sailed, every
inch of deck space was filled; the two women sat on
their bedding, trying to keep the baby quiet between
them, another family on each side grabbing at its
piles of bundles and jars, children wedged in and
crying, young girls, terrified, trying to veil themselves. At the last moment, Alxenor had the sense to
send Thrassa back with a jar to get some fresh water.
He wondered who the owner of the purse was, and
what he was feeling like now; it might be a woman
for that matter. At any rate, he would never know.
They got off in the afternoon with a light north-
westerly breeze; the sun on deck grew unbearably
hot, and every one spread cloaks for awnings, but it
seemed almost harder to breathe underneath them.
Night came mercifully at last, and then it was how
to sleep all jammed up together among the bundles.
They were all as tired as could be, but it was hard to
get any rest; when one was just going off, the ship
would give a lurch, one's neighbours shift about and
curse, something would begin to run into one's back,
or a baby close by would start on interminable wailing.
In the morning every one was dirty and stiff and
aching; they were out of sight of land.

About midday they sighted a sail to the north, a
small trader that drew up with them slowly, and at

last hailed. Every one who could crowded to the side, clamouring for news. It was much what they had expected, but sufficiently alarming for all that. Lysander was coming from the Hellespont, sweeping up the seas as he went, freeing the islands from Athens – and their own democracies – and driving every ship he could find that was owned by an Athenian or had Athenians on board, back into Athens: so that the starving out should not take so long. 'Where shall I be safe?' the captain shouted across. 'I'm bound for Samos.' 'Lysander'll be-after you then!' the man on the rail of the trader called back sharply. 'Get south – home for all you're worth! Chuck your Athenians out and keep in harbour and pray!'

That was the only thing to do. The wind shifted a little, and freshened; they ran before it, hour after hour, shipping a good deal of water, heavy laden as they were, every one's bundles getting soaked. All the time, half of them were staring out northward, searching the bare horizon for those first ominous sails of Lysander's fleet. Plainly, there was no chance yet of Poieëssa; they passed fifty miles to the south, and at last made Samos, on the evening of the third day.

For a man alone, the town of Samos was a gorgeous place to be in then, surging and roaring with the sailor democrats who would stick by the Lady of Athens and damn Lysander and let him come and snarl at them if he dared! They half knew that they were the only one of the Allies who would stay loyal; they were proud as hell, and cheered the ship coming

in from Athens! But Alxenor could not let his
heart stir and leap out to meet these brothers of
Chromon; he had to stop his ears to the shouting and
singing, the armed, splendid democracy. He went
to the captain: 'What about Poieëssa?' he said. The
captain looked at him sourly, knowing he had no
more money: 'Yes, and what about Lysander?
Risks of war, young man. Out you go!' 'You've
taken my money – it's against all law and right –'
'Chuck that!' said the captain, then, perhaps a little
moved by the spirit of Samos, perhaps just wanting
to get rid of him: 'Here, my cousin's bound for the
mainland – you can go with him, and a good rid-
dance! Take it or leave it – sharp now!'

Alxenor took it; he had no power to make the captain give back his money, and he would stand a better
chance of getting to Poieëssa from the mainland.
They sailed again, in a smaller and dirtier boat, and
after another wretched night, got to Ephesus harbour and were turned out on the quay.

'You stay here,' said Alxenor as cheerfully as he
could to the crying women. 'I'll go up to the town
and see if I can get work.' They had a little bread
left, enough for themselves and the baby; poor little
Timas was looking pinched and white, and his
crying had a horrid, thin sound now. For a moment
Alxenor thought how it would simplify things if they
all just jumped into the harbour and drowned there.
Then he kissed Moiro, left them, and started to walk
the five miles up to the town.

But though it seemed possible to spend any amount
of money in Ephesus, it was extremely hard to earn

any, and when he tried shamefacedly to beg from
one or two passers-by, the regular town beggars
turned on him and beat him with crutches. He looked
for some place to sell Belesys' ring, but knew it was
not very valuable except as a token: it was only thin
gold, and the crystal was flawed. The first two
jewellers who saw it would not offer him more than
enough to pay for a night's food and lodgings; and
that did not take him much further. The second one
asked him suspiciously where he had got it; Alxenor
told, and thought he saw a flicker of recognition in
the man's eye at the name of Belesys. 'Do you know
of him?' he asked eagerly. 'Is he here?' The jeweller
smiled a little to himself: 'Not actually – no. But
. . . m'm . . . if you cared to see his son? He might
be down here; he often comes about now.' He
craned out of his shop: 'Yes! You see? Fortunate
young man, go and show him the ring.'

Alxenor looked uncomfortably at the jeweller, not
quite liking the tone of his voice, the last hint of
mockery. Then shrugged his shoulders, and went
up to the Persian, a handsome, rich-looking man in
a fringed cloak, playing with a beautiful greyhound. He bowed low – Greek to barbarian! – saying, 'I have a ring, sir: I think you will know it.'

Good-humouredly, the Persian took it in his hand;
Alxenor had been so afraid of just being cursed at!
The people in the street went on past them at each
side; the hound fawned on his master; Gobryas
looked at the ring he knew perfectly well, much
amused. Alxenor waited anxiously. The jeweller
craned further out of his shop, filled with delicious

190

curiosity as to how Gobryas would treat a friend of
his father's; but he was disappointed, he had under-
estimated a certain essential pleasantness about the
son of Belesys, who still stood smiling, one hand
fingering the ring, the other resting on his hound's
neck. 'And how did you come by this?'

'It was given me.'

'By?'

'The wearer. Your – your father, sir.'

'H'm. Where have you come from now?'

'Athens.'

'Athens! Well, well. How do they take the news?'

Alxenor wondered if it would be safe to assume that
this man's political views were the same as his
father's; he decided on the whole it was better not to
commit himself yet. 'They were making ready for
the siege.'

'And their chances?'

'None – practically.'

'So you ran away?'

'I've got a wife and child.'

'I see. You're an Ionian?' (But did the man
want him to say he was an Athenian? – it was too
puzzling!)

'From Poieëssa.'

'So that is where you got his ring. It has been well
out of the war, your Poieëssa!'

Alxenor saw him frowning at the ring, thought
rapidly of Tissaphernes – the Persians were good at
changing sides – took the chance: 'I fought for
Athens two years.' Then, 'I killed a Spartan.' Still
the Persian stayed impassive, but at least not angry;

he ventured again: 'An enemy to the Governor.'
'Which do you mean?'
'Tissaphernes.' Then, as the Persian smiled, 'Not
Cyrus!'
'I see. So you did not altogether share my father's
views?'
'N-no.' (Oh, was the man playing with him after
all?)
'Difficult, isn't it?' Gobryas looked him up and
down critically; he tried not to be angry. At last
the other laughed outright: 'What a Hellene! Well,
where's the wife and child?'
They drove down to the harbour in a little open
chariot, Gobryas himself holding the reins, waving
his hand to friends as he passed; Alxenor standing
beside him, trying to feel the spiritual superior – or
at least equal! – of any Persian, in spite of being so
hungry and unwashed and penniless. It was late
before they got down to the quay again. Moiro
looked up, eyes big with tears of waiting, and then
down, blushing, as Gobryas first stared at her, then
took her hand. 'Well,' he said, 'I shall see what I can
do for you, ring-bearer.'
Alxenor could not help feeling he had been extraordinarily fortunate, first in Athens, then here; on
the other hand, it was not pleasant to be indebted to
a barbarian, and also Theramenes had not looked at
his wife in quite that way before helping him. He
decided to write to Poieëssa at once. Meanwhile he
found himself in an odd position in the Persian's
house. He did everything that came his way, wrote
letters, took messages, fed the greyhound, played

the flute, told Gobryas anything he could remember or invent about the private lives of Athenian politicians, read aloud to him, interviewed shopkeepers, mended chairs, mixed wine, and so on and so forth. Moiro and Thrassa helped the women about the house and at the looms; they all had good food and a place to sleep in, but of course no money. Alxenor was very much shocked at finding out, as he did quite soon, about Gobryas and his father; but what would you? Foreigners are always odd.

In the meantime, Lysander began to blockade Athens from the sea, King Agis from the land.

CHAPTER TEN

'Oh, why don't you work as the other fellows do?
How the hell can I work when there's no work to do?'

ALXENOR did write, to his brother, a friendly
letter, but not, he thought, unnecessarily
humble, saying that he was in Ephesus with
Moiro his wife, and asking if affairs went well in
Poieëssa. About the third week he found a ship that
was sailing for the island, and gave one of the sailors
his letter to take. They both went down to the harbour to see her off, but Moiro was crying so that she
could hardly watch at all, she did so want to be on
board herself, she was so aching for home. She
thought Alxenor might have borrowed the passage
money from Gobryas; but it was not her place to
say so.

In little more than a fortnight he got his answer;
Eupaides must have written at once, and Alxenor got
a quite unpleasantly violent thrill out of seeing his
brother's handwriting again. He broke the seal; it
was annoying to find oneself beginning to cry just
because some one that one really disapproves of
strongly, writes 'dear little brother' at the head of a
letter. However, as he read on he got angry again, so
that was all right. Eupaides said first of all how glad
he had been to get the letter – such a long time –
always hoping – and so on and so forth, very com-
forting as far as that went, and nothing about two
years ago. But then it went on to say that as for
Moiro, he had never got the consent of her guardians
who would doubtless want to have her back, anyhow
a marriage out of one's own city was a different affair,

194

he could pay the suitable fine for an abduction, and then it would be all over; he should marry Gello, his cousin – here Alxenor banged the letter hard on to the ground and stamped on it. He wished now he had put Timas into his own letter, only he had been somehow ashamed, it seemed ridiculous to tell one's brother one had got a baby! Well, anyway, he wasn't going back – not going to put his wife away at the word of a damned tyrant like his brother!

One evening Gobryas mentioned casually that there was an Athenian coming to dine with him, an official, said the Persian, who had been banished some time during the war, and was always anxious for news from Athens: 'So you can come, but just try and see what he wants said before you say it – oh, and remember to see we have fresh fish this time.'

So Alxenor got Moiro to wash and iron his only decent tunic, and was waiting punctually when Gobryas and his guest and one or two friends came in. During dinner he said hardly anything, but did the carving, laughed at every one's jokes, and thought the Athenian looked rather charming, a little old man with quick movements, always turning his head from side to side like a bird, wanting to listen to every one, a bit deaf but trying not to show it, by name Thucydides, son of Oloros.

When the food had been cleared away and the wine was going round, Gobryas motioned Alxenor over to sit by his guest; he gave what account he could of Athens, explaining that he had fought at Arginusae, and that his patron had been Theramenes. The old man nodded quickly and patted Alxenor on the knee

195

with his wrinkled, hairy fingers: 'Ah, Theramenes, he'll never live to be as old as me; you'll see, he's too good for them, a real statesman, a speaker to twist you round his finger, and last, well – a gentleman. If his government had stayed in power (six years ago – you wouldn't remember it), things might be different now. But there's always a tanner or a fishmonger jumping out of the gutter to upset it all – and make war again. Eh well, they've got their fill now by the look of things.'

'I'm afraid so, sir,' said Alxenor low, for the little man's talk had suddenly gone very bitter, his pleasant, shifting Attic voice had ground harshly down on to the words. Gobryas looked up quizzically and whispered to one of the other Persians; the servants tiptoed round; Thucydides the Athenian stared at the wall in front of him, his fingers twisted together.

All at once he turned to Alxenor again; his mind had gone on working since he spoke last, he took up the thread in a new place: 'But even so, though she is utterly lost, starved and beaten, under the heel of Sparta, yet it was worth while, yet my city is a star to the world! I feel now, I feel –' he shook Alxenor by the arm '– suppose this is the end, for myself I would rather have died before it came, but for the Gods there is no ending at all. A thing has been, the stuff of reality, it cannot perish; all the Spartans alive have no power over the idea. They may burn our temples and kill our men and make our women slaves, but we shall be remembered and other cities will spring up, in the clear air –'

'Things won't be as bad as that!' said Gobryas,

196

laughing. 'The King won't let Sparta have it all her own way any more than he let you!'

But though Alxenor bowed and smiled, he hated the barbarians, and the other Hellene beside him had not heard: he went on again: 'I am an old man, I seem to be standing on the edge of time, looking down on the ways of men. There have never been any years like these. Babylon – Egypt – they just went on. But we, we lived for the future: that's what history is, why I started writing: as soon as I saw what was happening, under my own eyes. For all cities have their time of growing and their time of dying, and the moment between; but with Athens the moment lasted long enough for me to know it.'

'You knew it *then*, sir? While it was there?'

'Yes,' said Thucydides. 'Yes! And, when I was banished, at first I was only full of bitterness and hate and plotting. But after a time I thought, it is not the place that makes the City, but the way men think, and if I still thought rightly – fairly – clearly – I would still be in an Athens of my own. Perhaps I shall never see this world's Athens again: it seems most likely. And when I think how beautiful she is, I can scarcely bear it, even now after so many years. But the other Athens –' He broke off, looking sharply and smilingly from Alxenor to his host and back again, shifted on the couch, drank and held out his cup again, scratched in his stubbly beard: 'Well, what a deal of nonsense we talk! But I wonder what your patron and his friends are going to do now; I wonder how long she can hold out – not one corn-ship coming through.' He screwed his face up pain-

fully: 'It doesn't bear thinking of. And I wonder
what Sparta will do to her. You know, young man,
I've had good friends in Sparta, for eighteen years
now; but I wouldn't trust them when it comes to my
City. I have gone back as much as all that. And
Samos holding out against Lysander; that can't go
on for ever; but it's been the key place this last dozen
seasons. I know it well; I've travelled much in my
time, seen most of the world that's worth seeing,
Asia, Egypt, Italy. Syracuse I saw, and the quarries.
And what shall I see now? But I say again, it has all
been worth while!' He turned round abruptly, his
back to Alxenor, and reached across for a dish of
radishes and began eating them by the handful, biting and scrunching and throwing the green tops
about over his shoulder.

He went on the next day, the queer little soldier,
with his secretary and his cook, and his lovely dap-
pled mare that he was so proud of, back to his estate
in the north. After he left, Alxenor found himself
fretting more for news of Athens; he used to go down
to the harbour sometimes, to see if the ships could
help him, but the blockade was firm round the City.
No news got out and no food got in: so till winter.

The baby flourished exceedingly on all the good
food he was getting now; he could walk and talk and
had deliciously fluffy dark hair, and his baby-blue
eyes were beginning to darken; Alxenor found him
great fun to play with and roll about, much better
than a puppy; besides, one was always making up
ridiculous plans about him, that couldn't possibly
come true, but still — Thrassa enjoyed getting back

into a big household with lots of others to talk to; except for Ditylas, she hadn't liked Athens much; she felt her little mistress wasn't getting her right chances there, particularly at first when she had been so much in love with Alxenor, not standing up for herself a bit! But Ephesus was a nice, comfortable Ionian town where women weren't treated like dogs; they could go out together here, and market, and make friends; there were plenty of other women about, oh, quite respectable, but friendly, ready to talk, not always having to hurry back home as if there was a thunder-storm! And if by any chance you did have a word with a young man, well, you didn't have the whole place after you, like it was in Athens. Nice, pleasant-spoken young men they were too, not just rushing off to the wars and as rough as bears in Spring! Not to speak of the Persian.

Gobryas had once or twice had a Greek lady friend, but they had tended to be a little elderly, and affected to look down on him. On the whole it had been more satisfactory to keep to his own race with their own methods of love, which he appreciated. But Moiro was a different, and much pleasanter, affair; the Gods had never before given him the chance of a free Greek woman, young and charming and sweetly grateful. And the husband was in no condition to complain.

However, Gobryas did not get on quite as quickly as he had hoped. Moiro was still very much of a country girl, for all her time in Athens, and more innocent than he quite realized. Besides, she was still very loyal to her husband, even though she

199

hardly loved him at all now. When Gobryas spoke
to her she was always very shy and fluttered, the
colour coming and going in her cheeks; she had let
him hold her hand because of the difficulty of doing
anything else, and she thought he was very kind and
rich and gentle. But she was not at all attracted to
him as a man, and she giggled to herself over his
Graeco-Persian clothes and his occasional misuse of
a Greek phrase. Thrassa was rather unsatisfactory –
she wouldn't laugh at him properly, and kept on
saying what a fine figure of a man he was, such fiery
eyes, such a passionate bearing, such a seat on a
horse! 'What a lying old cat you are,' said Moiro
simply. 'How much do you get out of him?' 'More
than Alxenor ever gave me!' Thrassa answered back.
'Even when he'd got it to give! The Persian's what
I call a good giver. And the things he's got for the
one who chooses to have them, pearls and rubies and
real emeralds – ooh, you wouldn't know yourself!'
'Well, it's nothing to do with me anyway, so you hold
your tongue, Thrassa. Silly old Trousers, he can't
fool me with a lot of coloured glass!'

But all the time of course she knew they weren't
glass. And she began to think about them, and
other things. It seemed as if the chances of getting
home were very small now. Alxenor had shown her
the letter; she had tried to persuade him to go back,
even so, saying that things were sure to come right in
the long run – what if her guardians did take her
for a little? It would be only for a few months; then
every one would be friends again. But she was
thinking of mother, Chromon, Aunt Pyrrhé and the

cousins, all the farm servants, the beasts – she began to cry about it. But Alxenor would be so proud. It was all because of the child; why couldn't he think of her a little – what she really wanted, not what he thought she ought to want! And if they didn't get back to Poieëssa, what was going to happen? And what was the good of being young and pretty if one's husband couldn't afford to be a husband? She'd just get older and older, and wrinkled and skinny, weaving and sewing and mending and washing, and scolding the baby and talking to Thrassa. Well, other women found other ways of living!

One day Gobryas kissed her, a long, slow, hot kiss; she knew it was coming and meant to let it just be the beginning, only then in the middle quite suddenly she hated the feel of his lips and got frightened and ran away, and at last, of all silly things, found Alxenor and told him! Alxenor realized that he had been all the time half-consciously expecting something of the sort, but had managed to smother it, so anxious to stay in this easy life. Now he must be up and off again, out into the bitter world, with her and his little son. It was winter too, or scarcely Spring; only a few crocuses beginning to break among the rocks. 'Keep him off for a week,' he said, 'and I'll get you away somehow. Dearest wife.' She was good, he thought, Chromon's sister; he could trust her; he must save her.

Archytas had been in Ephesus for three days before Alxenor heard of it. Then he went scurrying off to the house and waited about there for a couple of hours because there was no one in. He had not been able to hear of anything before; now he must make Archytas help him. At last the Spartan came in, older-looking than Alxenor remembered him, and his hair cut short to his shoulders after the fashion of Lysander's men.

Alxenor ran in front of him and knelt; after a minute or two Archytas recognized him with a laugh: 'Well, what do you want?'

Alxenor explained: work and pay. 'I'm a good sailor,' he said, 'and a good fighter. But they didn't pay us. Take me on, Archytas, and I swear I'll be loyal to you and Sparta – I can't afford not to be!'

'We've more men than we know what to do with wanting to serve now,' said Archytas. 'I'm sorry, I can't take you. Go back to Poieëssa.'

But Alxenor wouldn't leave go: 'Leon helped me before,' he said. 'For Leon's sake I beg you to help me now!'

Archytas hesitated, snapping his fingers together uncertainly; it was queer how Leon's name even moved him in this far Ionian town. 'Leon did a lot of silly things one time and another.'

'Not really, Archytas, you know he didn't. Suddenly sometimes: he'd got that fine, quick spirit – why he moved so lightly. Archytas, it would be throwing away his work half made to send me off now!'

'Well,' said the Spartan, 'perhaps I might do something. Have you got armour?'

'Not much.'

'You wouldn't! I suppose you can row?'

'I was Bow in Theramenes' ship.'

'Oh, then you ought to know about rowing and backing too! You can come.'

'Archytas, I do thank you – and Leon! He's not here?'

'No, in Sparta.'

'I'm sorry, it was beautiful to see him. Archytas, what shall I do about my wife?'

'You've got a wife, Alxenor? Oh hell!'

'It was her Leon helped to carry off. And a child. Let me come in and I'll tell you where they are.' Archytas nodded, and once they were inside out of hearing, Alxenor explained the position, down to that last kiss.

Archytas considered: he was rather well-off now, like most able-bodied Spartiates at the end of the war. Much gold had come lately into hollow Lacedaemon, the palish bars from Lydia stamped with their weights in Persian, heavy bright crowns from the Allies, minted money from the conquered cities. He could afford to be generous. In a way he had liked old Belesys; he would be glad to do any harm he could to the son who had murdered him. On the other hand, Spartan-wise, he disliked unnecessary expense. Finally, however, he decided he could take them all. 'My wife's Kleora,' he said. 'Leon's cousin: very like him. I'll give you half-pay; you can live on that and I'll have the rest for them: bring the lot to my ship this evening.'

It was close quarters in the warship; four bare planks from the side, and a curtain; they hadn't even been able to bring their bedding for fear of being caught. What a fool I am, thought Moiro, this is what comes of being faithful! Three times he's bundled me off in a ship like a slave-girl, and this time to go to Sparta at the end of it – Sparta where the women go about half naked and the men don't wash and there's no sort of comfort or decency! And if only, she thought, if only I'd let Gobryas have his way, he'd have given me rubies and pearls and set me up for life, and, husband or not, I could have gone back home to Poieëssa by and by, and lived happily ever after! And now we're going the other way, half across the world again, and perhaps I shan't ever have another chance. Oh, I wish I'd taken it!

Thrassa just gloomed and sulked; she had nearly told the Persian what was happening, but it had all been so sudden, she hadn't had time to use her wits. And now it was too late. Sparta . . . where every one knew slaves were worse treated than anywhere in Greece! Well, even old Ladas who was on board with them now, who'd served Archytas faithfully and helped him out of all manner of tight corners, and who'd been shield-bearer to his father before that, why, his back was a sight!

They saw rather little of Alxenor, as he was rowing – it was extraordinarily calm weather for so early in the year – and when they did see him he was not very welcome, and knew it. He found himself rather badly out of training at first, and ached for a couple of days. The other rowers were a mixed crowd, half-barbarian; he took good care not to say where he'd learnt the trade – he didn't want to spend all his time being laughed at or perhaps worse – and made

the women keep quiet about it too. And he tried
not to think all the time that he was working for
Sparta – nor about what was happening in Athens.
Anyhow, the pay was safe.

The only one who enjoyed it thoroughly was the
baby; he wasn't old enough to be shy yet, and he
made friends with all the men. 'Up-y, up-y!' he'd
say, dancing about on his little bare, brown feet, and
holding out his arms to Archytas, who couldn't help
picking him up and playing with him – he hoped to
have a son of his own soon. Then his father and the
Spartan would toss him about from one to the
other, and swing him by the ankles and pretend to
throw him overboard, till he squealed with pleasure.
'We'll make a man of you yet, little sausage!' said
Archytas, tickling him. Moiro hated it, that great
rough brute of a Spartan knocking her baby about!
She kept him shut up behind the curtain with her as
much as she could, but still she didn't love him
altogether, there was always the other coming
between. And Timas pulled at her skirts with his
mouth drooping, wailing for 'father,' even when she
smacked him for it, and went trotting and tumbling
off to Alxenor when he wasn't rowing, or else to
Archytas, or to Ladas who gave him a finger dipped
in honey to suck, and could make the funniest
possible faces.

By and by they came to Gytheion; here Alxenor
was turned over to another ship and said good-bye
very miserably to his household, hoping they'd be
all right, urging Moiro to take care of his son, till
she got quite angry, and would hardly kiss him at

the end. She was rather cross anyhow, because she was going to a fine house and a great lady, and – as usual – she hadn't got anything fit to wear, and no ear-rings, no necklace, no nothing! She refused to be interested in all the odd things there were to see when Alxenor pointed them out, not even in the shaggy black cows, though she'd never seen a cow before, nor ever tasted anything but goats' milk for that matter, and was really terrified. She just shrugged her shoulders and twisted up her pretty face, still thinking of pearls and rubies and how could she have been such a silly. And they all three went up into the green, sheltered valley of Eurotas, where already the earliest flowers were springing on the warm banks, and Alxenor went back to his oar and his shipmates, and night falling early over the sea that was Sparta's now.

He found the rest of the crew a very different matter from the men he'd known on Theramenes' ship; there wasn't a citizen among them, or ever likely to be. A few were barbarians, the others Hellenes – but what Hellenes! Some recruited from the harbour crowd of one or another allied town, some subject people of Sparta, the big-boned, strong-looking Perioeci and half-and-halfs, good, willing rowers but stupid as pigs, and some Messenians, still keeping together and singing their own songs when they could, still remembering a little after nearly three hundred years of slavery, and a good many helots, smaller and darker mostly, immense talkers about nothing in particular, screaming with laughter one moment, crying like babies the next, not so strong

206

as the others but very enduring. They got their
women-folk to bring them a couple of skins of an
odd drink of their own, which they hid under the
benches, and which had a very powerful and immediate effect. Alxenor tasted it once, and thought it
very nasty.

They had been knocked about a good deal, most of
these helots and Messenians; they cringed to the
others, particularly any Spartiate who came their
way, and half of them had broken teeth or torn ears
or nasty scars from some punishment. Alxenor
wondered why they did not revolt more; some of
them used to whisper about a rising two generations
ago – a hill-fort called Ithome – but mostly they
seemed in terror of the few Spartiates who ruled
them. A queer thing, Alxenor thought, listening,
for want of anything better to do, to the talk going
on all round him, first detachedly as the one civilized
man in a pack of savages, then gradually getting
dragged into it, against his will almost, but enough
to shiver with them at stories of the Krypteia whispered after dark from one bench to another between
the piled oars. There was one story that came out
again and again, oddly still keeping to the same
details from one telling to another, so that he thought
it must be true; and soon whenever it came he would
begin to see it for himself: the farm in the oak copse,
quiet and hot in the sun, the wood-smoke hanging
over it, and then the Krypteia, the secret killers, waiting a whole day behind the trees and only coming
into the open with the shadows – and that night –
and those two children – and the woman hiding in

the roof — and the next morning, the smell of blood
frightening the bees away. And there was the story
of the man burnt in the locked byre; it might just
have happened so, only as a matter of fact, he had
been going to do something against the Masters
the next day. They always waited till the last
minute; you might think you were safe this time,
but it wasn't any good: a knife in your back if you
were lucky, and if not, if they brought you to be
questioned by the Elders — Even the Gods watched
for them: Apollo of the market, who did loose his
arrows sometimes, an arrow all bronze following
you round corners, through the forest . . .

Alxenor began to wonder if slaves ever talked like
this in any other State; he had never thought much
about it before, but suppose their old porter Manes
had always hated him even when he was a little boy
riding on his back! It wasn't possible, though. And
at Athens — there'd been a slave rowing three down
from him one month, a very decent sort of man, and
he was always talking about his master and things
they'd done together, and how he'd been saving up
to buy his freedom and set up on his own in the shop
next door, but he'd taken his chance of being freed
sooner if he came as a rower. He had been freed too,
after Arginusae; Alxenor wondered what had happened to him now. These helots had nothing of the
sort to look forward to — or hardly ever. But if they
shirked their rowing they were whipped and chained
to the oars; then they howled all day, enough to
make one sick.

He found there were very few possible friends on

board; Archytas had spoken to the captain about him, so he used sometimes to go and dine with him and the other two or three Spartans on the fore-deck. But this was always rather embarrassing; he could not get as clean as he would have liked, either in clothes or person; his comb had lost most of its teeth, his hands were blistered and rough so that he hated looking at them, and besides he found himself always the one over when there was a joke or a story, and he could not bear the way they talked about Athens, though he knew he must say nothing and be very loyal for his wife's sake. And then, he knew what their slaves had been saying about them, and that was horrible enough. He preferred, when he could, to talk to the light-armed soldiers and the few best rowers, country folk from Amyclae way mostly, or else from the coast, not rich enough to be citizens, but decently bred and quiet friendly. None of them were particularly sympathetic, though, and he never got much further. He tried to amuse himself with making poems, but he had never had the feeling, even as a boy; the best game was to pretend Chromon was there and have long arguments with him. He found he had got quite used to a ship by this time, and hardly ever felt sick.

They were over by Asia mostly, sometimes quite close to Ephesus; once they put into the harbour, but only for a few hours, and then there was no sign of Gobryas. They were part of the fleet blockading Samos, but, as Lysander was off Piraeus all the time and could not be always sending them orders, very little was done. The news from Athens, when there was any, was horrible; they were still holding out, but if they went on much longer the whole city would be dead of starvation; many had died that way already. Theramenes was trying to get what terms he could from Sparta, anything short of utter destruction. As a matter of fact he was delaying a good deal about it, so that when he came back the people would be in no state to dispute whatever he said must be done. As for politics, he was a definite oligarch now; perhaps that was the only chance for Athens at the moment – if Lysander and King Agis thought the Athenian democracy had come to an end, they would let the City go on, sure that an oligarchy would be much more obedient to them. But of course none of the possible oligarch rulers could be said to be quite disinterested. Some of them were theorists, who really believed that they were the right, and only right, people to govern a State, Kritias for instance. But Theramenes himself was essentially a practical man and always had been. He knew that the democracy must go for the time being, but equally he knew that it was part of the genius of Athens, and would come back when the chance came; and he – God willing – with it.

However, Athenian politics were not a subject of conversation in the Spartan warship; Alxenor could only guess from an occasional scrap of news. Mostly they discussed suitable punishments for Athens – after Hellas was free – that was the phrase they used. Free! thought Alxenor, remembering the talk in old days at his brother's supper table, it's only big States that can ever be free – and then something terrible happens to them. We islanders won't ever get a chance; if it isn't Athens or Sparta it must be Persia, and that is really bad; one can bear other Hellenes, but not a man like Gobryas, a slave himself to his own King. All the same, he was being paid now in money provided by Persia! And then these people talked about smashing Athens as if they'd done it all by themselves. The things they wanted to do to her: even the helots began jabbering about it.

One April morning they lay at anchor off Samos. The sea was perfectly still, flat out for miles; whenever there was a ripple, one could see it coming for minutes before at last it touched against the ship's side. The sun had just pushed his way out of the mists, spreading clear, pearly light over all the water. Alxenor jumped off the rail, swam round once, and then climbed in again. He sat looking out till the day was well up, hot and cloudless, clear to the horizon on one side; and so completely without wind that he could hear a goat-girl singing from Samos on the other. There was nothing to do on board to-day; some of them went over for a bathe as he had, but most could not swim. They sat about, trimmed one another's hair, cleaned up, ate things, played dice and sang.

By and by they saw a ship coming towards them from the open sea, a little blot at first, crawling over the still surface, then precising herself more and more as they watched her, till suddenly there was a cry from two or three at once: 'She's a despatch boat – crowned!' Nearer and nearer she came, the little beauty, her oars in perfect time to the shrill flute tune that carried so far over the water. From her prow and mast hung two great green laurel wreaths. Her captain was garlanded too; he shouted the news across. Athens had surrendered.

CHAPTER ELEVEN

'Lord Finchley tried to mend the electric light
Himself. It struck him dead: and serve him right.'
– H. Belloc

THERAMENES had been right as usual. Whatever her Allies said – Corinth and Thebes and the others – Sparta was not going to destroy a perfectly sensible oligarchy, that was going to be good and work in with other oligarchies, and have instead that most dangerous of things, an oppressed and violently nationalist democracy, just five days' march away. Besides, they were Hellenes after all; and the war was over now; and another day it might be with some one else: let the Allies consider that if they liked! So the walls were pulled down and all the Empire that had once belonged to Athens was declared 'free.' And that was to be the happy ending for Hellas – till next time.

There was no gainsaying that the Thirty Oligarchs were intelligent, and most of them wanted to do their best by Athens; but unfortunately not in the way that Athens liked. Freedom, after all, was only three centuries old, and still very precious. So after a little the Thirty asked for a Spartan garrison to come and help them to govern. And about now Theramenes began to disagree with the others, and particularly with Kritias – Kritias the poet, the man with the queer, glittering, staring eyes, who believed in himself as ruler and teacher, and thought that the end justifies the means.

In the meantime Lysander took Samos. The demo-

crats were suitably kicked out with their wives and
children and one garment apiece, and their posses-
sions duly entered into by the good oligarchs (with a
Spartan governor), who then proceeded to set up a
statue of Lysander at Olympia, and to rename the
feast of Hera the Lysandreia, which was very
shocking to all right-minded and religious persons,
even in Sparta; and doubtless every little village in
Samos took care to have its Lysander Street for some
years afterwards. The Admiral himself sailed home
in triumph to Sparta, with all the ships surrendered
by Athens, the prows of those taken in battle, the
gifts and crowns from the cities, and four hundred
and seventy talents of good Persian gold that was
left over at the end of the war. It was autumn when
he came home, olive and grape harvest and the apples
ready to pick in orchards of Spartan houses, with the
war over and the men back, and long nights, not cold
yet, weddings and dances and songs, and plenty
everywhere.

In Athens, people were beginning to get over that
look they had worn during the siege. For a little
time afterwards, they had been numb, not fit for
anything, content to eat and work again, and offer
sacrifice to the merciful Gods who had saved them
and their children from slavery. Nikodike had her
baby boy, and for the time her mind was turned
towards him, away from the horrors and miseries
that had been happening outside in the world of
men and politics; her husband was kind to her on
the whole; she hoped some day he would talk to her
and teach her a little. The mother-in-law had died

during the siege, which made things easier for her;
her littlest brother had died too, of a kind of long,
weakening cold that had killed a good many children
that winter. Phrasikleia came to see her almost every
day now; the sister was married and lived down in
the country, on her husband's farm, so they hardly
ever met; but Nikodike had never been much interested in her young sister, nor ever liked her nearly
as much as she liked Hagnon.

Hagnon had shot up into a long-legged, sharp-
featured thing, quiet and watchful; he had lost the
grace of his boyhood, but seemed to have gained
instead a certain mystery, withdrawing himself a
little before as a man he plunged down on to the joys
and terror of life. He came to see his sister sometimes, and for want of anyone better he would now
and then talk to her about all he was learning and
thinking. And she would sit on her stool, looking
up and nodding, afraid to say anything or ask questions when she did not understand, for fear she
broke the spell and stopped him talking. As she
said nothing, he got quite a good opinion of her, and
often thought it a pity she was only a girl. He even
began talking politics to her; it was not everybody that
one could speak freely to that autumn. Her father-
in-law, for instance, was in quite an awkward position and had to be careful what he said; all his
political life, at least, he had been consistently oligarch, but yet not in the absolutely inner circle,
never more than an undistinguished member of one
of the Clubs; and he sometimes had friends – literary
perhaps – with the most deplorable opinions. Of

course, he had taken care to have no more to do with
them now, but still he might always be suspected;
every day he came in safely and ordinarily from the
market, he loosened his belt and gave a great sigh of
relief. He was not sure that he liked young Hagnon
very much; as to Nikodike, he never gave her a
thought except when she wanted housekeeping
money; above all, he would never have mentioned
politics to her. But her brother did more and more;
and what it came to was this: Kritias was running
away with the oligarchy.

He was putting people to death right and left, men
who were perhaps well thought of among the common
folk, but were doing no harm; he was always safeguarding and over-safeguarding. 'Just in case,' he
would say, and the hemlock cup would be prepared
again. He was killing the foreigners too, merchants
and bankers, Greek or barbarian, who had settled
in the city, trusting to the protection of Athene; of
course their estates would always be confiscated. It
seemed almost like plain tyranny, and ordinary men
began to think of the sword in the myrtle bough
again. And yet Kritias had always somewhere in the
back of his mind a beautiful, clear-cut theory of the
Ideal Constitution for Athens; only first one had to
get everything flattened and prepared and receptive.
People would keep starting up and worrying him and
stopping the Constitution from ever coming into
flower. That was what Theramenes did; Theramenes couldn't see that Athens must all be nicely
ironed out, and then the Constitution dropped
down on to her, and off she would go floating beauti-

fully into the future with it on her back, covering and binding her in, like a lovely, shining nautilus shell!

One morning Hagnon was coming home from school, and met his father in the Agora. Theramenes was excited and anxious; he caught his son by the shoulder and kissed him. 'Stay here!' he said. 'Something's going to happen. They've sent for me to the Council – that mad Kritias thinks he's got his Constitution started! I tell you, Hagnon, you'll see a change in ten days, or else – Son, they're after me now, because I won't go their road. Moderate I've been and moderate I will be; and they – they're making my Athens into a doll for Kritias to dress and undress! It's not for that we saved her from Sparta. They're weakening her every day, and hate's all the pay they get for it. I make a stand, and I'd have the whole City with me, only they're all as frightened as so many hares now, with all their arms taken away! If I could only get the Four Hundred back!'

Hagnon caught hold of his father: 'Oh, don't go! Kritias wants to kill you like he's killed all the others! Oh, father dear, don't go to the Council!'

But Theramenes laughed: 'I've saved my neck before, and by Zeus I'll do it again! They won't dare after I've spoken – I've got a sting or two for Kritias! Only – if it does happen – you get clear, son; they'll be after you as well. Out of Athens: you've got her in your heart, so it won't hurt you, and it won't be for long either; and take care of the others – you'll be eldest then. There, don't cry, it

217

won't happen. Wish me good luck like I've always had!'

Hagnon stayed there all the morning, one eye on the Council House, pretending to be looking at the stalls, wandering about, or sitting beside a pillar, as quiet as possible, eating fresh walnuts. He remembered his fight with Isadas a year ago, and how miserable he had felt after it; now he could look back quite detachedly on it all; he had grown up so much in these last twelve months that it was like being a different person. His brother-in-law passed and he nodded, frowning, and caught himself wishing he could tell Nikodike what their father had said: even a woman's advice would be better than nothing. But when noon came and not a sign of anything wrong, he began to think it was all a false alarm. And then he saw Kritias come out and start speaking to some men just outside the Council House. He came nearer, but they were speaking too low to be overheard; he thought he saw some of the rest of the Thirty among them. Kritias had a red cloak with black lines woven into it that followed the folds of the stuff: up and down. The Agora was still very full, though some people had gone to dinner. Most of the men went in again with Kritias; Hagnon remembered he wanted to ask his father about buying a pony, and began wishing he would come out quick.

Then there was a noise, and he stood stiff and white, listening. One or two others had heard it too, but as they came running up to the door they saw daggers half drawn and eyes on them from the little crowd in

front; their own arms were up on the Acropolis —
with Spartans guarding them; they were powerless
against tyranny. Hagnon did not know whether to
go on or not, till suddenly he was shoved roughly
on one side, and some one that knew who he was held
his arms to stop him hitting back. It was the Eleven
going in, with their ugly, well-armed Scythian slaves
at each side, grinning at the free Athenians. The
doors shut after them, so that no one could hear
much. Hagnon trembled, like a horse smelling
blood: 'They haven't come for father, oh not father!'
The man who was holding him — it was that eldest
son of Strymodoros, who had come through the war
alive and fairly well — whispered to him to be quiet,
it would be all right, not to be afraid. Already the
young men with daggers were beginning to look
their way.

Then the Eleven came out, dragging Theramenes
with them, and took him right across the market
towards their own place. Most people had seen the
Eleven at work before; Hagnon had seen them twice,
he had gone nearer to watch, pitiful and fearful,
wondering what the man felt like. Now he could
hardly believe it was his own father there, with his
clothes torn, panting, sweating, struggling every
now and then like a beast going to slaughter, and
shouting, screaming, calling on men and Gods with
the story of his wrongs. Horrified, the boy followed,
with his eyes on it all. The crowd had gathered
quickly and were trying to block the way, but as
every man was afraid to be seen doing anything himself, they were not much use. It was Theramenes

who held them back most, clinging to sun and air
and his luck that had never failed him yet – if he had
a chance. He was as tough as a wild cat, twisting
and straining and shouting so that all Athens could
hear him! Satyros, the chief of the Eleven, looked
from the prisoner to the space they had still to go, as
nervous as he could be; he had torn the man from
the Altar with his own hands, and the Gods must be
deaf if they didn't hear him screeching now! 'Keep
quiet!' he said, hitting out at Theramenes with the
butt of his sword. 'Keep quiet, God blast you, or
you'll be for it!' Theramenes looked round at him,
and suddenly grinned: 'Then shan't I be if I do keep
quiet?' and stood laughing in the middle of the
Agora with Satyros angrier than ever stamping at
him.

It was hardly longer than half a minute that he
stood there, laughing at his own grimmish joke, but
in that time he had pulled himself together, faced
the fact that his luck had definitely failed and he
was going to die within an hour or so, and found that
after all it was nothing that he had not been expecting, on and off, ever since he had begun to find life
interesting. Clearly, there was no chance of putting
it off any longer, by a day or a year; there were a
great many things he would have liked to do first,
but equally of course that would be so whenever
one died. It would do friend Kritias no good in the
long run: how pleasant it had been to remind the
Council of that incident in Thessaly! There'll be
another revolution before the year's done, he
thought, and then knew, with a queer blank shock

of realization, that he would not be in it. He went on without speaking, the smile still carefully on his lips, and all at once he saw through the guards to the face of the one he loved best in all the world, and as their eyes met at last, Hagnon made a rush and tried to burst through to him. He shouted 'Don't!' but it was too late, the boy was caught and held, and 'Stick to him!' yelled Satyros. 'We'll give him a taste of father's drink!'

But at that Theramenes began such a violent struggling and fighting that none of the guards could pay attention to anything else, and before they got him to the prison, Hagnon was out of their hands and into the friendly crowd, all ready to help him. Theramenes would have liked to kiss him once and say good-bye; he sat on a bench looking curiously at his own hands and feet, while they prepared his drink at the other end of the room; he wrinkled his nose at the smell of bruised hemlock. Suddenly the door was opened again, and he looked up and saw Phrasikleia; they let her stay for five minutes. He kissed her, but could not at once think of anything to say; he had lived with her so many years, and all the time they had talked scarcely at all. They both knew his estate would be confiscated; Phrasikleia said she would go at once to his brother, with the youngest boy and anything she could take; he agreed. 'Good thing the girls are settled,' he said. 'Give them my love, poor little piglings, it's all they'll get!' But he was thinking about Hagnon. Then, catching her glance and shudder towards the hemlock cup, 'I shan't believe in it till it's there!' He

kissed her again, gently, remembering the girl she had
been, and stroked her hair; she began to cry, painfully, trying to stifle it, but he stayed dry-eyed. He
began to wish it was over, this queer, inadequate
parting that moved them both so horribly, little love
though there had been before. And then all at once
it was over, they were taking her away. 'Phrasikleia!' he said, holding out his arms to her, and she
turned in the doorway, eager to come to him if she
could only help, but when he wanted to speak again,
he found there was still nothing to say.

They gave him cushions to lie back against on the
bench, but even with that death seemed quite remote.
Even when he had the cup in his hand, playing with
it, trying to make Satyros lose his temper again.
He wished he could see what was going to happen
about politics; he gave the Thirty six months at the
most — and how the next lot are going to manage
without me! Satyros made a movement as if he were
going to use force, that would put it all wrong. He
screwed his eyes up, and drank off the cup; there
were a few drops left in the bottom; he threw them
out, playing, thoughtless almost, like anyone drinking and giving a health at a party. 'And here's to my
beautiful Kritias!' he said, laughing gently all round
at the Eleven, a little warmth to his chilling heart;
and laughed again, and laughed . . .

Nikodike sat in her room, sewing a mourning dress
for herself, with her mother beside her. Phrasikleia
had already sent the little boy, and all the gold and
ornaments she could lay hands on, to his uncle in
the country, and now she was going to wait in the

222

house until they came to take it from her. Neither
she nor Nikodike knew where Hagnon was, only that
he had disappeared, but whether with friends or
enemies they could not tell: if with friends, the
less they tried to find out, the better. Phrasikleia
would be given her husband's body, to do with it
all the things which were needful, but he must not
be buried publicly; there must be no carrying
through the streets, no wailing or flute-playing, no
feast for the mourners. She went out now to hire
four men to carry the bier, by night; she would let
her daughter know in time to come to the grave with
her; there would be no one else. They were both
very practical, saying and thinking little about the
sorrow for themselves; both had the boys in mind so
much.

Nikodike went on sewing; the baby was asleep in
his cradle beside her; her maid slipped in, bringing
her cakes and a little hot wine; but she did not
care to eat or drink. She was very sorry for her
mother, going to be the unwanted woman in this
other household, to spin and weave for her sister-in-
law and take second place everywhere, and most
likely see her child get the worst of it with his
cousins; that would be hardest of all. How good
that she herself, and her sister, were married and
safe! The maid came in again, with a face full of
surprise and importance, but before she had time
to speak, the curtain was pulled aside a second time,
and Hagnon burst in, wild-looking, an old cloak
half across his face, and kissed Nikodike hard.
'I'm off!' he said. 'Father told me to! If you want me

ever, Strymodoros will know where I am — remember, Strymodoros, the stone-mason!'

'Oh, Hagnon!' cried his sister. 'You can't, you're only a baby! What do you think you can do?'

'I'm old enough for them to want me!'

'Oh, they wouldn't dare, they're not as bad as that, we'll take care of you! Stay here.'

'Wait and see what your husband says, pussy! I can take care of myself, I've got it all planned. I'll see you again some day. Don't cry, you silly, or I will!'

Nikodike swallowed her tears: 'Have you seen mother? Oh, do!'

'No, I can't. If I did, she'd make me stay, I know she would. And — and — it's not only them — I expect you're right and they wouldn't really want to kill me — but — oh, Nikodike, I can't stay in Athens now!'

She felt helpless against him, for all she was three years the elder; he was a boy, he knew things, he could do what he chose with life. 'Give me something nice to eat,' he said, 'it'll be my last for ever so long!' and he grabbed a cake. 'Won't you tell me your plans?' she asked, but he wouldn't or couldn't. And then he kissed her again, stuffed the rest of the cakes into his tunic, and was off as he'd come. Nikodike sat down suddenly and cried and cried and rocked herself about: he had gone out into danger, her little brother, hardly more than a child, and — besides — she realized all at once that she was crying mostly not for him but for herself, alone and deserted

224

by her own men-folk, with this husband who never talked to her, whom she hardly knew, and this tiny child who could not understand, companionless . . . The maid came in again, longing to talk and sympathize and ask questions; Nikodike sat up and smoothed her hair and took the sewing in her hands. The maid threaded the needle which had fallen on to the floor, and gave it back; and set the cradle rocking with a little push.

Before the next year was over a great deal had happened to Athens; and young Hagnon was in it all. First he had fled down to Piraeus, and stayed hidden there for a time, but then he heard that his father's old friend Thrasybulos was gathering an army of furious democrats, up in the hills at Phyle. He went there, one of a party of ten, whispering and stumbling in the dark, losing their way among rocks and rivers and thickets, crossing a watershed footsore in the dawn, and so up and welcome into the fortress. At first Thrasybulos said he was too young to bear arms; but the boy had grown so terribly earnest and fierce and manlike that there was nothing for it, after a time, but to give him his sword. No one bore him malice for being son to a man who had been one of the Thirty; if he loved freedom and Athens — they meant so nearly the same in Phyle — he was a friend to all, for one lost father gaining many brothers. Every week more came to join them, rich and poor, citizens and a few foreigners who had been long settled in Athens and were almost as anxious as the rest to put an end to the tyranny.

By that time it was nearly winter, but the weather

still held, bright and clear and almost windless; the
mountains stood up behind Athens in the calm
purple of distance. One day Nikodike, looking at
them too long, felt that her time had come for something to happen. She went down to the stone-yard
and asked for Strymodoros: 'Where is my brother?'
she said. 'You know.'

Strymodoros kept his eyes on her a moment before
answering: 'At Phyle. Where my boy is – and more
like them.'

Nikodike pursed her lips, feeling within her a
beautiful clarity of thought, everything quite simple
and straightforward. 'I shall want a mule,' she said,
'waiting in that thicket by the Ship Rock under
Lycabettos. Just after sunset. Be there yourself,
please, Strymodoros.'

'But –' said the stone-mason, and then, 'are you
sure you can do it? You'll need a lot of things, little
lady: courage mostly.'

'I've got that.'

'And then – I'd have gone to Phyle myself if I'd
been a young man, but old as I am I could do it
easier than you!'

'I know it's going to be hard,' said Nikodike.
'And I can't pay you till things are put right. Will
you mind?'

'If they ever are put right! But who's to do it with
your poor father murdered? No one to help us plain
folk.'

'They're plain folk at Phyle, – aren't they? And
you'll have the mule ready for me; I trust you,
Strymodoros. And I'll take any message to your son.

I know I'm only a woman; but it's my Athens too!'

Then she went out, and Strymodoros was left thinking of all the things he ought to have said. But Hagnon had asked him to help her when he could, so for the boy's sake he left off work and bundled himself off to see about the mule.

Nikodike said nothing to her maids; she did not even hear the baby laughing and cooing to himself in the next room. She took out a change of clothes, a comb, a pair of strong sandals, and a little oil flask, and laid them on her bed. Then she went to the box where the housekeeping money was kept, unlocked it and slid all the coins into a purse. She was humming to herself, rather tunelessly. The whole lot tied into a small bundle, not too heavy to carry. She put it on one side, waiting for the day to pass.

By and by the air began to grow chilly; she looked at the sun; it was time to start. She took her oldest and thickest cloak, muffling her face and body into a shapeless hunch over the bundle. Diokles and his father would not be back until late. She saw that the maids were all busy at their weaving; she sent the porter to look for something, knowing she could unfasten the door from inside. The baby was asleep; she kissed him gently; her cheeks were hotter than his. She did not even hurry through the courtyard; the road was so plain to Phyle and her brother. Only then, when she opened the door into the street, she came face to face with her husband.

She crouched into her cloak, trying to shape herself into an old woman; but before it was finished he saw her and caught her by the wrists and swung her back into the house. That done, he began: 'Where were you going, wife?' And again. She stared at him, unable at once to bring her mind back from Phyle where it had half flown. He shook her: 'Where were you going? Answer me quick!' And she: 'To visit a friend! I was, I swear I was, no wrong!' But when he pulled the cloak off and saw the bundle, he made her answer the truth. 'My wife!' he said. 'Mine! You dare! That's the trick you played on your father once, but now you're married to me. I'll teach you better, my girl.' Then he took her back with him to her own room.

Her mother came the next morning; she was still dressed in black and looked more bent than she had ever been. She found her daughter sitting on the chest opposite her bed, utterly miserable. All the servants were going about the house on tiptoe; they knew, and had told her, what had happened to their mistress. Nikodike winced away from her: 'Don't touch me, mother! It hurts still.'

But Phrasikleia's touch was so gentle, taking the brooches out, all along at the shoulder, slipping the linen away from the skin and looking at what the man had done to her own little girl. 'You should tell them to steep dittany leaves in warm water,' she said, 'and just a pinch of lime flower, and have it sponged on. That's the best thing. It'll be gone in a day or two.'

Nikodike looked away into an empty corner of the

room: 'I don't care about the marks,' – she pulled the dress up again over her shoulder – 'only the shame. Don't talk to me. Don't pity me. Oh, please, shouldn't you go away?'

'Darling,' said her mother, 'I'm not like that, – baby girl, little pussy, come and tell your mother – oh, littlest one, I do understand!'

And then at last Nikodike began to cry, knowing the utter baseness of being a woman – two women together clinging on to one another, oh shamed again and always! She spoke through her tears: 'He was quite right, of course. I'm his. Don't I know it. And things won't ever be different.'

Her mother groped about for any sort of consolation: 'But at least it does mean he wants you – he loves you.'

'But I only wanted to be free,' said Nikodike. 'Just a little.'

'Women can't be free – not our sort. It's always been the same, sweet, and we have to do our duty.'

'I meant to do my duty,' the girl answered, crying less. 'I wanted to be obedient to him and a good wife, as you were to father; and love him. But he never helped me. One can't alone. It was easier when Hagnon was here; there was something to look forward to – him coming. If Diokles was killed, I could go back to you and Hagnon would be my guardian.'

'He won't be killed, though,' said Phrasikleia, a little absently; and of course it was true.

Strymodoros waited all night with the mule, leaning against the Ship Rock, half asleep and coming
awake again suddenly – a bad night for an old
man. The next morning he took the mule back,
and said nothing to anybody. It must be getting
cold up in Phyle; but his son had plenty of warm
clothes.

One evening, very soon after, a messenger came all
breathless to them up there, with news that the
Thirty were marching at last against Phyle, bringing
their own forces, and some troops the Spartans had
lent them. The next day there was some sharp
fighting up and down the mountain paths, but not
more than a few on each side were in it. Hagnon,
longing to kill some one, never got his chance. The
Thirty planned to build and guard walls all round
them and cut off their food supplies; but Zeus – so
Thrasybulos said, anyhow – was with the Demos:
the weather broke in earnest for winter. Snow fell
all night and the next day. Kritias stormed and wept
at it, but there was no possibility of building walls.
The Thirty went back to Athens and their warm
houses, leaving only a few of the Laconian troops,
and some of their own cavalry – young men who
snowballed one another between times – to keep
guard.

Thrasybulos could see quite well where their camp
was; it made a dirty patch on the white. He knelt
up on his wall, peering down at them; Hagnon was
beside him, shivering with cold and excitement:
'You are going to take me?' he said. 'You do
promise?'   'Well, if you say you can do it: you

230

ought to know best. Try and get a little sleep first; we'll start at midnight. Oh, I'll wake you all right!'

Almost all the men at Phyle — nearly seven hundred of them — were ready to start that night, crowding together, stamping and whistling and flapping their arms. But once out of their fort there was no more noise, they must crunch their way very quietly through the thin, hard snow that did not give much under their feet. For an hour or two they had to stay quite still among the bushes, within ear-shot of the enemies' camp; Hagnon found it very trying at first, but by and by he fell asleep against the man next him, and did not wake until the light was beginning to change and they could hear voices and whinnying of horses; then they all stood up and stretched themselves, and got a good grip of their swords. Thrasybulos gave the word, and they all charged, yelling, into the middle of the camp. No one was ready for them or could reasonably be expected to do anything but run.

The first man Hagnon killed was a groom who got in his way; the sword just went into his neck and he fell over; it was so simple. Then he went straight for the tents where those young Athenian knights were only just coming awake, struggling half-naked and shieldless among their blankets. Most of them got away, but Hagnon killed one and took his helmet, for he had none of his own, only a borrowed thing with no crest. They chased the rest of them a mile and more through the snow, then came back, set up a trophy, and carried off anything they could lay hands

231

on, among them a good many horses. Hagnon was very tired and glad to be able to ride back; he looked at the new helmet and wondered if he had known the man it belonged to; somehow he had never looked at the man's face when he killed him. By and by he decided that killing was too easy as a way of dealing with one's opponents; it took one no further. Whereas, if one managed to convince them that one was right –

The Thirty were beginning to get uneasy; Athens was not so safe as it should have been after all their safeguarding. They went to Eleusis and managed to take prisoner and kill – of course in proper legal form – such of its people as they suspected; this way they got themselves a citadel, but it seemed to Kritias a step backwards from his Constitution of Athens. He was very gloomy these days, flying off into savage fits of temper when one of the others crossed him. Even his own poetry gave him no pleasure now.

But Thrasybulos led his men down to Piraeus one Spring night, and after a little fighting got possession of the hill Munychia. The army of the Oligarchs gathered in the market-place below them; the battle that was coming would decide everything. On the left were the Thirty themselves, the men who had driven them from their City, and killed their fathers and brothers; Hagnon had prayed for this day, and so had most of the others. The Democrats had the best of the ground; from the hill they could see their own Acropolis, their own Athene. Thrasybulos spoke magnificently, thoroughly in earnest, rising to

the spirit of the day; he bade them keep ranks until
he started the paean. They formed up ten deep on
the path, facing the enemy, well aware that there
were five times as many of them — but remembering that they had known it would be like this
before even they had made their first challenge from
Phyle.

Their soothsayer bade them not to attack until one
of their own side was killed; then they would go on
to victory. He thought that he himself would be
that man, and he was right. Later he was buried at
the ford of the Kephisos. But it all happened as he
had said: Thrasybulos and the democrats won the
battle. And somewhere in the middle of it Kritias
was killed.

Rather more than seventy of the oligarchs were
killed with him; by and by the victors began to strip
them of their arms, but not of their tunics, because
so many of them were fellow-citizens. Then the
friends of the dead came to ask for their bodies to
take back and bury, and this way there were many
meetings between men who had been not so long ago
companions in arms or in the market, and Hagnon
saw more than one of his old schoolmates. He tried
to keep his distance from them, holding hard on to
the reason why he was there, but first one and then
another came up and spoke to him, and almost against
his will he found that he did not hate them at all. He
himself had killed no one in this battle; that made it
easier. He was questioning one of them, asking
about his mother and little brother, when all at once
they both heard a call for silence, and stopped, and

233

looked round. It was the Herald of the Mysteries, a man with a very beautiful voice, one of the democrats, who was speaking. He called on his old comrades, by all the ties of friendship and kinship, by the Gods they had worshipped together, to cast off these utterly accursed and hateful tyrants, who for their own ends had murdered more Athenians, almost, than the Spartans had killed in ten years of war. 'And for many of those who are dead to-day,' he said, 'our tears are as bitter as yours.'

Actually, nothing was decided that day; but the new spirit was coming, freedom back to her old home in Athens. The Thirty were deposed, and went hastily off to their fortress at Eleusis; now that Kritias was dead, there was no one to keep them together and will them to go on. Half of them had no real wish to be tyrants.

But still the oligarchs in Athens were not ready to give in, though more and more citizens were going down to Piraeus to join Thrasybulos. He was very friendly with the foreigners too, and all who joined him were to have special privileges later on when the democrats were in power again; they were sure now that it was only a matter of time. But just here Sparta began to take a hand in the game. Lysander was not going to have his good work undone; he lent the oligarchs one hundred of the many talents of gold he had brought home with him, and took an army and a fleet to blockade Piraeus, one led by himself, the other by his brother. And in a few weeks things began to look very bad for the democrats.

However, Lysander was not the only Spartiate in Sparta. During the war he had managed to make an institution of himself, and up to now no one had quite dared to go against him. But the two Kings were getting anxious; Agis was an old man, and so rather disregarded in Sparta; but Pausanias began to talk to the Ephors. They authorized him to lead out another army against Athens, and Lysander had to take second place. Pausanias had worked it all out beautifully in his rather cautious head. If the Athenians were reconciled and no garrison needed by the oligarchs, then Lysander would not be able to make his own special head-quarters there, but must come back to Sparta just a little crestfallen. And once he's at home under discipline again, thought Pausanias, the Ephors and I can deal with him. But of course he said nothing of all this aloud, and when he called on the Allies to join him, Corinth and Thebes — worst enemies of all to Athens in the old days — refused to come, because they thought Sparta wanted to conquer utterly this time, and take all Attica for her own.

For a time there was fighting round about Piraeus, but nothing very serious happened, and all the time King Pausanias was trying to make terms between oligarchs and democrats. By and by he got what he wanted: both sides sent envoys to Sparta, and Pausanias saw to it that they were all given a good reception and persuaded into a lasting truce. Fifteen Spartiates came to Athens to give the award. Every one was allowed to go home except the Thirty, the Eleven, and those few oligarchs who had governed in the City immediately after the Thirty had gone. Anyone who was afraid might go and settle in Eleusis with the remains of the tyrants. This was all to the good for Sparta; both sides would have to be grateful to them, and in any case the place was far too weak now to be a danger for years and years.

Then Pausanias disbanded his army, and the democrats went up to the Acropolis, and sacrificed in their own temples once more. And there was peace in Athens.

Thrasybulos was of course leader of the democracy; he was a just man, but not so clever as Theramenes. He tried to get back the estates which had been confiscated by the Thirty for the heirs of the murdered men, but it was not always possible to get at or return all that was due. However, Hagnon got back most of what had been his father's, and Phrasikleia and the little brother could live once more in their old house with their old slaves serving them. He went to see Nikodike almost at once; she was quieter than usual, and somehow did not seem quite so glad to see him as he had imagined she would be. She would not talk of the winter that had passed, and did not care for him to talk of it either and she would not look forward into the future; he saw she was with child again. So he came away a little uneasy about her; but in the courtyard he met his brother-in-law, who explained all about it.

'Of course you were perfectly right,' he said. 'I should have done the same thing myself. Trying to get to Phyle! Utterly foolish. You couldn't have acted differently, Diokles.' 'I'm glad you agree with

me, very glad,' said Diokles, talking to Hagnon as
man to man, which was so pleasant. They walked
together down towards the Agora. It was a bright,
windy September day, with the first fallen plane
leaves blowing about the streets, still light and dry.
Country folk, coming in to sell their eggs and cheeses,
had posies of asters and wild cyclamen and scarlet
rowan berries, lying on their full baskets.

'She'd only have been in the way at Phyle,' Hagnon
went on. 'Women must keep to their own place.
Where would the State be otherwise?' Diokles
nodded. 'I felt sure that you would see it my way.
You know, Hagnon, I value your opinion a good
deal. It's been so hard for me, these last few months.
I'm not clever like you, and I didn't like to change
over from what we've always been, father and me.
Though we never did agree with Kritias – not in the
worst days. Well, it's all over now and I hope it'll
never come again. But about my wife; she's cured
now, don't you think?' 'Yes,' said Hagnon, 'or at
least she will be when there are two babies to look
after!' 'Best cure by a long way! And two won't be
all!'

They both laughed, coming out into the sunshine
and life of the market-place, full of talk and friends
meeting – dozens of men they both knew. Everything right again after all the wars and troubles.
And then, in the middle of it all, Hagnon saw in his
mind's eye a little picture of his sister shut up there
in her house, sitting disconsolate with her hands in
her lap, and her heart closed against him for ever.
But that was nonsense after all; and the Agora was

237

real all round him, and freedom had come back to
Athens! Only, underneath it all, it was as if he was
wearing a rough shirt, or something . . . just a little
uncomfortable . . .

CHAPTER TWELVE

'But they were *in* the well,' Alice said to the Dormouse,
not choosing to notice this last remark.
'Of course they were,' said the Dormouse, ' – well in.'
                                    – *Alice in Wonderland*

WHEN there was snow at Phyle, there was
snow almost all over Greece, swept down
before the north wind; though in Sparta it
only stayed fallen and heaped on the high ridges.
They breathed coldly into the valleys, but indoors
there were good log fires that warmed up the whole
place, and in the daytime there was often bright
sunshine for hours at a time.

Then Kleora would take her spinning outside into
the courtyard and the maids would spread a yellow
blanket with fringes, and the baby would lie out on
it, naked and kicking hard with his firm, solid little
legs, wriggling and clutching and cooing and trying
to roll over. Moiro thought it was dreadful, but
didn't say so; only she never let Timas go out until
he was well huddled up with woolly things, and then
she was always running after him to bring him back
into the warm. Kleora told her she was stupid and
the child would never grow strong that way, and
certainly Timas was apt to catch colds and be sick,
while Kleora's baby, only a few months old, was as
well as could be. Archytas would come home and
stand watching him, tugging like a young bull at his
mother's breast, with his hand spread out on her neck
and a wary blue eye cocked at his father.

They used to bathe him sometimes in water mixed
with wine to strengthen him, and his nurse would

239

carry him about in the open a great deal. Kleora managed marvellously not to spoil him or fuss over him; she was a big, tall, rather slow-moving woman, who smiled with mouth and eyes, but said little unless she really wanted to. She was full grown — eighteen when she married Archytas — with long yellow hair which she was very proud of; her maids had to comb it out and wash it in spring water and dry it with hot cloths and powder it with finely-ground flour that had been steeped in rose oil, and plait it and pin it round her head with small combs of gold and ivory, worked into flowers and bees and little trotting horses, till she seemed like Helen herself. Apart from the combs she had few jewels; only she sometimes wore the bracelet which Cyrus had given to her husband, and sometimes his gold laurel wreath, and she had a coral charm that hung always between her breasts. She wore the Dorian dress that had shocked Moiro so much at first, the straight woollen tunic, pinned once through the fold on each shoulder, with broad belt clasped with two golden swans, and no other fastening at all from arm-pit to ankle. Mostly she went barefoot, and she could knock any of her women down with one hand.

Their house was in the city of Sparta itself, a double square of wood and plaster walls, oldish and low, roofed partly with thatch, partly with broad tiles; there were poplars and apple trees growing all round it, and a good well in the middle. She had a garden, inside high hurdles, where she grew all sorts of herbs and salads, and roses, lilies, marigolds, larkspur and asphodel, with all the garland flowers. But in winter

there was nothing to bring one there except the
chance of a violet, or the faint scent still hidden in the
crisp thyme and rosemary leaves. On sunny days the
bees would still come out for a short flight, but
mostly the hives were silent.

Early every morning their food was brought in
from their farm high up the valley: great joints of
meat, cheese, butter and milk, eggs, corn, meal,
turnips and carrots in sacks, and sometimes wine in
tarred and stoppered skins. The farmer's son —
nephew to Ladas — used to drive in the ox-cart and
count the things out, wet or fine, to Kleora in the
middle of the yard; she took good care to see that the
weight and quality were good, and the best of everything always went over to Archytas for his Mess.
Moiro thought the cooking in the household curiously bad, considering the material, and offered herself or Thrassa to help; but nobody seemed to like
their cakes and stews and nice, buttery fried ducks.
Kleora said they reminded her of helot cookery on
the farms, and were no food for free Spartans; Dionassa said straight out they gave her the belly-ache and
she couldn't run a yard for hours afterwards; and the
maids just giggled. So back they went to porridge
and boiled mutton and haggis every day, with apples
and honey to end up with, all eaten out of the rough-
est pottery bowls — though Moiro and Thrassa were
sure they had plenty of money to buy nice ones!
And they heard it was the same for the men, even!

All winter Moiro felt it queerer and queerer; she
never could get to know the Spartan women, any
more than she could ever manage not to be frightened

241

when one of the cows swung its great horns towards her. Kleora never seemed to want to talk about the ordinary things of life, details of marriage and children, what to do with one's slaves, dresses and scents, marketing, charms and cures – or at least she did talk about them, but not, somehow, as if she took any interest in the things themselves, but as if they all had to be made to fit into some scheme of life, and were only worth thinking of in as far as they did. And there was Dionassa, her sister, younger than Moiro but a head taller, with beautiful broad shoulders and hips; she lived sometimes here and sometimes with her mother, almost as she liked. At first she had seemed quite dreadfully immodest, going about in the street with no veil for her bare head and arms, and her tunic up to her knee; Moiro had scarcely liked going out with her. But it had the most improbable effect. Nobody said a word that she could possibly have minded, the young men gave way to her, even the King's son bowed as if she had been a priestess, and any helots scuttled out of the way like rats. When an older man or woman passed, it was her turn to bow and make way; often they would stop and speak to her, and then she must give a short and modest answer, looking full at the questioner with hands at her sides. And there were dozens of other girls like her, mostly handsome and tall, often very beautiful, going openly about the town, smiling at one another, running together with a plan to go out into the fields and race or play at ball, with their short, plain dresses, and hair plaited and coiled low over the brow like a young man's.

No, thought Moiro after a time, this was not im-
modesty; but it might be something worse, more
against the order of nature. Oh it was all wrong and
horrible to an Ionian! Better to go out with Kleora,
who at least went decently veiled, though she held
herself so unwomanly, with proud, high head, walking as if she liked the air. Better still, perhaps, never
to go out at all, stay in with the child, like a modest,
gentle wife, try not to think of what she had missed
with the Persian, at least not give herself the chance
of walking down some street, and glancing round,
and seeing one of the Spartans standing at the corner,
with the sun in his hair, gold-brown and thick, glinting in his bright, deep eyes, curly beard like a bull,
strong, square shoulders . . .

Alxenor was only back for a few weeks that winter;
he was not a rower any longer, but doing garrison
duty as a light-armed soldier, sometimes in one place,
sometimes in another. He could hardly manage to
save at all on his half-pay, but at least he lived, and
his son was growing up — the thing he minded most
was seeing so little of the child. He was glad at least
they had not sent him to Attica; it would have been
terrible; he hoped he would never see Athens again —
now.

Most of that Spring he was at Melos; after Aigospotamoi, Lysander had swept up all the Athenian
colonists who were there, and had sent them back to
starve in their own City. Then they were replaced,
theoretically at least, by the original Melians. Now,
after a year and a half, the island was settling down
again, and it was likely to be a good season for the

crops. The town was being used as a naval base, and
the garrison was there chiefly to guard stores.

On a day late in April, Alxenor was up on the hill
behind the fort, sitting on a rock in the sun, cleaning
his shield. A dozen new men had come the evening
before; he heard their fresh voices from the quarters
below him, but he was not much interested. Life as
a whole was thoroughly dull; it seemed as if it would
go on just the same now, for years and years and
years. The shield was as clean as it would ever get;
it was rather an ugly shield. His own at home in
Poieëssa used to have his crest painted on it in blue,
and the rim was bright bronze with a lion's head at
the top.

One of the new soldiers came up to him and said:
'I know you, Alxenor; don't you know me?' Alxenor
looked up; after a minute's staring he suddenly
remembered: 'Isadas!' and made room on the rock
beside him. 'So you've come home,' he said, a little
surprised at himself for remembering that the boy
had been a Melian. Isadas sat down, smiling a little
one-sidedly, and looked away westwards, over the
slope of the hill. 'Home,' he said, rather ambigu-
ously; then, 'Tell me first, what are you doing here?'
Alxenor explained shortly, and asked what it had
been like in Athens during the siege. 'I wasn't
there,' said Isadas, taking his helmet off. 'I've been
soldiering for Sparta ever since that winter. They
pay well anyhow.' He began to pull up a tuft of
chicory from a crack in the rock; Alxenor watched
him — he was still not much more than a boy for all
his armour and sword; slowly he flushed red all

round to his neck and ears; he turned his head away. The chicory plant came out by the roots; he began to cry, shaken all over as the tears fell. 'Home,' he whispered again, and all at once it spread to Alxenor too, so that he began to think, if this were only Poieëssa and he could go back again with everything wiped out, able to start afresh! It took him by the throat and held him gripped and still with its vision of what life would never be now. A little time passed; then the Melian boy beside him mastered his tears and looked round. For both of them the sun shone again, the little bright beetles scurried over the warm, sandy earth, the sky-blue chicory flowers were wild scattered stars all across the hill-side. 'Stupid I am,' said Isadas, ashamed. 'Sorry. It's getting back.'

'Why haven't you been back before?' Alxenor asked, suddenly beginning to be interested.

'Well —' Isadas hesitated, looking at him '— perhaps it was this way. But it all started earlier; Alxenor, you don't know what it is being a slave! They were kind to me, you see; that made it harder to stay decent; there was nothing to fight against. If I'd been a man grown it would have been worse, I expect; there's less difference for a child; I don't think I lost much of myself. Only it was hard to remember; I wouldn't have but for my aunt. And she, poor thing — well, us two, that's all there was left of Melos!

'Then the news of the battle came that night. I didn't go out quite at once; I stood still, thinking of all the things I wanted to happen to Athens — I hadn't really pictured them till then. I wanted it to be the same for her. After that I went into the Agora, and I fought Hagnon, and hurt him; not that I hated him much, but he was Athens to me. Then I got out, and I found King Agis coming from Dekeleia for the siege, and I asked to be taken on. There were a good many more like me – out of the Grasshoppers' Nest at last.

'Well, it came to an end. And Sparta let her off – just because Lysander and the Kings were quarrelling! Or perhaps it wasn't that; but anyway I wanted to see everything smashed: and they didn't. Then I began to think of home; people said that Sparta was giving Melos back to us. I didn't know; they were and they weren't; it was difficult to get at the men who were really doing it. Then, when I did, they wanted to buy me out, but I wouldn't let them. And one thing and another. So that's why I'm only just come. But it's home. And – and – I don't remember it at all!'

'Then you don't know where your farm was?' Alxenor asked. Isadas shook his head; he was a little frightened and his eyes were red. 'You know,' said Alxenor, 'most of the people here now aren't Melians.'

Isadas looked down over the rocks and turf to where a house-roof showed between flat-topped pine trees. 'I've been thinking that already,' he said. 'Of course there aren't very many of us now. But still – Sparta does take things.'

After that Isadas spent most of his time trying to get his claim accepted. He wandered about the island, trying and trying to remember, kneeling on the ground wanting to think how some place would have seemed to a little child. There was a house he half thought might be the one; it was right inland, with vine terraces on the hill behind it, and a well with a great gean tree spreading over it. It seemed to Isadas that one of the things he remembered was long grass with the little, sour bird-cherries tangled in it. But there was a family living in the house, had been there for more than a year now. They did not like his coming and peering about their place.

No one he found on the island could help him much; he knew who his father had been, and there were a few people who could recall a man of that name, and things he had done, days they had met him even; but not just exactly where he had lived. Most of the actual Melians on the island now were either the few who had escaped the massacre by luck or money; or quite young men like Isadas who had spent all their boyhood as slaves; or women who were married to Laconians and were taking up their fathers' and brothers' inheritances; even a few older women with no men-folk had come back and were setting to work on their own, after the method of island Dorians, hiring labour and buying stock and building new byres for themselves. One or two thought they could help Isadas, but one put his farm here, another there, and a third had mixed him up with some one else. Then he said he would take any land, failing his own; but it seemed as if there was very little decent land to be had in Melos. Finally he was offered the choice of two bits of hill-side that would hardly do for goat pasture, even this with an air of extraordinary favours conferred.

That evening he met Alxenor again; they went out and had a drink together at a small shop facing over to the harbour; the serving girl brought them bread and wild strawberries. 'It's no good,' said Isadas gloomily. 'They don't want me, and that's all there is to it. I can't and I won't come back to starve all my days out on a bit of dry rock; it's all they'll give me. But I just won't take it. Melos shan't be made to be stepmother-land to her own children!'

'Sparta isn't good at making one love her,' Alxenor agreed unhappily; he was wondering when he would ever see his wife and child again.

'No,' said Isadas. 'She didn't help us before, and what's more she never will help anyone unless she thinks she can get something out of it! Not nowadays.'

Alxenor nodded and broke a crust of bread. There was a thing he had on his mind, he thought he had better get it said: 'And they won't want us soldiers much longer, now that the war's over. What are you going to do, Isadas?'

'You're right about that,' said the Melian, 'but I hadn't thought. Up to this last week I'd been so sure of staying here all my days. I wanted it so. You don't know, Alxenor.'

'I'm away from my island too.'

'Yes. But I thought I was finished with being away. The land knew me, the trees, the hills. They weren't less beautiful than I'd thought they'd be. Everything was right: except the Spartans.'

248

A few weeks later Alxenor was shifted to Paros. He was one of the guard of the Laconian governor, who had been sent there to consolidate Spartan interests and collect tribute and generally see that everything was all right. He found out accidentally that Alxenor was a good letter-writer, and adopted him as his secretary. Alxenor found it more interesting than the usual life, and made himself as useful as possible. It was a pleasant little town, too; there was always a breeze off the sea in the evening, and a short walk along the coast brought one to a grove of great plane trees with soft turf under them, where one could lie well shaded and watch the butterflies and the big grasshoppers with red and blue wings. Whenever he could, Alxenor wrote to Moiro, and twice got a letter back; but they were not, either of them, very good at expressing themselves in writing, and Moiro found she couldn't get anyone to help her over the long words; the Spartan women had never put pen to paper in their lives, and simply shouted with laughter at the idea of any woman they knew doing it.

One day the Governor, in the course of tribute collecting, decided to add a small boy to his collection; this was the younger son of a free woman, widow of one of the old democrat leaders, and he had the beautiful intense face of an Ionian who might be going to be a poet, and big, soft-coloured eyes under a high forehead. Alxenor had seen the Governor staring at this boy in the street, but thought nothing of it, and was shocked and horrified at finding him gagged and bound when he went into the inner room that evening for pen and ink. He wrote the letters as

249

carefully as usual, but he could not bear to think of this big beast of a Laconian hurting the young, fine thing in there. During supper he went out quietly and unbound the boy, gave him a drink, and helped him to climb up on to one of the rafters where he stayed hidden till early morning and then slid down and slipped out of the side door. Alxenor opened it for him and watched him running off, escaping like a bird into the grey empty dawn.

Nobody connected Alxenor with the boy's escape; he was not the sort of man they expected would do anything even so easily heroic. But the next week when he was in the plane grove, a slave put something into his hands and made off. 'Thanks!' the paper said and there was a gold cup with it. Besides that, he got something extra from the Governor for his work as secretary; he was careful to save it all. The mercenaries were being paid off now, more and more every month; soon it was bound to be his turn. Then – well, then he might go home, next Spring; and chance what his brother would say: or Chromon. He would not write again.

In summer the Eurotas valley got hotter and more like a garden day by day; Kleora would bid her nurse take the baby along by the river where the air was always a little cool under the poplars. Sometimes she went herself and took Moiro and Timas to see the dragon-flies darting over the great beds of rushes. Timas would stare and stare, quite quiet for minutes at a time; he never tried to catch them, and he did not ask many questions; he knew his mother was not good at answering them. He made up games to play

250

by himself in odd corners, and Kleora began to be
sorry for him and wonder what his future would be;
her own son's was so clear and straight and beautiful!
Moiro had never seen such a green place in summer;
Poieëssa was always burnt up by June, but here
there was still grazing for the cows in alder-shaded
water-meadows up the Eurotas, where the ground
was soft and warm to touch, and there were wide
fairy rings.

Dionassa was away most days, practising for some
ceremonial dance there would be in autumn; she
came back in the evenings pale and tired out; it was
hard work clearly, but she would not talk about it.
Once or twice at supper she seemed to have been
crying, and Kleora gave her the best of everything,
and put her to bed early and sat with her till she slept.
The young men were mostly up in the hills; they
came down sometimes fresh and cool with green
leaves on their heads and spears in their hands. One
saw them now and then in the market under the
shadow of Apollo's great bow; or in the street of
Sparta, a sudden laughter and running of hard light
feet past the house; or further off, standing in the
meadows.

Moiro walked up and down beside the loom, weaving a pattern of red and black squares ; she would
not look up from it, would not listen for any voices.
But if one had to remember, bit by bit, what one had
seen . . . could not help seeing . . . one day or
another. However hard one tried not. Memories
stick like thorns, long thorns that pierce right
through to one's inmost blood.

251

The Spartans, drooping
Heavy curls of long hair
On their brown shoulders: hanging
Beelike:
Heavy swarms of brown bees.
Goddess, be kind to me!
The swarm stirs, honey-sweet,
Brushing with soft, wild wings
My heart.

By and by the pattern would finish, the last square
woven off, the border and all; but life would go on,
and one would not be able to help what life did to one.

Leon was an Iren; he was good at doing almost anything, running and climbing and dancing, spear or
sword or bare strength of hands in an unarmed
struggle. He often came to the house to see Archytas, and Kleora whom he loved and respected, and
who laughed at him, and kissed him, and made him
garlands. He and her husband were splendid together, walking or talking or singing, the two fitting
into each other perfectly, setting each other off till
she had to run up to them and put her arms round
both together!

She was very fond of the little boy too, Erasis, the
twelve-year-old, Leon's own special friend, square
and solid and merry, not given to thinking much, but
a leaper at life, work or play as they came. Archytas
used to warn Leon often against spoiling him, making things easy for him at an age when boys can best
stand roughness. Then for a few days Leon would
be harsh to him, punish his lightest faults and make

him do the hardest and dullest work, trying to think all the time of nothing but his duty to the State. As for Erasis, he would shake himself and do his best, and wonder what was the matter with Leon. He liked so very much to be praised and sent with important messages, and to go about proudly with the Iren's hand on his shoulder. Once, when he had been feeling that more than ever, he began telling Kleora how he wanted Leon to lead him to battle one day, and how brave they were both going to be, childishly, not really knowing what he was talking about. Kleora gave him an apple and a great deal of good advice about friendship, and how to keep the same feeling, steady and beautiful, all through life. One or two other boys in the Class came sometimes, waiting stiff and straight in the courtyard for their orders. Moiro used to go away and hide herself in the women's rooms when she heard them – at first, anyhow. And none of them looked at her, not more than a glance, or spoke to her at all; until one day in autumn.

Kleora was in her garden with two of the maids, seeing to her bees, taking out the combs and talking gently to the warm, throbbing little winged people as they lighted on her hands, saying spells and bee-words to them, bidding them be at rest and go to their work again. Dionassa was in the house, but the time of her dance was come, and she must keep herself holy and not touch common things until it was over. And then Leon came in, very tired and queer-looking, and asked where Archytas was. The first thing Moiro knew was one of the helot girls coming

253   I

and whispering to her, begging her to take him food and drink. 'Why?' said Moiro, flushing. 'Why me?' The girl wriggled and twisted her hands together: 'We didn't want to, not any of us; and Thrassa's out with Nurse. Do, please, lady.' 'But why didn't you want to?' 'Ooh,' said the girl, 'it's because of what he's been doing. It won't matter though, not to you.' Moiro wondered very much, but she always liked doing what people wanted; and what was it Leon had been doing, and what would he look like? She took the things they gave her and went out into the court.

Leon had pulled himself up a bucketful of water from the well, and was pouring it over his hands. As she looked, Ladas came up to him and knelt, his grey, thin hairs level with the Spartan's knee. 'It wasn't at the farm?' he said. 'Not – not any of my folk, master?' Leon shook his head, tight-lipped, and put the bucket back; the spilt water trickled slowly towards her over the dust. She heard Ladas speak again, with an odd eagerness: 'We've always been faithful – all of us – haven't we? Never set ourselves up – my nephew, he's the same! They haven't said anything –' But Leon interrupted: 'I know, I know! Don't be an old fool, Ladas, it wasn't your lot. God, I am thirsty!'

Moiro hurried over with the wine and water; he drank two cups straight off. She shivered with fear and pleasure, knowing what he must have been doing, how few hours could have passed since he killed his man! 'Thanks!' he said, and then, 'You're the girl I carried off, aren't you?' She murmured some-

254

thing, not daring to look up higher than his chest —
his throat — his mouth — 'Well,' said Leon, 'are you
glad I did?' She felt herself getting hot, and suddenly the man was speaking right into her face:
'Would you rather I hadn't given you back to Alxenor?' Then he laughed and touched her neck, and
'Oh,' she whimpered, 'oh don't!' but could not
move any more than a rabbit. But then Kleora came
through to them, with a piece of dripping honeycomb for her cousin. Moiro was let free to run back
and find her child and cry over him, feeling herself
too weak to help whatever was coming. But Kleora
was thinking of her bees and had noticed nothing:
why should she look at Moiro after all? — it was the
man who mattered just then. 'I'm proud to think
how well our Leon's doing,' she said to Dionassa
afterwards. 'They're pleased with him. That was
the first time he'd been on Krypteia and it was a
difficult piece of work, but Archytas says he did it
perfectly.'

It was very soon afterwards that Alxenor came
back; he had been paid off and it was time to move
again; only Archytas had said he might stay the
winter in Sparta with them. Moiro welcomed him
very eagerly, as if she thought he could protect her
from something; he kissed her and spoke to her very
kindly, but was still careful not to risk another child.
It crushed all his senses too, living here among the
Spartans, tolerated; he could hardly feel himself a
man at all. Only it was very pleasant to have his
son's arms round his neck again. Timas was shy at
first, not quite remembering what father was like;

but they made friends again very soon, and Alxenor took him out into the woods and showed him birds and squirrels, and let him ask questions, and told him about when he was a little boy at Poieëssa.

'I want to do that too!' said Timas, after one story, but Alxenor was wondering what was the best way to spend one's boyhood, was beginning to look at the Spartan children. He held Timas in his arms, keeping him quiet, watching from behind a tree their game – or more than a game, was it? – six children on each side with a nine-year-old captain, marching, skirmishing, dodging for positions among the big oaks, and then the struggle, terribly in earnest, little fierce, frowning boys with eyes narrow and mouths hard shut, flecked with blood on hands and faces. Then, later on that day, he found one of the children down in a hollow, doubled up and sobbing with pain. 'Let me help!' he said, but the boy jumped up, his hands pressed over the cut in his cheek, staring out of his tears at the stranger. 'I'm not hurt!' he said. 'I hate you!' and ran off into the trees, back to the others. Timas hugged his father very tight. 'When I'm big,' he said, gasping and speaking very loud with the strength of his resolution, 'I will be brave too!' and then, 'I will be one of those boys!' So Alxenor went on wondering.

CHAPTER THIRTEEN

'Children of the future age,
Reading this indignant page,
Know that in a former time
Love, sweet love, was thought a crime.'
— Blake

By the end of October the harvests were all in; the fruit trees were stripped, the lightened vine branches tossed forlornly away from their elm boles; and Moiro shivered, coming up through the field paths, as the flying, spotted vine leaves patted her face and hands. But still it was scarcely cold, even in the hills, least of all when one had hurried there, panting and frightened through the dusk, not certain yet, not quite certain: if her husband should get to know . . . Over the ridge, pushing through a thicket of stiff wild pear and thorn all knotted together with creeping things that had to be broken – the dust rose, making her cough, warm dust between her fingers and toes; in a few weeks the rain was sure to begin, but not yet. Then the four pines just where she had expected them, then the little stream that flowed down into Eurotas, and the slope up with the goats all settling to sleep in one corner, and then the shepherd's hut, dark and square, with the first stars coming out round it, one by one.

Inside it smelt a little sharply of wild herbs and beasts' fur and pine needles; she groped her way over and sat down, shivering, and yet warm at the core, warm behind her eyes like a fire there, stopping her from thinking all the good things a wife ought to think. She could not tell how long or how short

257

a time she had been waiting; there came a moment
when she looked up suddenly.

Leon stood in the doorway, almost blocking it.
She could not even see if he was smiling at her.
Behind him moonrise was silvering the dark sky,
the jagged peaks of Taygetus showed blacker and
blacker; a white burnish was growing all round his
head as the thick curls began to catch the light.
She could hear her own breathing, and his, and the
river outside, and now and then a slow tinkle as the
belled he-goat lifted his head among the sleeping
flock. Again she shivered a little and felt the hard
edge of the mattress against her legs, and the thin
linen stirring coldly about her breast and arms. At
last he moved a step and shut the door behind him,
so that now the hut was dark and at once warmer
and full of rustlings and waiting for the first touch.
She thought he must be taking the shoulder brooches
out of his tunic; his beautiful deep eyes might be
searching the dark for her. Suddenly he was down
beside her, loosing the knotted ribbon of her girdle.
'Moiro!' he said at last, and his hands began to feel
about her, strong and hard, pressing into her young,
soft flesh. The hands lifted her further on to the
mattress, and he pulled his thick cloak over them;
his arms were round her, strange and delightful,
their mouths pressed softly together, and dank
fingers seeking, exploring, still uncertain. She was
not cold any more, nor frightened, nor thinking of
anything; pleasure and warmth and utter subjection
to him were gaining her altogether. For a few
minutes they lay quite quietly in each other's arms

like a big child and a little, sleepily given over to
their own bodies. Then in both of them the pleasure
grew and grew, and leapt to its climax and over-
flowed like a cup, spilling, spilling, spilling.

Now they lay close alongside of each other, peaceful
and happy, wrapped in the dark as in a mother's
arms. It was so still that a mouse came out of his
hole in the wall, and whisked across to the far side.
Moiro started a little, but Leon had hold of her too
tight; she settled down again, her mouth against
his neck, kissing slowly and heavily. Their eyes
shut for a little time on a dreamless half sleep.

By and by Leon drew himself away; it had been
such a queer violent thing, possession by so very
strong a God. She had been the same too. And he
had started it so lightly, just a word and a touch on
that day when he was anyway all strung up and not
thinking. Now it had come to this – with the wife
of a man he knew! Even though he was only an
Ionian. Better surely, he thought, to worship the
Eros one understands, the White One. Moiro
turned over towards him, clinging with damp, hot
fingers, murmuring his name. And he suddenly
thought of Erasis, and his young rough body, running into things, cool and clean like a sword. He
thought of him asleep now, breathing deep and still,
with cold autumn dew on his hair and cloak. He
kissed Moiro and went.

She could only come some nights, when Alxenor
was not there; often he was away for days at a time,
carrying messages and so on for Archytas. Then she
would be glad, and take her chance. Thrassa knew

her mistress had a lover at last, and was sure that in time she would hear his name; for the moment Moiro was dark and secret, nursing the flame in her heart. It was easier to get in and out of the house than it would have been in Athens, and not very far to the foot-hills above the crops, where no one came.

Moiro had never been afraid of the dark; as a little girl she used often to go out alone at night when her father and Chromon were up with the lambs, and she had to take them their supper, and then run back to the farm with the empty bowl, skipping along the turf tracks in the starlight. And now she felt a kind of power in her that glowed out and kept away the terrible things: she belonged to Leon, not to them. In the daytime she thought of him, silent and dreaming over her sewing in some shadowed corner. She could recall and linger over the beautiful, heavy square of his face, kissing again in memory all along his eyes and eyelids, the warmth of his cheeks, the ruffling of little curls about his ears and neck, his broad, untroubled forehead, and last his lips, clinging and fainting there; till even at the thought she grew dizzy, ready to sink and fall at his feet if it were only himself in front of her, instead of this moving, troubling image always in her mind whenever it cleared for a moment of the immediate things of the day! Every hour with him had been pictured, every touch quivered at by the willing flesh a hundred times before it came true. Some of the nights between, sleeping alone or beside Alxenor, she would dream of the hut and wake hot and throbbing

260

with desire. She had fought against the God as well
as she could, but when the fight was lost she let
herself go utterly. All other life lost its meaning,
it became a game of pretence, being a wife and
mother, working, talking at ease with other women
– she heard the words flow off her own tongue and
wondered sometimes where they came from, not
surely from her true heart and mind. With no one
there but Thrassa she could let herself be silent and
gaze with a little still smile at something invisible.
And Thrassa was faithful to her mistress of old days,
and took good care that nobody else should get to
know.

In the hut there was seldom much talk; all that they
felt was better said by kiss and touch, and the final
closeness of their two bodies; there was only one
idea to exchange, and that belonged to both. Afterwards they might whisper a little, but scarcely more
than one another's names, and broken love-words
like pigeons cooing drowsily together in the same
nest. But one night he had picked her up and carried
her a little in his arms, while she clung with both
hands round his neck, her breast just pressing softly
against his shoulder, her bare feet dangling, rubbing
his side as he moved. And all at once she was remembering the day in Poieëssa. She bit his arm to make
him squeeze her tighter on to him, and then murmured, smoothing her cheek against his skin all the
time, 'Leon, when you carried me before, that time,
did you like it, did you want to go on with your arms
round me, like this?'

Leon sat down, still holding her, rocking her,

nibbling the ends of her hair: 'No, I was only a boy. Little love, would I ever have let you go if I'd wanted you as I do now?'

She shivered, close up against him: 'I wish you had! Oh, I wish you had! If only you'd taken me –'

Leon suddenly laughed to himself in the dark, following up his own picture of how it might have been: 'There and then! I'd have killed Alxenor like I killed your father, all bloody –'

But she had moved quickly, away from him, slid to the ground, the floor of pine needles: 'It was you, then. You that killed him. I wasn't sure.' There was a minute's silence, Leon startled with fear in case he had said the unforgivable thing, wondering vainly what he could do now to get it right. He thought perhaps if he could get hold of her again – But as he was half risen, reaching out for her, he felt her fingers all at once on his feet, and then her lips. 'I would have been your slave,' she said, with a sob in her voice, 'all yours for you to do what you like with. I want you to do what you choose always, kill father, kill anyone, kill me! No, don't kill me, hurt me, beat me –'

Leon had been listening, drinking it in because it made him want her all the more, warming quickly at her fire. But then, as she was still speaking, his whole feeling about it changed over, like the heaped grain shifting across in the dark hold of a ship, and he pulled his feet sharply away from hands and kisses. 'Don't!' he said. 'Stop it, keep off me, get up!' And stooped down, pushing her away, her hair, her arms – he would not be dragged into the mud

262

she was crawling in! If that was how women thought of it — suddenly he found himself shocked, sick to the very depths of his body: the woman had no decency at all! This was how she thought of her father, the dirty slut; she wanted to be a slave, by God she ought to be, she wasn't fit for a free man to touch. And then in the instant he was out of it all, he did not love her, did not want her one minute longer: he would go! The filthy little Ionian!

It was cold outside. So much the better after the sweat and heat of that hut. A falling leaf flicked wet against him and clung. He gripped his clothes with one hand, and ran hard, frowning, knocking into things, stones and thorns and long, damp trails of vine. At the stream he turned and ran on uphill till he came to a deep pool, and jumped clear in, slipped on a stone and rolled over and over, ducking himself, choking in the chill, clean water. On the further bank he put his clothes on, soaked and dripping as they were, and started off again, bruised all over by now, still trying to run it off. As he went by birds fluttered shrieking out of the bushes; one moment a roe-deer stood in the path staring at him with big eyes and ears, the next it was just a fleeting rustle through the thicket on his left; and twice he saw a humped dark shadow that might be wolf or even bear. By and by there were no more bushes at either side, no more plunging under the dusk of a spread oak; the bare stone ridges lay plain and sharp before him, the wind bit through the wet wool of his tunic. And still he was running.

In the earliest grey of dawn, Moiro found her way back to the house, stunned. Thrassa was lying awake and heard and brought her into her own room. 'What is it?' she said, 'I won't tell, you know I won't. I can help you, mistress dear.' Moiro laid her head in Thrassa's lap; she felt as if the sky had fallen on her. 'He went away,' she whispered. 'He won't come back.' Thrassa began to stroke the delicate fine skin of Moiro's face, smoothing away wrinkles from eyes and forehead, tracing the line of nose and lips and brows with her broad, kind finger-tips. 'Who is he?' she asked, and started at the name her mistress murmured back: 'But that's Leon who killed your father, my dear master!' 'Yes,' said Moiro, and lay still in her guilt. The slave-girl went on stroking again: 'Didn't you know, then?' 'I did know,' said Moiro, 'but not for sure. We hadn't spoken of it, not till to-night; and then it was my own fault. I had to choose between them, when I was certain: between him and father. I chose him. And so father – then – father –' 'Oh, what?' said Thrassa, shaking her, she was so hard to hear. 'Then – I think the Ker came and drove Leon away. Because I ought always to be good and do my duty as mother told me, and be faithful to my husband and not look at Leon or any of the Spartans. I will be good now. I will never do it again.' And suddenly tiredness fell on her like a cloud, and she went to sleep with her hair loose on Thrassa's knees.

Winter came at last, the north wind to blow away the dust and heat of summer-time, the rain to flood Eurotas into a brown, tearing torrent, and soak the

meadows and the rush-beds and make everything
ready to grow again. The third month she was quite
sure; so was Thrassa. She tried to hide it, but already there had been some jokes about her looking
pale and not eating as well as she might; the Spartan
food sickened her now. One day soon – quite soon
– Alxenor would hear and know it was none of his
doing; beyond that she could not see.

She thought bitterly how careful she had been when
the first baby was coming, and she had gone about
softly full of anxiety in case she disturbed it; but it
was only a poor Ionian like herself, and this one was
a Spartan and wouldn't budge! Thrassa had thought
she knew ways of dealing with it; they were both
hopeful at first. But nothing was any use. Thrassa
would get hold of something, tell her how she'd
known it work before – she tried to believe, hard,
hard; at the beginning it always seemed as if it might.
But by the end she was back in her trap again, only
iller than ever between her fear and anxiety and all
those country poisons that would do nothing for her.
Just as she had thought of Leon all the time during
those autumn weeks, so now it was this other thing;
if she could manage to forget and be a little happy
for a few minutes, all at once there would be a jerk
and back it would come, more painfully than ever.
She became so conscious of time, that the very
passage of hours was a torture to her, nothing she
did or said was unrelated to the terror she was
drenched in. All day she and Thrassa were reading
one another's thoughts; without that companionship
she thought she would have gone mad. But often

265

now she remembered Nikodike, her clear eyes and sane mind, and wished for her desperately to come and be a sister: Nikodike whom she had never even said good-bye to.

Alxenor began to grow anxious about her; he saw she was ill and unhappy, and could tell she was not sleeping. He did not suspect what it was, knowing how careful he had been himself, but kept on worrying her with questions and suggestions of what drugs to take; she had to pretend to him that it was something else, but Thrassa helped her. She was most afraid of his going to Kleora and asking her advice; then she would have been found out at once. As it was, she could stave it off for another month perhaps.

A good deal of the time Alxenor had nothing to do; then he envied the Spartans going about their business, and felt more keenly than ever the loss of his State. Only a citizen could be truly a man, with a plan of his life that he could keep to, and the future, short of his City being destroyed, steady and fairly certain. If he had been a Spartiate the plan would be perfected to take in everything in life from childhood to old age; so that, as long as he remained a citizen, he could never be lonely, or wondering endlessly what to do, or ever have to face the fierce unfriendly world of nature and the barbarians except as one of a sure army of friends, armed and watchful, with their own Gods to care for them. If he had been a Spartiate he would have been strong and happy, still in the Class, an Iren perhaps like Leon. Everything would be made simple, he would have no responsibilities, no wife or child to look after and

266

be perpetually anxious for. He would be one drop in the stream, one leaf of the tree, part of some bigger scheme than he could ever make for himself. If he had been a Spartiate he would marry when he was old enough to be certain of his own mind, some beautiful, calm girl like Dionassa, who would never be ill or cross with him, or change from the self she had once been.

That winter Moiro made less fuss about Timas, and Thrassa as well was so unhappy that she did not take so much care of him as usual. But the rest of the women were all fond of him; the nurse let him walk beside her when she was carrying the baby; Kleora was kind and strong, and took him to ride on the cows, praising him when he was brave and held on to their horns, instead of screaming at him like his own mother. She encouraged him to do things which she would perhaps not have let her own son do. Eurotas was in full flood, grey-brown and cold with melting snow from the hills, but little Timas saw the Spartan boys wading and washing there, went in himself, and was nearly swept away. Kleora brought him back, chilled to the bone and crying; but all the same she was not quite sorry she had let him: he was such good stuff to try on! She put him on dry clothes, liking to touch his lean, soft, child's body – so many years till her own would have grown from a baby to a man . . . Then she gave him hot wine to drink, till he fell asleep on her bed; he kept it secret from his mother, just a lovely, exciting thing to laugh about with Kleora whenever they remembered, and he was none the worse for it.

But she wished he could go on like that; some day soon Alxenor would go home to his island and the child would be taken away from Sparta and grow up like any other Ionian. Such a pity.

Moiro never even noticed that the child's clothes had been wet; there was something now between her and all the rest of the world, a growing shadow. She sat in the courtyard with a thick shawl over her shoulders, bent low with her fingers moving on a fine strip of embroidery that should have had all her care. But one minute she was wondering if anyone could see her changing shape in the way she sat now; and the next minute she was trying to think of anything to say when the time did come; and then for a little she would hear nothing but the purring and rushing of the river two fields away, through the still, coldish air. She turned as Thrassa came towards her: 'You – you haven't thought of anything?' Thrassa shook her head pitifully: 'Nothing.' Moiro looked down at her work again; she did not hope for any help now, but it was still always a shock to know; a tear or two fell on to the embroidery. Then the slave-girl twisted her hands together, and bit her lips, and bent down and whispered.

Moiro sat up straight, white and then red again. 'Can you do it?' she said. 'Oh, Thrassa dear, if you really can!' 'I never have yet,' said Thrassa. 'I don't want to. It's only for you, my lamb. I won't have these people here laugh at you! And I won't have Alxenor hurt you. Not while I'm here to stop them. But – it's not safe.' 'Yes,' said Moiro, with her head lifted at last, 'I know. Only I'd sooner go into danger a hundred times than live another week like this.' She picked up the embroidery. 'Now – now at once! They won't miss us till supper-time. Thrassa, now, while I'm being brave!'

But was it right, was it? Had Thrassa been clever enough? What happened afterwards? Was the danger over – or not begun yet? It was terrible to go on, hour after hour, not sure, that night and the next day and the next night and the next day –

Kleora said to her sister: 'That poor thing's not well.' Dionassa shrugged her shoulders: 'She hasn't been all winter. But what are you to do? She's always sitting in the dark, she doesn't breathe!' 'It was worse to-day. Didn't you see at supper? She was in pain.' 'Pain? Is Sparta killing her then? She won't be much loss!' Kleora frowned: 'You are a hard little bear! Is that what you get from Artemis? Wait till you're married – you'll learn to be kinder to other women. Moiro doesn't like me, but I'm going to her all the same; I must find out. She's my guest, after all.'

Moiro was huddled up on the couch, crying faintly and shivering, twitching her fingers; her face was buried in the pillow, her knees drawn up under her. Thrassa was heating something on the stove; and she was crying too, all down her dress. Then Kleora came in, and the child ran up to her, terrified. 'Mother's so cold!' he said. 'She's hurt herself!' and he clung on to the hand held out to him. 'Quiet!' said Kleora, stiffening to look, and pressed him against her, thinking how queer it was, this sudden, violent anxiety for the mother who was in most ways so little to him. She came up to the couch; there seemed to be rather an odd smell about. Moiro turned half over and looked up at her with blurred eyes. 'Go away!' she said. 'Go away, Spartan!' and bit at the ends of her loose hair, and burrowed with her fingers under the pillow. Kleora knelt quickly and kissed the hot, dry cheek. 'What is it?' she asked, very gently. 'What happened? Can't I help?'

Moiro pushed her away, irritably, and shut her eyes: 'Where's Thrassa?' she muttered. 'It's all her fault — she's got to make me well. Thrassa! Thrassa!' she called, beating with her fists; but when the girl came running over, she only began to cry again and would not drink the hot milk or let herself be covered or have her face bathed. Kleora took Thrassa by the shoulder: 'What is the matter with your mistress?' And her hand tightened. 'I don't know!' said Thrassa, and then, frightened, 'It's only a chill, she'll get right! Please, please, let me go!' 'It's not a chill,' said Kleora. 'What is it? You'd better tell.' 'It's — oh, perhaps she's eaten something bad! I'll see to her, we won't disturb anyone. Please, lady, don't hold me!' Kleora let her go: 'I shall send one of my own maids in, and then I shall want you, Thrassa.' She went out, and called her sister.

Alxenor was not there, nor likely to be for a day or two; in any case it was a woman's business. Thrassa came in to them, looking, defensive and anxious, from one to the other; she was bigger than any of the helot women, and stronger, come of free barbarian stock; but all the time she knew, and they knew, that she was a slave and to be treated as such.

270

'Now tell,' said Kleora, going up to her. 'I don't know a thing more!' said Thrassa. 'Can't you leave us be, lady? We're not your folk!' But Kleora gripped one arm, Dionassa the other, their fingers closed like a trap. 'What did you do to your mistress?' Kleora asked again, and then once more, her arm, iron-hard, straightening, pushing the slave-girl to her knees. For a minute she struggled, trying to twist her arms free; the handkerchief fell off her head and the short, untidy plaits tumbled at each side of her face. It was no use; they only held her tighter, Dionassa laughed as if she were enjoying it. The other one repeated her question; Thrassa looked up at her and was very frightened, because she had never seen a woman look so grim before. They were pressing her arms back and up now, so that it was beginning to hurt a lot. She screwed her eyes up and bore it for Moiro's sake. If they got to know one thing they would get to know everything; she was keeper of Moiro's honour: Moiro with no one else to help her and guard her from the world and her husband. Moiro, her lamb. She would not be able to bear it much longer. She began to count: hold out to ten: and ten again: and ten.

The Spartans went about it quite quietly, hardly breathing faster than usual; they knew they would get their answer, that in another moment this dumb, huddled thing at their feet would come suddenly alive and do what they wanted. And so it did; for Moiro's voice came from the far room, calling, 'Thrassa! Thrassa, I want you! Oh, don't be so long!' And Thrassa turned and twisted madly, tears

271

running into her open mouth. 'Oh, let me go!' she said. 'Let me go! She's calling me, she's dying!' 'Why do you say that?' said Kleora. 'What did you do?' And again that terrible pressure and pain. Then Thrassa broke down and told them what she had done.

'Then if she dies, you will have murdered her,' said Kleora, and Thrassa's sobbing suddenly checked: 'Me! But it was to help her – I didn't want to! Oh don't you know I love her better than my own life! Me, murder her!' 'Alxenor will think so.' Thrassa threw herself down, clutching at Kleora's feet, 'Oh don't, oh I do beg and pray, not him!' Kleora stepped back: 'I shall tell him myself. You murdered his child, if not his wife. Listen, you slave, this does not go unpunished in my house!' Then Thrassa lifted her hands to her head in utter despair and confusion: 'Oh,' she said, 'oh, do what you want to me yourself, mistress, but don't tell Alxenor!'

Kleora looked at her closely, frowning. 'What are you hiding?' she asked, then, after a moment, 'was it his child?' Thrassa stayed silent, bowed to the ground. The Spartan women looked at one another over her head: 'Whose was it then?' Kleora asked, and her sister squared her young shoulders disgust-edly, staring out into the sunlight. Thrassa answered very low: 'I can't tell. It was her secret. Have pity on me, lady, and let me go back to her.' 'Go then,' said Kleora after a minute, and Thrassa fled out, wiping her eyes and nose with the back of her hand, and so to Moiro again.

She sat up all that night. Towards morning Moiro

got worse, not in great pain, but complaining curiously of headache; she was thirsty all the time, and very restless. Kleora's nurse brought dried herbs of her own to boil, and a pierced blood-stone to tie on with black thread; and just after dawn Kleora came herself and bade Thrassa get some sleep. She kept the curtain drawn across the door, and blew out the lamp, hoping that Moiro might sleep, but it was no use; the fever was boiling up in her too strongly, and every little while she asked for a drink and gulped it down, and then turned over again, pulling at her dress and moaning. Once when she was quieter, Kleora combed back her hair, and plaited it out of the way, and sometimes sponged her face and hands. She wished Alxenor were back, but was yet not sure how much to tell him. She wished far more that her own husband would come; he was with her for a few hours at least most days, but sometimes he had to stay away longer on duty. If this went on getting worse she would send a message to him; she had never seen anyone die, and she was a little frightened.

Moiro herself had stopped being frightened hours before, stopped struggling against what was happening to her. Death had been real and terrifying the day before; she had held tight on to Thrassa, strong, live Thrassa, crying to be saved; but now that was all past. The night went by slowly; short spaces of whirling darkness, falling into deep pits of dream; and then the return to life and consciousness and thirst, the yellow blink of the lamp, the ache in her head, the sour taste in her mouth. And then the drink, and Thrassa's kind hand and voice; and by

273

and by darkness again. Some one had said – or was it only in a dream? – that she would be better in the morning. But dawn brought no relief. Dimly she heard the Spartan voice, and then found Thrassa was gone. Through blurred and sticky eyelids she saw the line of light above and below the curtains, and the gleam on Kleora's piled hair. For a little her mind was filled with the idea that Kleora was turning into a wild, shaggy cow, with horns to pierce into all the pain spots of her body. The idea turned over and over, sometimes serious, sometimes clearly fantastic, and after a time it went. Still Thrassa was away. She was beginning to slip more and more into her dreams, and the headache stood away from her, something hard and knobbed, outside. It turned into a stick; it turned into Alxenor; it turned into a ship, one could watch it turning, quite calmly; it turned into Gobryas. It turned into Leon.

She wondered if she had said his name aloud or only in a dream. It was so hard to tell. She must not speak, not while Kleora was there. She fumbled at the edge of the blanket and got a corner into her mouth; while it was still there she would know she had not spoken. It was full day now. How long, how long, how long.

Thrassa slept solid for three hours, then woke, suddenly remembering everything. She could still feel where the Spartans had hurt her. She looked into the courtyard and saw little Timas, one hand in Dionassa's, pointing up at a bird on the roof. He didn't know, poor innocent. She remembered the day of his birth and how she'd helped put up the

olive wreath; and telling Ditylas. How proud she'd
been! And when he'd said her name first, calling at
her all over the house. Oh well. She didn't want to
think about what Kleora had said, being a murderer.
That would mean – oh no it couldn't! Some things
can't be true. She shoved it down, out of thought,
got a drink and a piece of bread from the kitchen,
and went back to Moiro; the fever was much about
the same.

It was so terrible not to know what it was. Any
woman could tell you it went wrong sometimes when
you did – that. If it wasn't just right. But what was
the God who would help now? Again she felt her
mistress' burning skin, and smelt the horrible breath
of spent fire coming from her mouth; and she was
more and more afraid.

By this time Moiro was getting very distant, floating off by herself, giddily. She slid down dark, closed
ways back to Poieëssa, and played there till her
father's Ker came buzzing round the corner of the
house, like a hornet, and chased her back and back.
Then Thrassa gave her a drink. Thrassa was crying.
She laughed at Thrassa. There was a crack in the
plaster of the wall; it was beginning to open. She
could see through it, there were stairs, going up and
up. Things were coming in through the crack in the
wall. A cow came in – she shrieked and found herself clinging to Thrassa and the cow gone. Her bed
was sliding about over the floor, jarring her: 'Stop!'
she cried. 'Stop!' but it went on. Grey sheep began
coming out of the crack, sheep and sheep, piling up
till the room was full of them; they weighed on her

with their thick fleeces, oh so hot. She tried to push them away, they melted into mist under her hands; Leon came out of the crack. She heaved the mist away and cried to him: 'Leon, oh, Leon, my love, you've come at last!'

It was evening then. Thrassa and Kleora were both there, and when she cried out so clearly at last after all the vague talking and singing of the day, Kleora turned to the slave: 'Was it Leon?' Thrassa did not answer, but Moiro from the bed called again: 'Leon, Leon, come nearer!' And then, as though she were whispering with a lover: 'Stay now, I've wanted you so, Leon, Leon, Leon!' Kleora blushed slowly and painfully, and her eyes filled with tears. 'It must have been!' she muttered. 'Oh, my house is shamed!'

Her nurse brought in another wise woman; they said charms and did what they thought fit to Moiro. Kleora gave them all they wanted and bade them come to her for anything else, then went out. She had sent a message to her husband, who might know where Alxenor was, and how to get at him. In the meantime Dionassa came and sat with her; the sisters held hands, talking low about this stain on the honour of their house. 'My guest,' said Kleora, 'and the wife of my guest!' 'Yes,' said Dionassa, 'but most likely it was her fault.' 'Perhaps,' Kleora answered, slowly. 'But Leon must answer for it as well as her.'

Archytas came after Mess, hurrying; he knew his wife would not send him a message for nothing. Ladas went off on a pony to find Alxenor; he was very sorry for them both; like most of the household,

276

he suspected, without quite knowing, what was the matter with Moiro. Kleora told her husband the whole thing; he was very angry and ashamed, and said that everything possible must be done for the woman. 'Don't tell Alxenor what it is,' said Kleora. 'Why not?' Archytas asked, and then: 'Very well. Not till it's over, anyhow. You know best, my lady.' He kissed her hand, and then her lips.

Moiro slept a little that night, but not for more than half an hour at a time. And when she was awake she was talking and crying out and laughing, without any stop; sometimes she knew Thrassa, but often not. She would seem to be talking to Leon, arguing and entreating and calling to him. But her own consciousness was dissolving; she no longer felt she was herself; she was separating up, getting vaguer, hardly held together by the sick body, in which the fever was worsening every hour. By the afternoon of the next day she had grown quite quiet, her eyes scarcely moving, her fingers scarcely fretting at the blanket. The fires in her were burning out, the glow sinking and crumbling to ash and finish.

Alxenor came at last; he had taken the pony from Ladas, and ridden it up hill and down as fast as it could go; his clothes were stained with foam from its mouth, he shook all over with anxiety and hurry. He knelt by her bed, kissing her hands; she did not look at him for a long time; when she did, it was emptily, unaware of him, a stranger. He began calling her name, a little wildly, till the women stopped him; she moved her head, frowning, and then lay still again. He stayed crouching beside her,

277

watching her; he remembered old days at Poieëssa,
and how he had taken her away from everything she
loved, carried her off, sure that being his wife would
be reward enough for her; and then it had all gone
wrong. Athens had killed their love, and now Sparta
was killing her. If only he could take her home.
He kissed her hands again: so hot they were now,
but once they had been cool and easing and dear,
the little fingers he had played with. He thought of
that gold cup of his, still hidden away against the
time he should need it most, and vowed it to Apollo,
Sender and Stayer of sickness, if only these fever
arrows could be loosed from his wife. Kleora vowed
too; she felt it was her fault, through her cousin
Leon; she knew that really there could be no blood-
guilt on the house, and yet, if Moiro died it made
the whole plan of life wrong.

But Moiro did die; she came up out of her depths
for a moment first, and saw, obscurely, the room, and
Thrassa, and her husband – his face, terribly troubled.
She knew she was dying; as far as she thought at
all, she was glad: the fight had been too hard and
too long. 'Don't mind,' she said to Alxenor, with a
faint surprise at hearing her own voice again, and
smiled just a little; and died.

CHAPTER FOURTEEN

'Bolshevik Russia has never failed to produce a violent
reaction in the spectator, either of enthusiasm or of hatred.
The authors of this book . . . were fortunate in that the
fury led them in completely opposite directions. . . .'
— Dora and Bertrand Russell

STILL Moiro's body lay there; Thrassa had
washed it and weighted its eyes, and put on it
the white funeral linen; she moved about the
room now, heavy and dull with tears, desolate for her
little mistress. Alxenor had cut his hair short for
mourning; he had been crying too, his mind felt
washed and blank and very sad. He would go
straight back to Poieëssa, with the child. Timas
came up to him, white and big-eyed in his black
tunic, and got on to his knee and curled up there,
sucking his thumb, not quite understanding. For a
moment Dionassa stood in the doorway, watching
them, then went on, frowning, and saw that there
were no servants listening at the door where those
others were.

Leon stood with his hands twisted in front of him
and his eyes on the ground; every word that Archytas
was so slowly throwing at him hurt like a stone. And
he knew that his lover was hurt too, bruised to the
heart by what he had done; the two hurts jangled
about in his mind, making each other worse. Because there is nothing sorer to the spirit than falling
below what one's lover thinks of one. He had made
what excuses he could at the beginning; now he was
beyond that, he was nothing but sorry, and still
sorry. 'I should never have lived,' said Archytas, 'if
this evil thing is all I make of you!' And he looked

279

away, shivering, looked at anything but Leon, the spirit of his own teaching, with this flaw in him. Leon rubbed his hands over his eyes angrily: it was not by easy tears he must get his pardon — if he did get it. He went and knelt in front of Archytas, keeping his hands with a great effort from touching him, keeping his eyes away from his face. Shortly and truthfully, he said how sorry and shamed he was, and how he was punished by what Archytas thought of him; he laid his soul at his lover's feet for a better moulding. After a time Archytas put one hand on his head in forgiveness, and kissed him. And out of shame happiness began to rise.

Kleora got up from her chair and came over and looked at them, a little coldly, the distaff still in her hand. 'All this time,' she said, 'you have been thinking about yourselves.'

'No,' said Archytas, 'I thought of the State. If he lives badly, so does it.'

Kleora swung the spindle angrily. 'It's others besides the State you hurt; will you do nothing?'

'She's dead.'

'She's not all.'

'Well — you've a plan: tell.'

'Let the State take Timas and bring him up as a foster-child.'

Archytas thought a minute. 'Yes, that's fair. Leon, you shall have him in your Class and make a Spartan of him: the best way you can clear yourself.'

Leon bowed his head, knowing that Archytas was right, but angry all over, hating the thought of that Ionian child, hers and Alxenor's, always there to remind him of something he wanted so badly to forget. Besides, he had no liking for the foster-children; there was one in his Class now, always getting in the way, spoiling the beauty, the wholeness of the thing, not being a Spartan! And now there was to be another.

'I'll take him for the next three years,' said Kleora, 'till he's old enough for the Class. I think – perhaps I can help to make something of him.' She looked down, shyly, suddenly aware that she was the youngest of the three, in spite of feeling so old and sensible. But Archytas came and put an arm round her: 'You will if anyone can,' he said, and then to Leon: 'Now go! That's over.' Leon kissed both their hands and went; but it's not over, he thought, as long as I've got to have that child in my Class, shaming me . . .

He went out of the City, on to the Amyclae road; here he took his sandals off, and went barefoot through the mud to save the leather. Then he cut himself a stick and walked on, jabbing at things and muttering under his breath. He had begun to think of Moiro herself, those warm, soft legs and arms, all cold now and stiff: and the sweet smell of her breasts and hair, gone bad. And he thought of the thing he had made himself, the child growing inside her: dead too. But it wasn't real, not real as she had been, to touch and fondle. There was a loaded ox-cart creaking along in front of him, its wheels slowly following the two ruts of the road. 'Out of my way!' he shouted, and the helot driver looked round and ran to the beast's head, pushing on the yoke to get it over; but the wheels were too fast in the rut to move at once, and Leon had to push past, so that a bramble caught in his hair and tugged it. He let fly with his stick at man and beast; the slave was hit on the arm and cried out, and the ox swerved a little, and swung its beautiful, heavy head, lowing at him. He wished they would send him on the Krypteia again.

By and by he saw Erasis a little way ahead, and ran up lightly behind him. The boy had a sack over his shoulder; he was rather dirty, particularly about the legs, because of the mud; his winter tunic was nearly worn out, all in rags round the hem, and, after the habit of small boys, he had not brushed his hair for some days. Suddenly he looked round, and grinned delightfully at Leon through the dirt. 'I knew it was you,' he said, 'I know how your feet sound. I've got meal in there, for the Mess, and a hare; I killed him myself – with a stone. Are you pleased, Leon?'

'Yes. Where was he?'

'On the way – a mile past Summer Market. He was playing on the ploughland, round and round, with his friend. First I watched, then I threw. He's heavy.' And Erasis gave a little jump of satisfaction, then looked round again: 'Oh, Leon, I'm sorry, I've been talking too much!'

But Leon shook his head: 'No, go on. It's not you, it's me.' He was trying hard not to cry in front of the boy.

'When you're not happy, I'm not happy either,' said Erasis, timidly putting his hand into Leon's; then, finding it was all right, he took courage to go on: 'Tell me what it is, Leon. I think I could help.'

With a great effort Leon found he could stop the tears coming. 'I did something bad,' he said, 'and then it got worse. Things do. I'll tell you some day, Erasis.'

But Erasis rubbed his head consolingly against Leon's arm. 'I don't think you'd do anything very bad.'

When the time came, they buried Moiro. Alxenor called her name three times across the fresh grave-mound, and bade her rest; the child pressed against him, staring and clinging to the handful of earth he had been bidden to throw. They went back and purified themselves and the house with sacrifices, and Alxenor made ready to go down to Gytheion with his son and Thrassa, and find a ship to take them home.

But the Spartans were talking about him among themselves. It was sunny, and the maids had their spinning outside in the court. Kleora sat on the step of the colonnade where she could see that they kept to their work. Her sister stood on her right, leaning against a pillar, fingering and smelling the thick-budded vine beside her. On the wall at the back, the red, painted swans were a little faded; last year's swallows' nests still clung to the eaves; soon, soon the swallows would come again. Archytas stood with one foot on the step, his back to the sun. 'No,' he said, 'no. I've waited long enough. I must tell him now.'

'Ah,' said Kleora, looking up at him, one hand on his bent knee, 'why need you? He has it in his head it was fever: men don't see. Let him go on thinking the best of her; let her rest, poor thing.'

283

Archytas stroked her hand. 'When were you so fond of lies, little wife? Here's another thing: Thrassa is his – will you have no punishment for her?'

Kleora frowned uncomfortably, saying nothing, but Dionassa nodded: 'Yes, that has to be done.'

'And yet,' said her sister, 'she only did her mistress' bidding.'

'She is a murderess!' said Dionassa, 'it is terrible still to have her in the house!' And she shivered all over, with a curling back of lips and fingers from the Unclean Thing.

'Yes,' said Archytas, 'the House must be cleared; for Leon's sake she must die and take all blame from him.'

'Tell, then!' said Kleora, flushing and looking herself not unlike Leon, and she buried her face in her hands till her husband went away.

Dionassa bent over her, and kissed the back of her neck lightly. 'Big sister,' she said, 'you've got to stay strong still, haven't you, as we were made? Because of the sons we're going to have.'

Alxenor looked up as the Spartan came in; he had been putting his clothes and things into a sack, ready to go. There was an old red cloak stitched with black, plain along the hem and two cocks with a flower between at each corner; he remembered Moiro stitching it, in the evenings, at Athens, close to the lamp always – that bright haze of light through her hair. And now – yes, he must listen . . . Archytas was speaking, telling him horrible things, standing still there by the wall with his terrible straight eyes!

For nearly a minute Alxenor said nothing; it was all clearly and dreadfully true; that was why Moiro had been so queer, since autumn. He went on fingering the red cloak with her embroidery: at least, nothing changes the past. Archytas was expecting him to say something; he folded the cloak gently. 'It is best that I should know,' he said. 'I am going home now, away from Sparta; I should have gone before. I thank you for your hospitality, Archytas.' Said the Spartan: 'We owe you something. We offer, if the Class and the Elders think well, to take your son and bring him up as a foster-child of the State.' 'My Timas!' said Alxenor, 'would you –? Oh, it's been in my mind, seeing the boys here!' 'He would be the same,' said Archytas gravely. But then Alxenor was swept with uncertainty: 'Only now . . . I can't tell. It seems too rare a chance to lose. And yet –' Then Timas came in himself; he had been too unhappy to stay playing alone; he wanted father.

Alxenor picked him up and explained the offer; he felt he would accept what the child said. Himself, he was all unblessed; he could come to no lucky decision; but his little son, not knowing, might yet have surest knowledge. Timas listened. 'I want to stay here,' he said. 'Please, father, I do want to play with those boys.' That was decided, then; Alxenor found he was glad, he had been hoping the child would make it go this way. 'You shall,' he said. But, 'If he passes,' Archytas added, and then went out.

Again Alxenor started taking the things out of the chest and putting them into the sack; and he kept on looking at his little son. He was big and strong for

his age, that was all in the last year or so. And clever
– no question of his passing. And then, he'd grow
up with the Spartans, learn to be the best of everything, master the world, as they did in Sparta. He
would make vows to their Apollo, the Bow-bearer,
who had more power than the little Apollo of Poieëssa
ever could have; the Twin Gods would be his shield
and help in battle, the Twin Gods who had been
stronger than Athene. All this the child had gained.
Better so, oh surely better; though it was hard for the
father. How lonely he would go home now, he
thought, with even the picture of seeing Poieëssa
again almost dead in him, how lonely, oh, Moiro, my
Moiro, if you could have been faithful a little longer!

Timas, copying his father, had begun pulling things
out of the chest too. 'Look!' he said, 'there's mother's
new dress! – isn't it?' Alxenor took it out and passed
it through his hands, wondering if she had made
it for her lover to see; it was queer not to be angry
with her at all, just because she was dead. As for the
rest, he scarcely thought about Leon at all; any more
than as the lightning, the hand of God, blasting his
house.

Thrassa came in with some of her mistress' linen
laid across her arms, all washed and darned and
folded, with the borders turned out to show; she put
it down carefully. Her eyes were red and her face
pale from tears and want of sleep; she, too, had cut her
hair on Moiro's tomb, and her cropped head showed
an odd shape under the handkerchief. Alxenor
watched her laying the things out in piles. 'It's all
there!' she said, 'all. Don't look at me that way! I've

286

done my duty by you, master. There's no one can say I'm not honest!'

'No,' said Alxenor, considering her still. 'Honest you've been, Thrassa. But you killed my wife.'

As she heard, Thrassa's hand went fluttering to her heart: 'They told you,' she said. 'God's curse on them!' And then, rather slowly, she sunk down on the floor at Alxenor's feet.

'Why did you do it?' he said, low and strangely; and Timas ran out again, frightened.

But Thrassa answered, from the ground: 'For her honour's sake. She asked me.'

'And you hadn't even the skill to do it right!' said Alxenor bitterly. 'So she's dead, my Moiro!'

Thrassa lifted her head a little. 'Master, I did what she thought best. She was so afraid!'

'Of me.'

'You were her husband, master; and I – I just loved her. Like I always did. I'd have died twice over rather than this happen. But the Gods wouldn't have it.'

'Get up!' said Alxenor harshly. 'Who are you to talk about Gods and love! You murdered her, you shall get your punishment!'

Thrassa stood up, her hands clenched on her breast; she drew in her breath on a half scream, facing him. 'I hate you!' she said. 'Oh I do hate you! You took her and hurt her and frightened her, and she'd got no one but me! She was so good, she wouldn't take Gobryas, and then this blasted Spartan comes and has her, and it all goes wrong! But it's your fault, you wouldn't even earn enough to keep her decently,

nor you wouldn't take her home, nor nothing! And
it was always me that had to put things right! And
now I'm to take all the blame, but before Zeus, and
my own Zeus too, it's your fault, you beast, you
brute –' And she broke down, sobbing noisily, her
back to the wall.

Alxenor had been too miserably surprised to stop
her; he looked at her now, with her hands up to her
eyes, and her mouth pulled down and ugly with crying: his slave. Through all these years she'd seemed
more like a friend. Could he judge her now? His
mind was all unjust, twisted with passion; he must
get straight again first. He walked out and left her
among the half-sorted clothes. Time enough before
he went away from Sparta for ever.

Two days later he had made all his preparations; it
was simple to go on a journey alone. And yet he had
done nothing to Thrassa. He could not make up his
mind, and he would not let the Spartans make it up
for him, though they told him plainly what he ought
to do. And Thrassa stole about the house, doing her
work, looking after Timas, watching her master from
corners with a scared face. She thought of running
away, but what was the good in Sparta? – she'd heard
stories enough of the things that happened to slaves
here. Better to trust to her master's mercy or at
worst take the death he gave her and maybe find her
mistress somewhere in the underworld.

Archytas came home that afternoon with a guest, a
tall man, grey-bearded and wearing only the Spartan
cloak of bluish wool wrapped across him. Kleora herself ran and opened the door to him; Dionassa

288

brought him wine and oat-cakes and honey; they all
stood, like children, while he sat and ate slowly.
'Now the child,' he said, at last, and again Kleora ran
to do his bidding. Alxenor knew that this was one of
the Elders; he was questioned as to his State, standing there, and what he had done since; he tried to
answer shortly, Spartan-fashion, but usually before
he had finished the old man was asking the next
question. Then it was the child's turn; Kleora stood
him in front of the Elder and took his tunic off. He
was asked his name; very shy, holding on to Kleora,
he whispered it: 'Timagoras, son of Alxenor, sir.'
Then for a minute or two the old man handled him,
seeing that bones were straight and muscles well
started. Alxenor looked on uncomfortably, thinking
there was a touch of the slave market about it, but
for some reason Timas was amused and looked up,
grinning, at the Elder, who grinned back: 'If you
saw a big goose coming to bite you, what would you
do?' 'Hit it!' said Timas, then, confidentially, 'They
don't really bite, they only make that funny noise.'
'Good,' said the old man, and nodded to Alxenor,
who took the child away again and dressed him. It
was queer to think of the long years ahead before
ever he could see or feel this small, fresh body again
. . . it would have grown out of all knowledge, to a
young man, hard and sun-browned. And he would
be old himself – a stranger. Yet he was glad and
proud that his son should look so well to the Spartan.
  'He passes, sir?' said Kleora a little anxiously. 'Yes,'
said the Elder, 'and yours grows?' 'Oh, would you
care – to see him?' 'No.' The old man stood up,

looking from her to her husband. 'Full time you had another.' She and Archytas both went red and said it should be so. Then Dionassa stood up to be questioned; she was full-grown now, fit to be married and start her work for the State. 'You shall have a son before the twelve-months is up,' said the Elder, and got to his feet, refusing more food and drink, took up his long stick and set off, with Archytas. Dionassa knelt down by Kleora, and suddenly began to cry with her head in her sister's lap.

The next day Timas was brought out again, naked, into the courtyard. The sun was really hot for the first time that year, the mud had dried to dust, the flowers were coming. Kleora had made him a wreath of wild irises, that shed their sweet scent round his head. His eyes were just the same deep violet as the petals, his brown hair sprang up in little soft curls under the wreath – darker than the Spartan children. Archytas had put on his finest clothes to honour the Class, scarlet and white, and the flat, beaten gold of his laurel wreath; his wife, too, wore all her best, with a blue veil over her hair and breast. Dionassa had a clean tunic, but not new; being a maid, she had no gold or jewels, and went bareheaded. The two women had food ready, bread in flat loaves strewn with poppy seeds or salt, or baked with honey, dried fish soaked overnight, and bowls of lettuce and garlic and dandelion leaves. They had made garlands, stripping the garden bare of bud and blossom, and sending out the maids for wild evergreens, rosemary, laurel and thyme, the first young leaves of beech that fade so quickly, catkins of hazel and pink cones

of larch, and scented pussy willow from the banks of
Eurotas. They were still making them when the
Class began to come.

Of course there were only the boys, and a few of the
men; most of those over twenty were away with their
Brigade, each year-class marching and messing
together. Those who were left were the Irens, the
teachers and captains of the boys, picked and fine-
looking, with their brown curls and thick short
beards; they would only go to the Brigade if there
was actually war and need of them. They came in
first and greeted Archytas, and Alxenor still in
mourning; then came the rest, crowding and laughing and hitting one another, but in good order all the
same, quiet in a moment at a glance from their captain. As they settled down along the four sides of the
court, there were short and violent games of touch-
last and tripping and pinching among the smaller
boys, and scrambling for a good corner and climbing
up the pillars on to the roof. All round there were
friends sitting together, the best of them mostly in
twos. They passed about the food baskets and the
big water jars; none of them had eaten yet that day,
and they bit into the loaves, the hard bottoms first,
keeping for a last treat the top crust with its lovely
brown sprinkling of seeds. The Irens had the first
pick of Kleora's garlands, and those that were left
went to the others; there were only enough for some
of them, and soon one could tell who was best liked
by who was garlanded. Erasis had one, but Leon
would not wear his; Kleora had asked him not to
show himself, so he sat right back in a corner among

some of the little boys, who made room for him, pleased and surprised, and he was so well hidden here that Alxenor never saw him.

When they were all in, the courtyard was packed. Alxenor looked round at them, smelling their strong, rough bodies beginning to sweat in the sun. They had bathed on their way in the Eurotas, still running strongly with cold March flood-water, and the shock heads of the elder boys, who were letting their hair grow long, was still wet, flopping over their eyes and cheeks till they shook themselves and tossed it back again. By this time of year their tunics were often worn through, and half of them were thrown off now and used as cushions. They hunted one another quietly for thorns and fleas, or stared at Alxenor and Timas.

The Irens looked Timas over and talked to him and his father; they were very careful what foreigners they took, there were only quite a few in any year who were given the privilege of the Spartan training, and they had to have some special qualities. Kleora, looking on, thought it was lucky she and her nurse had been having so much of the child's bringing-up in the last year. Timas was naturally very shy at all this, but the Irens thought no worse of him for that; by this time they were good at telling what children were really like. This Class was nearly all Spartiate; there were just a few Laconians and half-and-halfs, and one foreigner. He was called up to talk with Alxenor, a boy of about fifteen, tall, with reddish-brown hair and no wreath, a Phokian, they said. One of the Irens pushed him forward, a hand on

292

his shoulder. 'Now, Kratis, tell what it is.' The boy
stood quite straight, looking into Alxenor's eyes in
the disconcerting Spartan way. 'We are all one
blood,' he said. 'Your son and the Kings' sons will
equally have the training – the Crown of Sparta which
is the Crown of Hellas, making bad into good, better
into best. There are steep paths between Eurotas
and Taygetus, but who learns to climb them, can
climb to the top of the world.'

He ended, with his mouth shut firm; Alxenor asked:
'But at first, it was hard, to be in the Class? – hard to
get like you are now?'

The boy answered, with the Iren's hand still on his
shoulder: 'Not easy winning; but worth it.'

'Yes,' said Alxenor, vaguely unsatisfied, but seeing
he would get no details out of the boy, then: 'Are you
the son of Harmokydes?'

'Yes.'

'I met him in Athens, four years ago. He said you
were here, and how wonderful it was. He told me it
was the best thing he had done in his life to get you
taken. And now I've seen you, and – and everything –' he looked round at the sun and the flowers
and the Spartans, and his own child in the middle of
it '– and I know he spoke truth!'

'He did,' said the boy, and was sent back to the
others with a pat on the back from his Iren.

Alxenor was pleased and excited now; he felt that
meeting the young Kratis was another good omen.
How fine the Class looked! He began to compare it
with his own young days; there was Chromon of
course . . . But apart from that he remembered the

293

soft clothes and bed he always had except just for the
time of his soldiering, and all the pretty things, the
sweet food and warm water, the mother and nurse to
run to if one hurt oneself — oh surely if he had lived
hard and under discipline like these boys, he would
have been a different man now! He would have been
accustomed to think quickly, take the wisest and
bravest course, instead of the easiest . . . what seemed
the easiest . . . and never was. But at least he had
done well by his son. One of the Irens picked Timas
up and set him on his shoulder. 'Shall we have him?'
he asked, walking all round with him, so that every
one could see. 'Yes!' shouted the Class, and Timas,
half understanding, clapped his hands and shouted
too.

After that Kleora took the Irens to see her own
baby, who was talking quite a lot now, and running
about and climbing over things. As they came in, he
tumbled off a bench on to his nose, but the nurse had
been taught not to scream, and the baby was so
interested in all the new people that he forgot to cry.
The Irens were pleased and laughed, and wished
Kleora good luck for another dozen like that, and
Kleora was glad he had shown off so well, and kissed
the Irens all round.

Then the whole Class went out again, singing
altogether, a marching song that stirred the heart of
any Spartan who heard it. None of the slaves had of
course been in the courtyard, but they knew what
was happening. Ladas came up to Alxenor afterwards, and asked if the child had been chosen. 'Yes!'
said Alxenor gladly. 'He's to be a lucky one — like

your master, Ladas.' 'Like my master,' Ladas echoed
him. 'Well . . . he's got another three years first.'
And he looked at Timas, a little queerly, Alxenor
thought, and later went and told Thrassa, who had
not dared to ask. 'Oh, what would my dear mistress
have said!' she cried miserably. 'Oh, the poor lamb,
the poor blessed little lamb! What'll come to him
now! Oh, my poor innocent!' 'Yes,' said Ladas,
looking on.

These last few nights Alxenor had slept with the
child in his own room; Kleora's nurse had offered to
take him, but Alxenor only had him for such a little
while longer. Only a day now, or at most two, before
it was good-bye, he said to himself that night, and
remembered he had not yet given his judgment on
Thrassa, and there she was, making the Spartans'
house unclean, after they had been so kind to him.
And yet . . . he could not bring himself to give her
death; the more he thought of it, the less guilty she
seemed, and the less guilty anyone seemed, Moiro or
Leon: it had all just happened. Somewhere there
must be justice in it; or the whole universe would
have to alter. And how uncertain his own justice
was, compared to that of the Gods. Puzzling over
all this, he went to sleep, and began, uneasily, to
dream about it; only in his dream it was not Thrassa
he was judging, but Timas.

Suddenly he sat up, wide awake, staring and listening into the room. The shutter was still fast against
the moonlight, only the thinnest white line slipt past.
'Timas!' he whispered, 'go to sleep!' But the child
breathed on quietly, yet stirring the air so that he

could not be sure there was not a third person in the
room. 'Who's there?' he called. And the answer
came quietly out of the dark: 'Kratis. Don't move,
please.' For a moment the moon-line was broken
by a shadow, then he felt, and almost saw, the boy
settling down on the blanket beside him. 'Why have
you come?' he whispered back, catching at a hand,
to assure himself of its reality.

Kratis pushed it away angrily. 'Don't leave your
child in Sparta,' he said.

'What!' said Alxenor aloud, startled.

And, 'Oh can't you be quiet!' the boy said in a fierce
whisper. 'Don't leave your child in Sparta if you love
him.'

Alxenor was blankly astonished: 'But you said
yourself –'

'What else could I say this morning? But it was
them speaking through me! Now I speak for myself
– and your child.'

'Wasn't it true, then?'

'In a way it was true. In a way I suppose it is the
best you can make of a man. But it is not the best a
man can make of himself! It may be very well for
the Spartiates; that's their life, they only want to
think of themselves as part of the State – they're
willing to give up their own selves for that. But I'm
not, and that child – you're Ionian, aren't you? –
why, it's in his blood to think for himself!'

'But surely it's half the Training, to learn to think
for oneself?'

'No: to think through oneself for Sparta. And then
– he'll care for art and music and philosophy, as I

296

might have cared, as, God knows, I'd care now if I had the chance! But it's all lost. I remember, when I was little, before I came, beautiful things, shapes and colours and softness: I dream of them now.'

'Kratis, you do get beauty here! The better beauty of friendship and fine living and the mountain tops!'

'For a year. For two years. And then, if you're not a Spartan, you'd give it all for one lovely, kind picture, one poem. I had a book of poems; I could read when I came; I didn't understand them then, but I loved them. The Spartans took it away. People who'd do that to a child –! They make nothing beautiful themselves.'

'Except their lives, and their State.'

'Oh, I give you that; but is it enough? There are no poets here! How could there be? They'd never have the quiet time alone for their minds to grow. We're always herded. And there's nothing new ever allowed; it's all frozen: living in ice!' He threw out his arms violently, as if he were trying to break something, then went on: 'If you still believe Sparta is worth all that, then think what your child has to face. The rest of the Class will know he is a foreigner and want to make him like themselves. All in goodwill, but the way they do it! They're bad enough to one another, but it's utter hell to be a stranger child alone among the Spartans! And when they've driven you dumb with fear and hate, they're pleased with you and themselves, and they say they've got you used to it – and you must be grateful! That's what Leon said to me: when he'd driven me nearly out of my mind. And it's under him your child will be, Leon

297

who's such a good Spartan that he's forgotten he's a man! As if he were a God: not knowing what they suffer down on earth. So that one worships and hates. Think how he'd treat an Ionian!'

'Yes,' said Alxenor, 'yes, I see.' It had brought him up with a jerk, this about Leon; he had never thought of him as having anything to do with Timas.

Kratis went on, speaking more calmly now, 'Leon knocks Erasis about too: to make him a good man! But it does make Erasis a good man; so there's no harm in it. There's no harm in pain if both giver and taker think it's good; but, if one of them doesn't, then there must be wrong somewhere.' He turned to Alxenor, peering at him through the dark, trying to show it all clearly. 'You see, the whole thing is that the Spartans feel differently about things, and what's right for them is not right for me or your child. We find it too hard to get friendship or love from them. Perhaps if one had that it might all fall together somehow and be beautiful. Because it is beautiful to them. But they won't make friends with me; they don't know how I feel. And – when you spoke about my father – they wouldn't let me ask –'

'Wouldn't let you?'

'Didn't you see? – his hand on my shoulder. But – how is father?'

'Well; and happy about you. But that was four years ago, and I didn't know him much; he was friendly, though. But don't you hear?'

'Sometimes. But they don't like it. And there's something else.' He moved close to Alxenor so that he could whisper right into his ear. 'The Gods. Tell me, your Gods, they're kind, aren't they? – and – and like all the good there might be in you? And they stay Gods, they don't do anything terrible? But it's different here. It's like old days, stories one's nurse told one, when the Gods used to do things. Apollo here – oh, I can't tell you!' His voice dropped and he shuddered, making the bed shake.

Suddenly Alxenor remembered all those things he had heard as a rower among the helots; a current of understanding passed between him and the boy. 'I think I know,' he said. 'Go on.'

After a minute Kratis did go on. 'Even if the Spartans accepted us, He would know we were strangers. Here: and at Amyclae: and at Thornax. He is one great awful Spartan stone out of the hills up to his arms, and then – then it breaks out into that terrible head, and the hands with the Bow. And supposing He were to follow, stone and all –' The boy broke off, and then again, as Alxenor stayed stiff and still beside him: 'He must bring suffering, hat is his being. And Artemis is his sister. There are games we have to play at the Altar, and sometimes – sometimes you get too much hurt . . . The Spartan boys want it; however much pain there is, they have chosen freely, and for them it is good. But if you are not a Spartan you do not choose it, and then it is horrible and nothing else! Do you mean that for your son?'

'No,' said Alxenor, 'no! But surely, surely, that's only one side?'

'Yes,' said the Phokian, 'the side you hadn't heard. Now, I must leave you to choose.'

299

'But go on, I must hear more!'

'I've no time. I only wanted to tell you the truth, as I would my father had been told.'

He got up, but Alxenor caught hold of him. 'But what do you do all day? You can't always be thinking this! You weren't the whole of this morning!'

'I wish you wouldn't talk so much!' said the boy. 'I'm in danger of my life coming here! I don't think this always, I've never put it into words before, but you can believe me all the same.'

'How are you in danger?'

'I'm a traitor to Sparta, traitor to her spirit! Isn't that enough? Oh, don't be a fool!' said Kratis, and in a moment was gone.

Timas had slept through it all; Alxenor went and sat by his mattress, and touched and held his limp, soft hand. So easy to hurt. But the child had wanted it himself, thought his father, from those quite first days when they had gone together and watched the Spartan children at play in the wood. Alxenor turned it over and over in his mind, sometimes thinking the Phokian boy must be mad, or else that he must be himself, and sometimes thinking that this was right and seeing the whole fabric of Sparta crumble away under his eyes. Morning came, and he was yet not sure.

About midday, Archytas saw him with the child, and stopped him. 'Kratis was with you last night,' he said.

Alxenor tried to look utterly surprised: 'Kratis? That boy I talked to yesterday? I promise you, I haven't seen him since!'

'Don't lie to me, Alxenor,' the Spartan said, 'it is no use. I tell you as a warning – to you both! Things can't be hidden here.' Alxenor was silent, rather afraid. 'He was not worthy of the gift we made him,' said Archytas.

'And so?'

'And so he has gone to Thornax, to worship Apollo.'

Said Alxenor, humbly, 'He only spoke out of kindness – what he thought was kindness. Lies, I know, but not on purpose! Have mercy, Archytas, he is only a boy!'

But Archytas turned sharp away: 'Be quiet, Alxenor, you fool! And think about what I have said!'

Alxenor did think about it; he was afraid to the bottom of his soul, but more afraid for his son than himself. He knew he was feeling like the helots felt on that ship; he fought against it, trying at least to be rational enough to make a plan. He took the gold cup out of its hiding-place, and any other gold he had, also a small dagger that he could hide under his tunic, a sling and some bullets; but he dared not even take a thick cloak, nor any food except a piece of bread that was over from breakfast. Then he went hand in hand with Timas, and found Kleora spinning. 'We're going up into the fields,' he said, ' it's my last day with him, and I want to talk to him before I go.' 'Surely,' said Kleora, and then, 'I'll take care of him as if he were my own, Alxenor.' The two of them went wandering out into the fields at the back of the house, getting further and further from the city. There seemed to be no one about. 'Where are we

going, father?' asked Timas suddenly. 'Just up into
the wood,' said Alxenor, 'that's all.' He was making
for trees and high ground, covert of some sort,
though he knew it would be no good, supposing
they really wanted him.

Once in the trees, he went quicker, north-east and
up; very soon the child was dragging behind and
had to be carried. There was very little leaf yet, but
at least that let one see ahead; and there was plenty
of thick evergreen undergrowth, box and ivy and
butcher's broom. Dusk began to fall before they
were more than a few miles from home. 'I'm cold,'
said Timas, beginning to whimper. 'Run then!' said
his father, and so they went on for another hour,
with alternate running and carrying, till it was quite
dark. Then Alxenor gave Timas half the piece of
bread. The child was beginning to cry with tiredness now, so Alxenor took off the light cloak he
always wore, and put him to sleep on it. Then he
saw that the gold cup, the purse and the sling were
safe in the breast of his tunic, and, as soon as Timas
was really fast asleep, picked him up with the cloak
rolled round him, and started to walk with the bundle
in his arms. There was all the difference between
carrying him this way and on his back; he had to sit
down and rest fairly often with the child across his
knees, mercifully still sleeping sound. It was fine,
starry weather, and he could guide himself by the
Dog; if he kept on thinking about stars he found he
did not think so much of worse things behind him.
There was a fairly good path, and he did not trip and
stumble too often, but whenever he stopped for a

moment it was very cold, and his arms ached all the time from the strain of carrying.

By and by the moon rose, which was lucky, as there was a broad, stony strip of pasture beyond the trees, very hard to find one's way across. After that trees again, and the continuous splashing of a small stream; but the slope was getting steeper: he could not go on. He turned off the path for some way, and pushed into a laurel thicket. There he found a hollow with drifted leaves where he could lay Timas, still quite warm, without waking him; he lay down himself beside his son, covering both with leaves as much as he could. He thought he was bound to stay awake with cold and fear, but he was so tired he fell asleep almost at once, and slept heavily till near dawn.

He woke with a thumping heart to hear voices quite close to him, and the laurel bushes rustling; he hardly dared to open his eyes, though when he did, it was too dark to see anything, as the moon had set. After an age the voices passed; they must have been wood-cutters going early to work. He got to his feet, with dew dripping coldly from his hair, and a light sweat of fear on his hands. Before it was more than faintly day he woke the child and halved what was left of the bread with him. And they started again, climb-ing now, through oak and laurel, dark and creaking and evil-looking in this half dawn. 'Where are we going?' asked Timas. 'Why? Where? Why?' But Alxenor would not answer him, thinking that if they were caught it might be best for the child to know nothing. At last it was day again; they were well up, but still in woods; all round there were flowers that

303

would turn into food by summer, thickets of rasp-
berry, small waxy buds of blaeberry and crowberry,
tiny white strawberry blossoms, and now and then a
drift of blackthorn where the sloes would be. But
nothing for them, till, about the middle of the morning, he came on a patch of yellow tree fungus which
they both ate. Once they were seen by some children
herding goats, who shouted at them, but nothing
came of it.

When the sun was up, Alxenor began to think
reasonably again; it seemed very doubtful that anyone
could be hunting them; why should they? There was
all the difference between them and poor Kratis; they
were not betraying anything, only refusing a gift,
very foolishly, the Spartans would say. He could
not believe they would do more than say that, not
Archytas, not Kleora! But yet – he wasn't sure.
Sparta was an unaccountable place. It began to be
clearer to him that he was not so much afraid of men
as of Gods – Gods who might be angry and send
their Messengers, the following Arrow, the terrible
long Bear of Artemis. But at least Timas had done
them no harm, he was innocent, utterly innocent!
Though Gods do not always punish the guilty alone.
Well, it was no use thinking of that too much. He
began to talk, as cheerily as he could, interesting
Timas in things to help him on, flowers and birds
and beetles.

He managed to hit a squirrel with his sling; at first
Timas would not eat it raw, but he dried some pieces
in the sun, and they were both hungry enough for
anything before the end of the day. Soon he found

he had to put the child up on his back almost all the time, and got on very slowly. He kept high up, so that there should always be a shoulder of hill-side between themselves and the easy pass with the road across it. It was difficult going through the pathless oak scrub, but when he got out on to the open hills he was afraid of being seen. There were plenty of small burns and springs, and they had enough to drink, and once Alxenor stopped to dig up some doubtfully eatable roots. It occurred to him that he had done nothing about Thrassa before he left. Oh well, the Spartans would do it. Poor thing.

That night they slept on the hill-side, under a big rock; Timas had bad dreams because of all the odd food he had eaten during the day, and kept on waking and crying. Alxenor gave him his own woollen tunic for an extra wrap and slept bare himself, or tried to sleep, for he was too cold and hungry to keep still even. He began to be afraid now that this was more than the child could stand, and more than once thought of turning back and trusting to Kleora, or even hoping to hide in some small farm. But in the morning he went on again. Now the high ridges were ahead of him, steep and lonely and dark in shadow between him and Tegea. He could have crossed them in a few hours by himself, but not with the child to help along and carry and be gentle with. Again they lived as best they might on raw bird flesh, and some eggs he found, but Timas was violently sick several times, and had to be carried all the way.

Then, at the head of the valley, Alxenor saw a tiny house, a square lump of rough stones, roofed with

305

turf, and a goat tethered outside it. He took his chance, and walked in. There was no one there but an old woman, very deaf, who gave them acorn-bread, and milk that tasted of peat smoke. Timas was sick once more, but then drank some milk and went to sleep in his father's arms, pale and exhausted, with damp rings of hair sticking to his forehead. Alxenor put him down on the bed, and waited, sitting beside him. It was evening. The door opened, and a man came in, who started violently on seeing Alxenor. 'There's nothing to fear, shepherd,' Alxenor said, 'I'm not one of the masters.'

'Who are you then?' the shepherd asked, a little reassured by his un-Doric voice.

'A stranger, in trouble.'

'With – with them?'

'Must I say?'

'No,' said the shepherd, then, to the old woman, 'Supper, mother.' Alxenor shared their soup and bread; no one said much. When it was dark they slept.

In the morning the child seemed well; Alxenor asked for a loaf and a little jar of milk, then paid for them fairly. At that, the shepherd picked Timas up. 'You're for Tegea?' he said. 'I'll put you on your way.' Till midday he carried Timas on his shoulder, then he stopped and pointed to the high, wooded slope in front of them. 'There's the frontier,' he said, 'for men and Gods.'

They crossed it in the evening, very tired. There were more ridges ahead, and Alxenor thought it best to sleep here; they had still enough bread for to-

306

morrow's breakfast. The next day they started, down and up again, and down, at last into a small, winding valley, There suddenly they met a man with a spear. Alxenor went up to him boldly. 'What State are we in?' he asked. The man grinned at him: 'This is Tegea. You're safe.'

CHAPTER FIFTEEN

'But where is the penny world I bought
To eat with Pipit behind the screen?
The red-eyed scavengers are creeping
From Kentish Town and Golder's Green;

Where are the eagles and the trumpets?'
– T. S. Elliot

BEFORE they sighted Poieëssa, Alxenor had used up almost all his money, and the gold cup was gone too. It had taken him a little time getting to the coast and finding a ship; now it was April. He stood on the deck, staring; it seemed now like yesterday that he had left his home, there was nothing between him and the deep line of downs above the City. Then Timas pulled at his hand; child-like, he seemed only just to have realized what was happening. 'Father,' he said, 'aren't we ever going home?' 'Home?' Alxenor answered, half to himself, 'this is home!' 'But I don't want to come here!' said Timas, fretting, 'I don't like it!' 'You'll like it soon,' his father said, but the child's mouth began to drop for a wail. 'Aren't I ever going back to Kleora?' he asked. 'Aren't I going to see those boys? Oh, father –' And as the boat made Poieëssa harbour, Timas started crying bitterly for Sparta.

They landed; it was late afternoon with a kind of glow about everything, a foreshadowing of summer without the heat and dust. It seemed to Alxenor that perhaps it had been like this all the time since he left. He stood for some ten minutes on the quay, half afraid to go into the town, his bundle dragging from one hand. Every one's voices sounded familiar,

308

he looked quickly from one man to another, wondering if he knew them. The child pulled at his arm: 'Let's go on, father!' He went straight up towards his brother's house; there was no trace anywhere of fire or destruction. Timas wanted to go through the market, but his father avoided it, skirting round by back streets, and so into Red Walls Passage at the bird-seller's shop, where they both stopped to look, and Alxenor to gather heart to take him to the house, and hear whatever news there might be for him.

He knocked; it was a new porter who opened, and he nearly said 'Where's Manes?' but then thought it better to stay a stranger, and only asked if he could see Eupaides, son of Timagoras. The man looked at him doubtfully: 'He's at supper now, with guests. Of course if it was anything very important –' Alxenor slipped one of his few remaining coins into the porter's hand: 'I've news for him; go and see.' 'Well, sir, I think if you could step this way,' said the porter, 'he might see you. But there's quite a little party to-day. Who? Well, there's Chromon, son of Thrasykles: you know him, sir?' 'Chromon!' said Alxenor. 'Here!' But checked himself, because they were just coming to the supper room. 'Ah,' said the man, 'you're thinking of five years back, aren't you, sir? That's an old story now.' 'I see,' said Alxenor, then, 'I'll wait here till they're ready. You needn't say anything.' And he quieted Timas, who wanted to ask questions.

The curtains were half-drawn; he stood in the opening, nearly hidden. The room had been dark-

ened, so that there should be no daylight to put out
the softer and friendlier shining of the lamps, and
there were flowers everywhere: hyacinths and jon-
quils, single red tulips like blown bubbles, branches
of fruit blossom hanging on the walls, and sweet
pinks strewing the table. His brother looked quite
unchanged, sitting there with his garland well
down on his head, eating roast larks. And Chromon
was on his right, Chromon . . . grown-up. Not
talking quite so much, nor flinging himself about.
Chromon leaned across, frowning, saying something
in a low voice to Eupaides. They had only just begun
supper; slaves came hurrying by with the roast lamb,
the salads and the sauce, jostling past him with eyes
only for the dish they carried. Some one told a funny
story, and they all laughed.

'Oh,' said Alxenor, stepping out into the supper
room, 'won't either of you speak to me!'

Abruptly the laughter dropped. Eupaides stared,
smiled, and jumped up from his couch. 'Well,
Alxenor,' he said. 'Here you are at last!' But
Chromon, half sitting up, clutched at the cushions
by his head. 'Is it you?' he said, very white. 'Oh, is
it?' 'Yes,' said Alxenor, 'it's me.'

Then his brother was hugging him, and he was
suddenly so full of mixed emotions that he could
hardly breathe. All these familiar things, the room,
the voices, the faces, closed on him, beating on him
with memories. For a moment time swept backwards, like the afterwash of some great wave on a
steep beach, and he was a boy again, five years
younger. He clung on to his brother, blindly.

Then Timas began to feel all this emotion spreading to him; he got frightened and hit his father as hard as he could, to make him attend. Alxenor freed himself, a little ashamed, and picked up that small, dear son of his, realer by now than Poieëssa and Chromon and everything. He began to be slightly conscious of the servants, and one or two of the other guests, whispering and staring at him. 'Chromon,' he said, 'this is her child.' 'A boy?' said Chromon, flushing, and came near, his eyes on the death-coloured tunics: 'And she?' 'She died in Sparta.' Still the two men stood quite close, but yet not touching, nor looking directly at each other. The silence went on, growing worse for both of them. Then Eupaides began tickling the child's bare foot, till he wriggled round, grinning softly, still clinging to his father with arms and legs, but ready to make friends; and by and by slipped down, stood in front of Eupaides, and looked up at him. 'Is that supper?' he said. 'Yes,' said Eupaides. 'Come and see what you'd like to eat.'

Then Alxenor moved a little, enough to touch Chromon, shoulder to shoulder, and in a moment they were holding hands again, after so long, and weeping. Eupaides glanced back at them a moment, smiling to himself, and then sat down again, with Timas on the couch beside him, very straight and grown-up, with his brown legs sticking out in front of him. There were eggs and shrimps and honey and dates, and lovely sticky cakes, as many of them, apparently, as one wanted to eat; and funny sweet stuff to drink, out of a cup with little boys running races all round it; and such a smell of flowers that one's eyelids got heavy, one nodded and began to dream, with somebody's arm to lean up against . . .

'Alxenor!' said Eupaides at last, 'what am I to do with this nice baby of yours? He's fast asleep.'

'Oh,' said Alxenor, 'I didn't see!'

'He's quite happy. And you two now?'

Alxenor looked at Chromon, and Chromon nodded: 'Yes.'

'Well,' said Eupaides, rather softly, 'shall we tell him?' And again Chromon nodded.

'I know I'm a fool,' said Alxenor, 'but I do want to know what you and Chromon are doing in the same house!'

'Gently, gently!' said Eupaides, 'I'm coming to that. But first we must hear what you were doing in Sparta.' Alxenor told. 'So you don't love the Spartans much,' said Eupaides meditatively, at the end.

'No,' said Alxenor, very short.

'And neither do we.'

The servants were all out of the room now; Chromon and the two brothers and the other guests were all close together so that a whisper would carry. By and by Alxenor realized what was happening, and why democrats and oligarchs were united against the Laconian garrison and the governor who was treating them with a properly Spartan contempt for Ionians. Eupaides put the case, dispassionately, crumbling a piece of bread between his fingers: 'You see,' he said, 'I don't admit that we were wrong before, whatever Chromon says. But now things are different. Sparta has won, and she's not the State to settle down and keep house after that. So it's time we cut clear before she goes over the falls.'

'But surely there's not another war coming now?' asked Alxenor, frowning.

'One never knows. Did you think her Allies all . wanted to stick to her for ever?'

'No. But if you do get clear – the barbarians?'

'They'll have their hands too full to hurt us, with the Great King dead. We needn't count Persia for anything either way – yet. Keep it to Hellas. Sparta has lived for nothing but war these twenty years; it's in the nature of things that she can't change all at once. Maybe there'll be nothing for a little –'

Chromon broke in, with a fierce, impatient whisper: 'The Spartans are tyrants and that's all there is to it! You're with us, Alxenor?'

'Yes,' said Alxenor, 'what's your plan?' They came closer still.

Alxenor nodded: 'I'm back just in time. And after this what happens?' Eupaides laughed. 'Then you'll have to make up your mind again between Chromon and me!' Chromon shook himself angrily in his old way: 'If you'll only be reasonable, Eupaides –!' They sat down again; Timas was still asleep. It must be dark outside, night falling over Athens and Sparta and the long, empty waves of the sea, all those places where he had been so unbelievably lonely for five years. This, this alone was real, friendship and kinship, the old house, the same curtains and silver vases and paintings on the walls, and being a citizen again in one's own City! He ate and drank, sinking back

into it all, not trying to compare it with other houses
he had seen. At last he felt he could let himself go,
not have to try so hard all the time to be a reasonable,
grown man and father, not have to fend for himself
and think ahead every moment. He could be young
again, young as he really was; he would cut off his
beard and have a long, hot bath, with fine oil and
scent, and fresh linen to wear; and afterwards
Chromon would play ball with him and they would
walk out on to the downs and hills of Poieëssa, and
talk themselves back to the days before anything
happened.

'There's one thing,' said Eupaides, by and by,
'that I've wanted to say, Alxenor. I'm sorry I had
you knocked down by that Laconian. I had to decide
in a hurry, and of course he was more violent than I
meant. I'm afraid you were hurt – I didn't ever
mean that.' Alxenor laughed, but not quite wholeheartedly, for he hated having to remember that
day. 'It's all right,' he said, 'and Damagon was
drowned at Arginusae. Archytas told me later.'
'I'm glad,' said Eupaides; 'he was a brute to have
about the house, you know.'

That night Alxenor could not sleep at first, but
when he did it was long and soundly, right into the
morning; he only woke when Timas got in beside
him and began pulling his hair. The curtain across
the doorway was half drawn; from outside he heard
the noise of the mating pigeons, and voices in the
sunny court, the pleasant, soft Ionian voices, full of
laughter and high notes, and beyond, some one
whistling a dance tune. 'I want to go out!' said

Timas. 'There's a big dog – I can see him! Wake up, father!' Alxenor stretched himself sleepily, pushing the blanket off and taking deep breaths of the morning air. 'I'm so happy,' he said. But Timas only lay on his middle at the end of the bed, kicking his feet about, and casually asked: 'Why?'

Eupaides had married quite lately, a niece of his old friend Tolmaios, plump and soft-skinned, with long eyelashes and easily flushing cheeks. She got shrill and excited over Alxenor, and a little jealous; and she was not very successful at mothering Timas, who did not like her much, and clung to his father in this new house, scarcely realizing that from now on it was to be his home. She began at once planning to marry the young widower off to some nice girl – this was naturally a great subject of conversation with her friends and maids.

Alxenor found himself at once plunged into the middle of things, and was glad of it, because this way he avoided all the fuss and talk and questioning, and good advice five years too late that he had been dreading ever since he made up his mind to come back. Eupaides and Chromon were both too busy to do much more than love him; the others took him for the moment as a matter of course. Questions were bound to come later, but in the meantime he could establish himself, perhaps do well in this business . . . On the fourth evening they went to supper at the big, yellow-painted house under the Citadel, where Tolmaios lived now. It was to be the simplest kind of party – with just the Governor and his four chief officers.

They came rather late, when everybody else was there and waiting for them. The Governor himself was a Laconian from the hills above Amyclae, very anxious to impress the islanders, and with that curiously violent passion for Sparta that those who were not citizens often had, the feeling, perhaps, of wanting to do even better than the best. Because of this, he was always rough and harsh, and deaf to any persuasions, no friendlier to oligarchs than democrats, though he would sometimes ask them to his own unpleasant suppers of black broth at its most traditional. This party was a return – a poor, a mere Ionian return, as Tolmaios explained – of his hospitality.

After the wine was going well, Alxenor was introduced: the young brother just back from Sparta, with a Laconian trick of speech here and there, even if he'd got nothing better from the greatest State in Hellas! Nervously he mentioned Archytas, and the Governor was delighted; he had known Archytas just a little on service, and this gave him the opportunity of showing these Ionians what a gentleman he was. He beamed and drank – would Alxenor not sit beside him? And Leon? 'Why,' said Alxenor slowly, 'he's a Spartan. Need I say more?' The Governor laughed and drank again, and Alxenor felt the sheath of his dagger rubbing against his thigh under the heavily stitched tunic. It was odd to hear the Laconian voices again, and rather terrifying. But he was a citizen now, in his own City, not alone to face it. He signed to the wine-boy to fill the Governor's cup, and began to talk of the poplar

groves by Eurotas, the fruit trees of Amyclae, and
the spring flowers, the crocus meadows, the gentian
on the hills you could see a bow-shot off, blue as
paint . . . Home-sick, the Governor grew very
silent, and sighed. Then came the awaited flute
note, and Alxenor, thinking of Sparta too, stabbed
him under the ribs.

It took hardly any time to clear the bodies out of
the way, and wipe up the blood; everything had been
arranged beforehand. Eupaides laughed quietly and
took a drink. 'I don't want to hurry you,' said Tolmaios, 'but this is only the first step – and the
easiest.'

There was a beautiful precision and success about
the attack on the garrison. That had been left
entirely to Chromon; they knew his hatred was as
practical as it was strong. In the dawn Alxenor met
him limping down the steps, a little tired; he was
not so well as he used to be. 'It's finished, then?'
said Alxenor, still rather shy and awkward with his
old friend.

'This is,' said Chromon, stopping and slowly
sheathing his sword. 'At last. But now there's the
old game to play.'

'Ah!' said Alxenor, 'must it all happen again? I
thought you and my brother would be friends after
this.'

Chromon smiled just a little: 'You were always the
hopeful one, Alxenor!'

Ahead of them, morning was coming across the
sea; from up here they could see lines and lines of
waves, just touched with light, glimmering far out,

beyond and below the pale rose-coloured dawn
clouds: no wind, and no noise now that the fighting
was over. Alxenor wanted everything to be right.
'How can you hate one another?' he said, 'now that
you've saved Poieëssa together?'

'Poieëssa,' said Chromon musingly. 'Maybe we've
saved her body together. Now we must fight each
other for her spirit. And I shall win, Alxenor.'

Said Alxenor: 'Are you so sure you're right?'

And, 'Yes,' answered Chromon; then after a
moment, 'Haven't you made up your mind between
us yet?'

Alxenor stood still, looking out to sea. 'It was
always you I thought of, Chromon, all these years.
You I wanted. In spite of your cursing me. But
now I'm back, and my brother is so – so reasonable –
and good to me –'

'And I've not got Moiro now to bribe you with,'
said Chromon, bitterly, finishing the sentence for
him.

'Ah, Chromon, don't! Can't you see I'm just an
ordinary man, I don't feel about this like you! It's
not right and wrong to me, not black and white! I
want to be just, I want to see both sides of things!'

'You can see both sides as much as you like,' said
Chromon, 'you've had time . . . But then you must
choose.'

'Ah why?'

'Because if you're not for the light you must be
for the darkness.'

'I can't see that either way has all the light! Why
need I choose, Chromon?'

But Chromon was tired of fighting and talking; he began to limp down towards the City again. 'If you want us to be friends still,' he said.

Alxenor sat down on the edge of the steps; before he quite knew it, the cool, bright morning was come. Suddenly he felt very sleepy and unhappy and dirty; now that he saw them in the light, his hands were filthy with blood and mess. There was no more to do up here; he went back to his brother's house, and washed, and lay down on the bed; Timas was still asleep.

He woke four hours later and went through to find Eupaides, who was busy sending off letters to various friends, in Sparta and elsewhere, giving suitable accounts of last night's doings, and asking for certain help. In Poieëssa, they were largely trusting to the fact that, even now, Sparta was bad at using her fleet, and, though quick to punish on the mainland, she could be bribed and persuaded into overlooking the doings of a small and far-off island. It was not as if any Spartiate had been involved, only Laconians or allies, and the Governor, as Eupaides had taken care to find out earlier, was not in great favour with the powers at home. With any luck, things should be all right, and Poieëssa free – to go back to home politics.

It was all quite plain to Alxenor that morning; it was all going to be just like it was before, and this time he would have to decide. Not quite like, he thought bitterly, for then we were young and hopeful and eager and – oh, again, young, when all was said! He went down into the market, where every one was

talking about last night and pointing up at the citadel. After that time in Sparta, he did enjoy a book-
shop, the flute-maker with his strange, smooth ivory;
the jewellers, the carpet importers, the inlayer at
work on a lovely pear-wood couch for Tolmaios –
Looking from one to another, he wandered down
towards the harbour, and, all at once, found himself
n the Street of the Ship-builders, just passing Chromon's uncle's house. He stood there for a long time,
looking at it. He could see where it had been rebuilt.
Just opposite, between two houses, was the way in
to the narrow, twisting lane where he had carried
Moiro, drooping over his shoulder . . . the rose
smell of her hair. Half blind with tears he saw
Glaukias come out of the house, and a moment afterwards felt the hand on his arm. 'Come in,' the old
man said. He could not answer, but followed.

Inside, fresh paint hid almost all the marks of fire;
he stared at it all the same. 'No,' said Glaukias, 'you
won't see anything now. Tell me about your son; is
he like Moiro?'

'A little,' said Alxenor, shaken. 'His mouth, perhaps. I don't know. I could bring him if you liked.'

'Yes, do that, Alxenor. It would please my wife.'

'Oh – how is she? It was not – not too much for
her, all that happened?'

Glaukias shook his head. 'We begin to forget. At
least – almost all. The girls are married.'

Alxenor looked down. 'I am sorry, Glaukias,' he
said. 'I feel as if it was all my fault.'

'We heard afterwards,' said Glaukias, 'you weren't
what we thought. You did your best.'

'I wish I had!' said Alxenor. 'I was a fool, I didn't think. And you? You were wounded?'

'Yes. It took six months to heal.'

'Oh, I'm sorry!' said Alxenor, inadequately again. And then a boy came in, a boy of eleven, lame with a twisted foot, rather pale and unboylike. 'Your son?' Alxenor asked.

Glaukias turned to the boy very tenderly, and then to Alxenor, as if he could not think what to say. 'Yes,' he said at last, very low. 'You dropped him that day.'

Alxenor remembered. 'Oh God,' he said. 'Oh God!' And turned and ran out of that terrible house.

At supper that day he and his brother were alone together for the first time since he came back. 'By the way,' said Eupaides, 'I paid your debt to the banker, and a nice lot of interest too, silly cuckoo you were!'

'Well,' said Alxenor, 'you've been saving on my keep for five years! I'll pay you back some time, though. Eupaides, I'd be glad not to live in the city now. Will you let me run the Twenty-Acre for you? I know you don't think much of your bailiff there, and I'm honest anyway. I could learn farming – it's more common sense than anything.'

'Do you think you've got much common sense?' said Eupaides. Alxenor shrugged his shoulders and said nothing. He wanted the farm – he could not bear living in the same town as that twisted foot. But his brother was being just as difficult to deal with as five years ago! Eupaides also apparently recognized this: 'Sorry!' he said, laughing. 'I mustn't say that sort of thing now. I believe you only didn't like me in old days because I wasn't treating you as if you were grown-up!' Still Alxenor said nothing; he didn't want to lose his temper. 'I wouldn't go out to the farm if I were you,' said his brother. 'Stay here and take your place in the City. I won't interfere.'

'But what is my place?'

'Your fathers have been among the rulers of Poieëssa for ten generations; that should have worked itself into the blood.'

'I'm still a democrat, Eupaides.'

'Well then, suppose you were at the head of one party, and I of the other, how would that be?'

'But Chromon –'

'I wonder if you won't find your Chromon a little grown-up too since old days.'

Alxenor did not answer for a moment; he felt the poison of those last few words working in him. 'Anyway they wouldn't have me,' he said at last, 'and I'd rather be out of it if I could – alone and quiet on the farm, trying to make my son into a good man. You don't know how I want that, Eupaides.'

'We'll see at the end of summer,' said Eupaides. 'Wait till then.'

As the weeks went by, Alxenor found himself in a curious position. The oligarchs were all very friendly; no one seemed to remember old days. And they were mostly pleasant people, who gave the nicest parties, the only houses where he could see, and talk over, the newest books, a painting or vase by some master from the mainland, a foreign embroidered hanging, or what-not. There was music

too, better than he had heard for years; Tolmaios
had taken to it as he grew older – there were always
flute and harp players, or singers, among his guests.
It was so kind and lovely after the chill of Sparta,
and all the arts frozen to death there!

But all the same he wanted to go to meetings of
the democrats, the Club that met by the Temple of
Poseidon at the little harbour; he wanted to hear
Chromon speak, and become himself completely
persuaded that this was the right way. But the
democrats were shy of him. His relationship with
Chromon was not, after all, perfectly plain sailing.
They wanted him to say straight out that he was one
of them, and would follow their leaders through
blood and fire. And he would have liked to be able to
say it; he would have liked to rest his troubled mind
in a party. Only always at the last moment he could
not agree with everything. He kept thinking of the
Athenian democracy, the cleverest people in the
world, and yet they had almost come to ruin, and
even in the end – well, it was hard to tell what
Athens was like nowadays. And he remembered the
trial of the generals after Arginusae. Though that
was better, a hundred times over, than what the
Thirty had done, if half what one heard was true.
Only one did expect so much more good from a
democracy! Chromon got angry with him after a
time, and no wonder. Somehow that friendship had
not lasted through the five years; just at first they
thought it had, but soon they found there were too
many things they could not talk to one another about
– most of all, Moiro. It seemed to be only when

323

Alxenor brought Timas with him that things got
better.

Timas got very fond of both his uncles; he found
his way about the town, and could trot by himself
from one house to the other; no one was going to
hurt him, there was nothing to be afraid of. And
he learnt how to play with the sea again after his
two years inland in Sparta; and he learnt to run
among the sheep and pull the cistus gum out of
their fleeces, to bring home and burn and make a
sweet smell; and he learnt how to buy sweets in the
market, and he even learnt to pretend to his aunt
that he didn't mind her kissing him. But sometimes
he remembered Sparta, and asked when they were
going back, and of course Alxenor began to wonder
whether it had been right after all to take him away,
whether perhaps Kratis had been mad all the time.

So it went on till autumn. There was no Spartan
vengeance for the garrison; Eupaides had managed
that. And there was more and more bitterness
between the parties, till things stood much as they
had been before Notium. And Alxenor was very
uneasy. The worst of it was that, apart from politics
even, he was not really happy in Poieëssa; the island
seemed very little and unimportant after Athens or
Sparta; whatever one did, he could not feel it
mattered intensely; nothing really exciting happened. So when the question came up again, he
found he scarcely wanted the farm; he began to
wonder what he did want. And then, at the beginning of winter, a seaman came up from the harbour
with a letter for him.

He opened it, very much excited; it began formally:
'Hagnon son of Theramenes, to Alxenor son of Timagoras, greeting!' At once he became glad and excited,
holding tight on to the letter as he read it. 'I know
you meant to go home,' wrote Hagnon, 'so I send
this on the chance that it may find you. I have paid
the bearer. Do you remember what Athens was like
when you were there? It is different now. We try to
think it is the same, but not in our hearts. Sparta
did win the war for all we can say, and something
was killed then, something that used to make Athens
the most wonderful place in the world. We shall
never be quite sure of ourselves again now. A few
people say that is wrong, Sokrates the stone-mason
among them. He is a queer man, Alxenor; he makes
me disturbed in my mind. They say that Cyrus, the
brother of the Great King, has a rebellion to put
down among his own barbarians; he may want
soldiers from Hellas. Anyway, I am going east early
this spring. Perhaps I may touch at Poieëssa; if
so, I hope to see you, though I do not know even if
you are alive. But if you are, be happy! Perhaps it
is best never to have belonged to a great City.'

That was a queer letter to get on a still, grey
December afternoon in Poieëssa; he read it through
again. His brother had been writing at the far end
of the room, and now looked up at him questioningly: 'What's the news?' Alxenor spun the letter
from his hand by its string. 'It's from Hagnon the
Athenian. Tell me, have you heard anything about
Cyrus wanting Hellene troops for anywhere?'
'Well,' said Eupaides, 'he may be having a tougher

business over the siege than he thought.' 'Miletus?
But that won't last long. Well, he'll have plenty to
pick and choose from now that the war's over and
half Hellas with no money and nothing to do!'
'Quite,' said Eupaides; 'is that what you were thinking of?' Alxenor stood frowning. 'It's in my mind,'
he said, 'I might do worse.'

He said nothing to Chromon yet, but in himself
he was much happier; he saw a way out if things
went on as they were. By the next ship that was
sailing for Athens, he wrote back to Hagnon, thanking him for his letter, and telling him to be sure to
come, scarcely able to say how much he looked
forward to it. It was one of the last ships to sail for a
long time; in winter the little islands in the Aegean
settled down, sinking deeper and deeper into themselves, losing touch with the outside world, going
back into ancient, self-sufficing days, each one a
folded flower nursing its own seeds.

Tolmaios had a painter staying with him, a refugee
from Miletus, very anxious that Cyrus should win
back his town for him from the Satrap Tissaphernes,
whom they all hated, but with a much too thorough
dislike of war to do anything about it himself. He
had painted a frieze in the new dining-room Tolmaios had built that autumn, and by and by there
was a supper party to see it. 'Splendid!' said
Eupaides, standing back to look: 'That shadow –
just right. And the pheasants among those rocks.
You've got the balance and the variety. Yet sometimes I wonder if the older men hadn't more power
over their subject; what do you think, Tolmaios?'

They settled down to supper. The two men on
Alxenor's right began talking at once; and on his
other side they started a lively argument with the
painter; he joined in at first, but not very keenly, and
soon lost the thread of the talk. He was still thinking
of Hagnon's letter. Later in the evening there was
music, and a picture dance by the flute girls – the
Nine Muses and Painting crowned by Apollo.
Alxenor applauded, but he liked the singing best;
he had been drinking a good deal, which made
things sound exquisitely sad and fleeting; he felt as
if he was the only one there with sensibilities . . .

'Oh my guests, my friends, be gay!
Let no talk nor cup go by you,
Where the couch is softest lie you,
Is there naught my love can buy you?
Flute-girl, lift your pipes and play!
(On my roof the dawn is grey.)

Now the swallows wake and say,
Downwards from their roof-tiles peeping,
"Ah the light while we were sleeping,"
"Ah the feast that men were keeping,"
"Freed from bonds of night and day!"
(On my roof the dawn is grey.)

Oh my dear companions, stay!
If you knew the joy you gave me –!
From the lonely morrow save me,
In your deeps of laughter lave me,
Not so soon, so rash away!
(On my roof the dawn is grey) . . .'

327

Alxenor began to cry quietly and pleasantly; before those swallows came to Tolmaios' roof-tiles, he would be away, sailing east with Hagnon the Athenian, leaving his little son . . . and suddenly he sat up, whispering to the slave behind for a cup of water, and steadied his rocking mind to consider the question of Timas.

The next morning he said to the child: 'I'm going away in Spring; perhaps for a long time.'

'Where?' asked Timas, anxiously.

'To a war,' Alxenor answered slowly, realizing how little he himself knew of the where.

'Back to Sparta?' the child asked. 'Oh, father, am I going too?' And Alxenor wondered for the hundredth time when his son would lose that Dorian accent he had picked up when he was first learning to speak. 'Oh do take me!' said Timas again, 'please, father!'

But Alxenor shook his head. 'I'm going to Asia, to the barbarians' country. You must stay here and learn to be a good citizen.'

'Oh, father – you took me with you last year when I was little! Why can't I come now?'

'Because you're little still – really, Timas. And I've got somewhere to leave you now; all Poieëssa is your home.' For a minute Timas looked as if he was going to howl. 'I've got to go,' said Alxenor, 'anyway; and when I come back I'll bring lots of money and Persian things, and we'll have a house of our own to put them in. Let's play I'm back, and I've brought you a peacock and a monkey and one of those lovely blue stone boxes full of dates, and one of the Great King's gold whiskers!'

'And what else?' asked Timas.

'I'll tell you if you'll tell me which uncle you've been staying with while I was gone.'

'Both uncles. And they gave me a pony to ride on – they did really! And I went in a boat by myself. Now you go on, father!'

But it was not so easy to arrange in real life. Chromon and Eupaides both wanted the child. Only here Alxenor stood firm and insisted, and they were both so much surprised that they gave in, and agreed that he should live half the year with one, and half with the other. He was to see two sides of life: and try to be fair. So his father pictured it; and so he told Timas, that miserable last day in March, after Hagnon had come. . . .

CHAPTER SIXTEEN

'I wish one could know them, I wish there were tokens to
tell
The fortunate fellows that now one can never discern;
And then one could talk with them friendly and wish them
farewell
And watch them depart on the way that they will not
return.'
                                        – A. E. Housman

URNING his head a little, Hagnon could see
the bushes on the ridge outlined against
the glow from all the camp fires behind, but
looking west over the sea it was not yet quite dark.
He spat out the fern stalks he had been chewing,
and jerked his head towards the camp: 'They're a
decent lot,' he said, 'my men get on well enough with
them.'

Alxenor agreed. 'I suppose there aren't more than
thirty Athenians here, counting yours, and the rest
all Spartan Allies.'

'Well,' said Hagnon, looking straight in front of
him, 'that's all Athens is now. Besides – they were
soldiers in the war, not Generals; I wouldn't care to
meet Lysander. But these men are different, they've
had bad times too. They want to be friends with us;
we ought to take it.'

Alxenor admired Hagnon a good deal more than
he cared to say, he knew he could never be so splendidly reasonable himself. 'You look at the future all
the time,' he said.

'Where else?' Hagnon answered. 'I have to remember now, not that I'm an Athenian, but that I'm a
Hellene – and they are.'

330

'Do you think,' said Alxenor, 'it's partly being in Asia that makes you feel that?'

'Maybe. But while there's the sea I'm not too far from home.'

'They say we go up to Sardis soon.'

Hagnon pulled his cloak round him, because the land wind was beginning to blow cold. 'I wonder what Cyrus really wants us for.'

'But surely to put down his rebellion?'

'Most likely. But yet – I wonder why he can't do that for himself; I wonder why he's so anxious to get us. And they say he's holding up the siege of Miletus till afterwards. Alxenor, have you heard anything at all certain about this rebellion?'

'Well – no.'

'Nor I. Nor any of the officers. I don't care where he takes us, though, so long as there's something to do.' He got up. 'Come on, Alxenor, let's go back and see if there's any news.' They cut back across the ridge, pushing their way at first through tangles of wild peony, then, further up, pressed in among the gleaming of white, scented cistus flowers, light and thick on the bushes. There seemed to be fewer birds on this Asian coast, not a nightingale anywhere; but perhaps it was only the nearness of the camp that frightened them.

Hagnon, as captain, had a small tent to himself. Alxenor shared a larger one with two other heavy-armed foot soldiers, free men and citizens, all with a thorough contempt for the light-armed troops, and still more for the barbarians. They were cooking supper now; to-morrow it would be Alxenor's turn.

He leant over the pot and snuffed at it: hare, he guessed, and took a turn at stirring. It had been very pleasant out all day with Hagnon, talking and sitting about, and a swim from the beach further along. He hoped desperately that Hagnon would go on liking him; he wondered what he could do to insure this continuance. Friendships were such lovely, brittle things, they broke unless one was very, very careful. And Hagnon was so much younger than he, not old enough to have found out yet what an ordinary man he was. Alxenor caught himself being terrified lest Hagnon should find a better friend and leave him: well, that was a bad thing to be thinking! If Hagnon was not to make friends with the better man then he must be the better man himself.

The light-armed troops had less pay and less food; they often came round to the others' quarters, hoping for a share of whatever was going. The smell of the hare had lured up two or three now; they stood just outside the circle of the fire, making loud remarks to one another as to the goodness of the cooking and how large an animal a hare was – large enough to feed half a dozen and still enough for to-morrow. Alxenor looked up, the spoon in his hand, meaning to send them off with a flick of hot gravy in their faces; suddenly one of them called his name: 'Alxenor! I never knew you were here!' And Isadas the Melian came smiling into the firelight, with hands stretched out to him. 'Oh!' said Alxenor, 'nor did I.' And he thought rapidly and crossly that now he would have to feed the three of them.

In the meantime his own two friends came back.

'What's this?' they asked, and Alxenor rather reluc-
tantly explained that it was a man he'd known once,
and suggested that they should all share supper.
'Very well,' said one of the hoplites, 'and next week's
drink on you.' The two men Isadas had brought
with him came forward shyly, delighted at their luck,
and sat together, rather silent and eating hard. They
were Peloponnesians, country folk and simple, not
wondering very much what was going to happen to
them or when they were going home. Isadas sat by
Alxenor, eating the hare stew out of the bowl. 'I am
glad to see you!' he said. 'I never thought you'd be
here. Didn't you get back to your island?'

'Yes,' said Alxenor, 'oh yes. But one can't stay in
the same place for ever.'

'Can't one? I could have if I'd found the place to
stay. But I didn't. Alxenor, where are the wife and
child?'

'My wife died,' said Alxenor shortly, 'and my son
is at Poieëssa.' He quite liked Isadas, but he wished
he was anywhere else just now – supposing Hagnon
came!

Isadas laid a hand on his knee, with rather too
much feeling. 'I'm sorry about Moiro! She was so
kind, so gentle . . .' He thought of the wedding,
and Moiro as he had seen her among the Athenian
women, such a child – and an islander. But Alxenor
did not respond, only moved away a little, and stirred
the fire. What was the matter with Alxenor? Why
wouldn't he be friends, like last time? Isadas stopped
eating, felt as if it would choke him. 'Alxenor,' he
said, 'I'll go. You needn't be friends with me if you

333

don't want to, now you're a hoplite with your fine
armour and fine friends and all! Come on!' he called
to the others, 'we're not wanted!' and got up, blushing to the ears.

But Alxenor pulled him by the arm. 'Nonsense!'
he said, violently uncomfortable, and feeling already
that he quite liked the man after all. 'Sit down!
Don't be a fool, Isadas!'

'Really?' said Isadas; then, very glad, 'Oh well, if
you like me to, I want to!'

'Of course,' said Alxenor, 'here, come and have
some more meat!'

Isadas sat down again, smiling uncertainly, still not
quite sure if Alxenor meant it. The difficulty was
that Isadas never knew if people despised him just
because he was poor and young and had no City, or if
they knew somehow that he had been a slave, by
some look about him, some tone in his voice, something he could not see himself. But Alxenor knew
already. Perhaps he had made a mistake about what
Alxenor thought, only – 'I suppose you found everything all right at home?' he asked. 'You're rich,
aren't you?' He looked at the fine, beaten-out cable-
work round the rim of Alxenor's shield, and the good
stuff of his tunic.

'No,' said Alxenor, 'not rich. I'm only a plain
soldier.'

'Yes. But you look like a captain.'

'I'm not. But I'll tell you who is – bread, Isadas?
It was fresh made yesterday – and that's Hagnon the
son of Theramenes.' For a minute or two Isadas
said absolutely nothing and stopped eating. Alxenor

looked at him, irritated, thinking what an idiot he was, and then suddenly said, just to see what would happen, 'Well, shall I take you to see him?'

And Isadas took it seriously! 'Yes,' he said, 'yes, do. Thank you, Alxenor.'

None of the others of course saw the point, only that Alxenor was looking extremely cross and embarrassed. 'You'd better not, really,' he said.

But Isadas quite firmly wanted to; he felt that if he could face Hagnon, he would be able to face anyone. 'When?' he asked. 'To-night?'

Alxenor answered sulkily that he would have to ask Hagnon first: 'And he mayn't want to see you.'

'No,' said Isadas, 'I don't expect he does. But I'll come round to-morrow about midday and see what's happening.'

'Well, I'll see,' Alxenor said roughly, hunting about in the pot for another piece of meat, 'but if he doesn't want you, you shan't go, Isadas.' He was not at all decided yet whether he would actually say anything at all about it to Hagnon.

But the next morning he thought he would. Hagnon had started it by talking again about all the odd Dorians and allies there were in the army; he seemed to find them curiously interesting. And Alxenor said: 'There's one here – I don't know what you'll think, Hagnon, he's – he's a Melian.'

'Well?' Hagnon did not remember.

'He was your slave. Before all this.'

Then Hagnon did remember. 'Isadas? Is he here? Free?'

'Yes,' said Alxenor, watching him uncomfortably.

'He seems a decent sort; he's with the light-armed lot.' Hagnon did not answer; he was trying hard to feel that now he had nothing to do with that boy – himself – who had fought, and been beaten, three and a half years ago. Alxenor went blundering on: 'I saw him at Melos – when I was doing garrison there.'

'Why didn't he stay, then, if he really was a citizen?'

'The Spartans had taken all the land.'

'They would! Well, it's odd finding him here; but sooner you than I, Alxenor!' He laughed and shook himself, not wanting to hear any more of a rather unpleasant subject.

But Alxenor had one of those sudden, awful ideas – that he must test their friendship – that it was no good unless it could stand the test! 'Will you see him, Hagnon?' he said. 'Try what he's like now? Oh, I wish you would!' And then stopped, horrified at himself.

Hagnon got up and walked away. 'No,' he said. And then, angrier, 'How can you say a thing like that, Alxenor! Haven't you any sense? Can't you tell what a man feels like when he – when his State – when Athens – oh, get away and don't come near me till you've got some decency again!'

'But –' said Alxenor, following him round the tent, '– but – you said yourself, about being a Hellene –'

'Anyway I don't come from a rotten little island that no one's ever heard of!' said Hagnon savagely, and hit Alxenor, who hit back. Then they both tripped over the tent ropes.

Alxenor got to his feet first. 'All right,' he said, 'good-bye.'

But Hagnon jumped up; the fall seemed to have shaken something in his mind too, for he was laughing. 'No!' he said, 'don't be a baby! I'll see your Melian if you want me to, Alxenor. Don't go away! I will; but I bet you a month's pay he won't like it any more than I do!'

It was nearly midday by then. When Alxenor got back to his own tent, he found Isadas waiting. 'You can come,' he said rather loftily. 'I've managed it.' 'Oh!' said Isadas, and fidgeted with his belt, then, 'Have you got any oil, Alxenor? Could you let me have some? I must wash!' Isadas washed with some care; being a Dorian, he was fairer-skinned than Alxenor, and the dirt seemed to show more; even so he took a very long time. At last he was clean; but he began to look uncomfortably at his tunic. 'It's torn,' he said. 'Alxenor, couldn't you lend me –' But Alxenor lost all patience. 'Oh, come on!' he said. 'You aren't going to wait at table this time!' Isadas got very red, and followed without a word, only shoving back his hair nervously once or twice.

Hagnon saw them coming. He got up and then sat down again, and went on doing the pay accounts of his company with tallies, a way he had learnt from Strymodoros. He was very anxious not to seem the least bit different from his ordinary self; after all, he had only just to ask the man who his captain was, and whether he had good quarters, and perhaps give him some money – yes, that he would certainly do – and then send him away. Nothing to get flurried about. Hagnon wished his beard would start growing soon; he would feel so much more dignified.

337

Then the two came up; he grinned and nodded to
Alxenor, and tried not to look at the other – better,
he thought, to be surprised and very gentlemanly; he
waited for Alxenor to tell him.

But Isadas spoiled it all by speaking first, all in a
rush. 'Hagnon!' he said. 'Oh, I wanted to see you!
I'm as good as you now, I'm a free Hellene, I can say
what I like to anyone! And – I do want to say – it
wasn't you I meant to hurt that time, it was your
City – I did hate Athens then, but I don't now! And
anyway I didn't hurt you, I can see by your face,
you're still in the stars, I didn't shake you out, you
can look the whole world in the eyes – let me go,
Alxenor, he can, he does – oh, I do wish you'd say
something, Hagnon!'

Hagnon gripped the tallies, looking at them, rather
than Isadas: 'You don't give me much chance, do
you?' he said, then, trying to get back to his first
idea of the talk: 'Who is your captain here?'

'I don't want to talk about my captain!' said Isadas.
'I want to know I can face you – and you me if it
comes to that! And I'll say I was wrong if you like,
Hagnon. I'll say you're better than me, made finer.
Will that do?'

'What's all this got to do with me?' said Hagnon,
getting up, fretting with his fingers on the tallies.
'Of course you're free. You didn't think I meant to
claim you? I'm glad you're free, if that's what you
want. It's no good to anyone having Hellene slaves.'
He turned rather angrily on the other: 'Alxenor,
can't you tell me what he's after?'

Alxenor answered quickly, 'I think he wants to

338

get back a bit of himself that he lost when he was a slave.'

'What do you mean?' asked Hagnon. 'Can't you speak plainly? I'm not a poet!' And he frowned at them both.

'It is that!' said Isadas, twisting his hands. 'I'm left now all unsure, so that I don't know if I've really got the whole of myself to give, to an army or a friend or anything! I say I'm free – and – and I am, only I think there's something wrong still. Hagnon, it's not because you were my master, but I know there's some fine thing in your spirit and not in mine, and I know you can't ever be friends with me, really, but if you could just a little, that would make it right.'

'One can't be friends like that,' said Hagnon, looking away. 'You're free all right. Don't think about it so much.'

Isadas came forward softly and touched Hagnon, who drew away. 'Was it the fight?' he said. 'I wish I hadn't. It was the sort of thing a slave does. No free man would hate that way. I'm sorry, Hagnon.'

'Oh, do stop!' said Hagnon, his voice rising. 'I'm not thinking about the fight! I never have!' And suddenly he burst into furious tears. 'You've turned me into a baby!' he said, sobbing gustily and fiercely, with wet cheeks and fists clenched at his sides. 'Aren't you pleased!'

Alxenor put both arms round him, regretting the whole thing with all his heart. 'It's all right,' he whispered. 'It's all right, Hagnon. I'll take him

straight away, you shan't ever see him again.' Then,
sharply, to Isadas, 'Come – quick!'

But Hagnon gasped and rubbed his eyes, and
stopped crying as suddenly as he had begun. 'Stop!'
he said, and they both stayed still. He came after
them and took Isadas by the wrist. 'Listen!' he said.
'I will be friends with you! I told Alxenor we were
all Hellenes together, in this barbarian country, and
I will not say things unless I mean them! I will take
it out of words into life, I will forget all that has
happened, I will make the world right for you,
Isadas.'

Isadas looked at him a minute. 'Thank you,' he
said, low; 'it is right now.' And they took each other
by the hand. Alxenor looked on from a little way off
and thought to himself that it was better to be neither
of them – high or low – better to be unshaken by
these violences, to take the middle way. And yet he
was not sure; and he wished he could feel about
Poieëssa as Hagnon felt about Athens. Only that
was all wrong: because Athens had fallen out of her
pride and was broken . . . He was going back to
his tent again, when Hagnon called him, bidding
him come to supper that night, saying Isadas would
be there.

Just before sunset he came over, wearing his best
tunic, and a fine embroidered cloak that Chromon
had given him. Hagnon wore his best too. 'You
were right, Alxenor,' he said. 'Now I am sure that
Hellas is more than Athens.' Isadas and two or
three others were sitting about on the grass under
the great plane tree by the tent, eating young green

spring onions from a pile in the middle. They were all talking, Isadas still rather shyly, but at least like any other free man, and the Athenians were accepting him and being friendly. Hagnon brought up the last of his guests, a Laconian captain, newly joined, a big, heavy-jawed fighter; he seemed rather uncomfortable, looking round for some other Dorian. Isadas was the only one, and he backed away, into the shadow of the tree; but anyhow the Laconian was probably not the sort of man to start a conversation with one of these light-armed out-of-works. Then Alxenor came up, queerly attracted, as always, by that harsh, unsubtle talk, the accent of Laconia; he thought for a moment of Timas, safe at home; then sat down beside the captain, and asked him if he'd heard anything new of when they were moving. No, there was still nothing certain. But what could Cyrus want with all this? Well, that was his own look-out, and at least he paid well.

'Where did you land? – Ephesus?' asked Alxenor. 'Any news from there? I used to know the place.'

The Laconian shook his head; then after a minute rumbled with laughter. 'Yes, by the Twins, there was though! I'll tell you. It was one of those dirty barbarians –' He paused to laugh again, and spit, and take another mouthful; it was just the beginning Alxenor would have expected! '– always doing his best to muck up our landing and lodging, always shoving his nose in and asking questions!'

'A friend of Tissaphernes?'

'Shouldn't wonder. Gobryas he was called. Poi-

341

soned his own father – sort of thing they all do.
Well, we were getting about sick of him, but we
didn't like to do anything: never do to get these
foreigners nasty.'

'Yes,' said Alxenor. 'What happened?'

But the Laconian never noticed his strained, hungry
voice; he went on: 'Well, by and by we had a bit
of a turn-up in the market, and one of us – not like
me, I mean, he was one of the Masters, all right, all
right! – he just walked in and knocked friend Gobryas on the head, and that was the end of him: all
squashed in! A nice row there'd have been too, but
Archytas – that was his name – got up on a bench
and gave those dirty Persians something to chew
on. Oh, a proper telling-off they got – that's how
to get on with it!' He laughed again, so loud that
Hagnon glanced across, with an eyebrow cocked at
Alxenor.

But Alxenor did not notice. 'Archytas, you said?'

The Laconian nodded; he was full of pleasant
thoughts: the way those barbarians had been sat on!
– and now this capital free meal he was getting. He
wondered vaguely why this young Athenian captain
should ever have asked him, coming along before
he'd got his tent up, even, and bidding him welcome
and inviting him, without so much as knowing his
name! Well, he supposed Athenians were like that;
he'd never had much to do with them himself, except
– he grinned into his beard, sensibly deciding to say
nothing about the war.

As they were talking, day dropped out of the sky.
The young plane leaves showed marvellously pale

and veined against the level torches. Hagnon had been silent for a little time; then he stood up, pushing the garland higher off his forehead, pressing with his hands against the great round bole of the plane tree, flaking the bark off as he sang. The others grew quiet, listening to him.

> 'Gather, Hellenes, on the shore.
> Troy is taken; now once more
> Into Asia goes the war!
>
> Here forget we strife and hate,
> Here is none too proud or great,
> Here is none to challenge fate.
>
> Here at last let all be wise,
> Deep the sacred truce-time lies
> On our hearts and lips and eyes!'

He looked round at his guests, lying on the grass, or leaning forward, their faces in the light, thinking of home, as they mostly did when anybody sang to them. Isadas sat very still, with his eyes fixed; he had the idea. The Laconian drank and fidgeted; it was not the sort of song he was used to: on the whole he disliked it. One of the Athenians was looking very sad, so, he thought, was Alxenor. He sang again.

> 'Now's another debt to pay,
> Salamis lies west away:
> There our prows were crowned with bay!
>
> Yet no looks to that far west,
> Now the soldiers' way is best:
> Wine from grapes that others pressed,

343

Bread from corn that others sowed,
Lances make the lightest load,
Eastward lies the Persian road!'

Isadas jumped to his feet and shouted. Two of the Athenians followed his lead, then Alxenor. And the Laconian captain, who was very sleepy after his long march up from Ephesus, came over and said good night. The party came to an end.

'That was a bad song!' said Hagnon gloomily.

'Oh no,' said Alxenor, 'it was better than I could have done, anyhow. And Isadas liked it! But tell me something; we're going up now, to help Cyrus, to help the Persians. Why did you sing as if we were going against them?'

'It came to me like that,' said Hagnon. 'People can't be brought together except against something. But it's no good. They may feel that way now, for a day or two, even; but tears and songs don't last. Well, good night, Alxenor.'

'Good night and good luck, Hagnon.'

It was nearly a week before they marched, after all; they were glad to get off – the camp had never been more than temporary, and it was really filthy by now. It was cool and fine, just after daybreak, when they started; some one had seen an eagle ahead of them; each lot was singing its own songs. Hagnon turned once in his saddle to look at the sea, before it was lost, out of sight, for how long he could not tell. He wondered what it was like in Athens to-day, whether anyone was remembering him; for a moment Nikodike came into his mind. He did not think about her much nowadays; she was a good wife to Diokles,

344

doing her duty in every way; but after one is grown-up, one does not talk to women, not even one's sister – what good would it be? He rode forward to the next bend in the road, to see how the land lay ahead.

They found Sardis full of Greeks already, camped in great armed squares outside the town walls. Cyrus came over and inspected them all one day; he was a splendid looking young man, he rode a great, trampling bay stallion, his Persian officers thundered magnificently after him, with swords drawn and cloaks tossing out, and heavy gold necklaces; every one cheered. He gave them fresh equipment, new tunics of the best crimson cloth, and anything else they wanted. It was a fine thing to be a Hellene!

There was plenty to see and do at Sardis, new things to eat and drink and stare at. Hagnon enjoyed it all; he was still young enough to love anything fresh for its own sake. With his captain's pay, he had money to spend, and he liked Alxenor to help him over the spending. Both of them bought things to send home by the merchants who travelled between Sardis and the coast. Hagnon sent a bundle of embroideries in a sandal-wood box back to his mother, and Alxenor sent Timas a carved ivory fish and three puzzles and a snake-skin belt that was a charm against fevers, and a long letter, all about everything. As he wrote, Hagnon was looking over his shoulder. 'What a nice father you must be, Alxenor!' he said.

Alxenor was making a drawing of a Persian priest with his funny hat, on the margin of the letter. 'Yes,' he said, 'it's about the only thing I'm a bit good at, and this is all I get of it! I do wish I knew what he's growing up like, between the two uncles; I suppose it's bound to end in his siding with one of them. I meant him to see both sides, but that's too much to hope!' He finished his drawing off minutely, bending right over the paper and sticking his tongue out.

Hagnon was nibbling at the sealing-wax. 'It might work', he said. 'My father used to see both sides of things.'

'M'm . . . yes,' said Alxenor.

'You mean, he was killed in the end? But no one lives for ever. He always knew it would come some time. And before that he did so nearly save us!'

'Yes: so nearly! But it's the men – and the States – that believe in themselves and their own right and nothing else that really win and get what they want.'

'Do they?' said Hagnon. 'I don't think so. They make things go all their way for a little, and then the Gods get angry – or the people – or their Allies – or whatever it may be; and they are broken and swept aside. But if one could truly take the middle way, oppressing no one, the Gods would stay their hands.'

Alxenor was drawing an antelope's head now; he frowned over it. 'The Gods might be merciful, but not men. You would be hated from both sides – crushed by the millstones.'

'Yes, into bread! Oh surely that would be better. Alxenor, this is what I think. My City used to be all one side, Athene mirrored in her own shield until her

pride rose above the bounds of justice and she was
taken and made poor and little again. But now I
think she could stand half-way, between other prides,
holding the balance of right thinking. Sparta – I
don't know, I can't see yet. But if my Athens could
be like that, it would almost be worth it all.'

'But, Hagnon, you told me Athens was so queer and
sad now, something wrong.'

'Perhaps that's because I'm young and easily made
sad. And because so many of my friends are dead.
And perhaps Athens isn't going to be like I want her.
Perhaps it's only a dream.' He moved away and
began humming a tune to himself, pushing open the
flap of the tent to see out into the sunshine.

Alxenor finished the last of his pictures and sealed
up the letter. 'I'm glad these things are going off at
once,' he said. 'Do you think we're really going to
march to-morrow, Hagnon?'

'I expect so,' said Hagnon. 'Cyrus is a quick
mover. Look – here's our man coming!'

The merchant bade him good morning, and then
waited patiently outside the tent for the two packages
done up firmly with cords and straw, and the red-
sealed letters. Hundreds of the Greeks were sending
something back from Sardis; he had hired an extra
dozen pack-mules; what a lot of different places their
homes were in! Queer folk, but good for business.
Alxenor handed over the things, telling the man to
take special care of them, lingering as if he did not
want to see the last of his letter to Timas. Then
suddenly he turned and called out cheerfully to
Hagnon; they went over together to the stores to

see that everything was ready for to-morrow's start.

And in the morning Cyrus set out from Sardis with all his troops. And he marched through Lydia three days' journey, a distance of twenty-two parasangs, to the Maeander river.

Lightning Source UK Ltd.
Milton Keynes UK
28 January 2011

166524UK00002B/1/P